PHRASEBOOK • DICTIONARY

Terry Kawashima
M.A., Harvard University

Crown Publishers, Inc., New York

To Kishiro and Mitsuko Nagahama

For their help with the preparation of this book, the author would like to thank Kathryn Mintz, Living Language Director; Jacqueline Natter, Editor; and Victoria Su, Editorial Associate. The editors wish to thank Lindsey Crittenden, Peter Davis, Linda Kocur, and David Natter for their contributions to this project. Thanks also to Fodor's Travel Publications, Inc., for portions of this book taken from *Fodor's '92 Japan*, available in bookstores nationwide.

Copyright © 1992 by Crown Publishers, Inc.

All rights reserved. No part of this book may be reproduced or transmitted in any form or by any means, electronic or mechanical, including photocopying, recording, or by any information storage and retrieval system, without permission in writing from the publisher.

Published by Crown Publishers, Inc., 201 East 50th Street, New York, New York 10022. Member of the Crown Publishing Group. Random House, Inc. New York, Toronto, London, Sydney, Auckland

LIVING LANGUAGE, LIVING LANGUAGE TRAVELTALK, and colophon are trademarks of Crown Publishers, Inc.

Manufactured in the United States of America

Library of Congress Cataloging-in-Publication Data

Kawashima, Terry.

Living language traveltalk. Japanese : phrasebook, dictionary/ Terry Kawashima.

1. Japanese language—Conversation and phrase books—English. I. Title.
PL539.K35 1992
495.6'8321–dc20

ISBN 0-517-58733-5

10 9 8 7 6 5 4 3 2 1

First Edition

CONTENTS

3 FINDING YOUR WAY 33

4 ACCOMMODATIONS 47

5 SOCIALIZING 55

6 DINING OUT 68

13 ACTIVITIES AND ENTERTAINMENT 180

14 GENERAL INFORMATION 196

15 GRAMMAR IN BRIEF 214

ENGLISH-JAPANESE DICTIONARY 228

JAPANESE-ENGLISH DICTIONARY 252

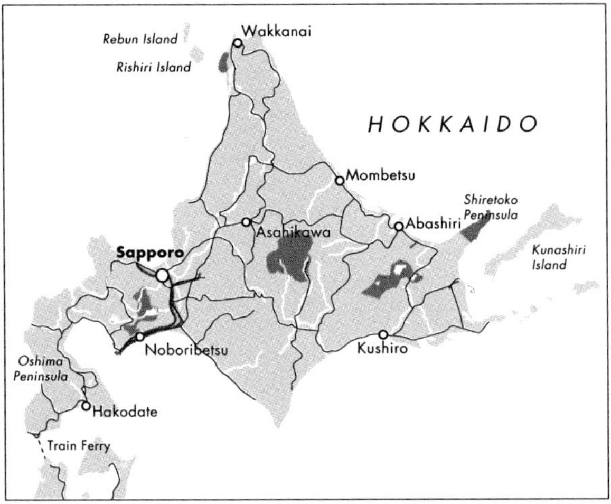

Rebun Island
Wakkanai
Rishiri Island
HOKKAIDO
Mombetsu
Shiretoko Peninsula
Abashiri
Asahikawa
Sapporo
Kunashiri Island
Noboribetsu
Kushiro
Oshima Peninsula
Hakodate
Train Ferry

Oki Islands
N
Matsue
Tottori
Tsushima Island
Iki Island
Yamaguchi
Hiroshima
Okayama
Kobe
Fukuoka
Takamatsu
Awaji Island
Osa
Goto Islands
Matsuyama
Beppu
Tokushima
Wakayam
Oita
Nagasaki
Aso
Kochi
Kumamoto
Kii Peninsula
Amakusa Islands
SHIKOKU
Shimo
Shimo-Koshiki Island
KYUSHU
Miyazaki
Kagoshima
Kuchinoerabu Island
Yaku Island
Tanega Island

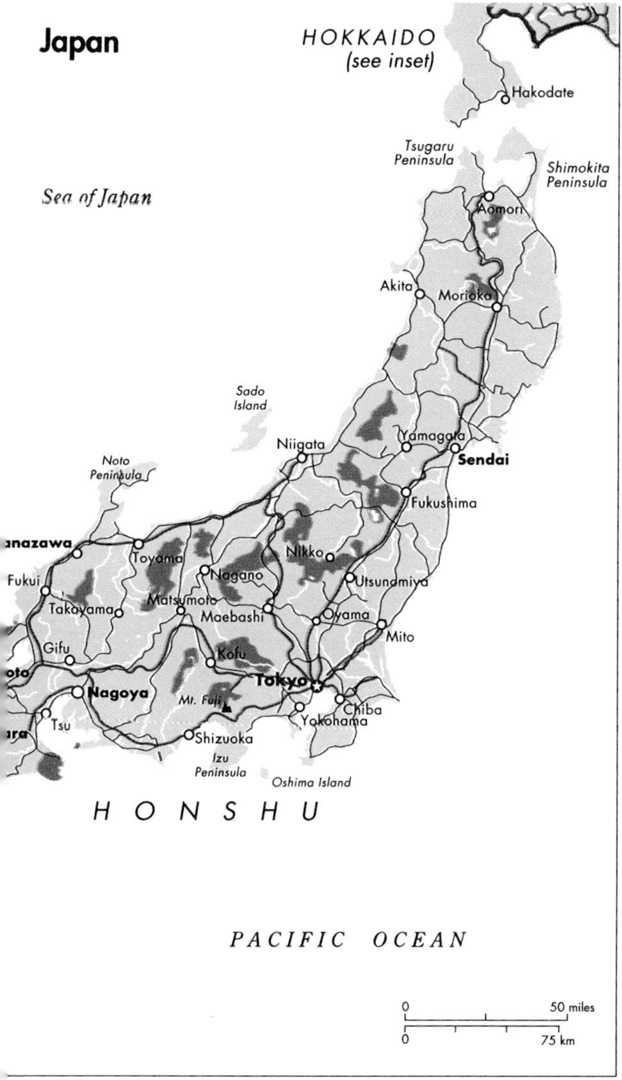

Japan

HOKKAIDO
(see inset)
Hakodate
Tsugaru
Peninsula
Shimokita
Peninsula
Sea of Japan
Aomori
Akita
Morioka
Sado
Island
Niigata
Yamagata
Sendai
Noto
Peninsula
Fukushima
anazawa
Toyama
Nikko
Nagano
Utsunomiya
Fukui
Matsumoto
Takayama
Maebashi
Oyama
Mito
Gifu
Kofu
oto
Tokyo
Nagoya
Mt. Fuji
Chiba
Tsu
Yokohama
ara
Shizuoka
Izu
Peninsula
Oshima Island

H O N S H U

PACIFIC OCEAN

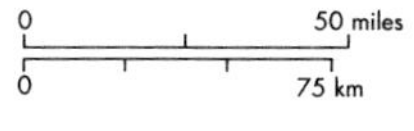

Tokyo
0 1 mile
0 1 km
N
Mejiro
Mejiro-dori Ave.
Koishikawa Botanical Gardens
Hongo-dori Ave.
Hakusan-dori Ave.
Uguisudani
Ueno Park
UENO
Ueno
Showa-dori Ave.
ASAKUSA
Kappabashi-dori Ave.
Asakusa-dori Ave.
Takadanobaba
Waseda-dori Ave.
Kasuga-dori Ave.
Korakuen Garden
YUSHIMA
Suidobashi
Okachi-machi
Kiyosubashi-dori Ave.
Kuramae-dori Ave.
Okubo
Shin-Okubo
Seibu-Shinjuku
Iidabashi
Ochanomizu
AKIHABARA
Akihabara
Asakusa-bashi
Ome-kaido Ave.
SHINJUKU
Jimbocho
JIMBOCHO
Yashukuni-dori Ave.
Shinjuku
Ichigaya
Kanda
Shinjuku-dori Ave.
ICHIBAN-CHO
Yoyogi
Shinjuku Gyoen Garden
Yotsuya
IMPERIAL PALACE
HAMA-CHO
Tokyo
Nihombashi
NIHOMBASHI
Sendagaya
Shinanomachi
Akasaka Palace
Uchibori-dori Ave.
Meiji Shrine Inner Garden
Meiji-dori Ave.
Meiji Shrine Outer Garden
Chuo-dori Ave.
Showadori Ave.
Akasaka-mitsuke
Sotobori-dori Ave.
Aoyama-dori Ave.
Yoyogi Park
Aoyama-Itchome
AKASAKA
Hibiya
YURAKUCHO
Yurakucho
EITAI
Harajuku
HARAJUKU
Hibiya Park
Sumidagawa River
Eitai-dori Ave.
Meiji-Jingu-mae
Gaien-Higashi-dori Ave.
GINZA
Tsukiji
Shin Ohashi-dori Ave.
Omotesando
AOYAMA
SHIMBASHI
Shimbashi
ETCHUJIMA
SHIBUYA
Sakurade-dori Ave.
Hibiya-dori Ave.
TSUKIJI
Kiyosumi-dori Ave.
Shibuya
Roppongi
ROPPONGI
Hama Rikyu Garden
HIROO
Hamamatsucho
Shiba Rikyu Garden
HARUMI
TOYOSU

PREFACE

Are you planning a trip to Japan? If so, this book will help you make the most of your trip. The *Traveltalk™ Japanese* phrasebook/dictionary features more than 2,200 Japanese expressions to use in the various situations you may encounter as a tourist. Each word has a phonetic transcription to help you with pronunciation.

No prior knowledge of Japanese is necessary. All you have to do to make yourself understood is read the phonetics as you would any English sentence. We also recommend using the *Traveltalk™ Japanese* cassette so you can hear Japanese spoken by native speakers and practice your pronunciation. However, this book is useful on its own, as it offers the following features:

Pronunciation and Character Guide The phonetic transcription system is presented in this section through the use of simple English examples and explanations. Reading through it first will enable you to use the phrases in subsequent chapters with full confidence that your pronunciation is comprehensible. A complete character guide is also included, with transcriptions of simple and complex Japanese consonant and vowel combinations.

Chapter 1: Useful Expressions Many common phrases are used over and over in a variety of contexts. For your convenience, these phrases have been grouped together in chapter 1.

Chapters 2-14 reflect the full range of the visitor's experience. From arrival at the airport to saying farewell to new friends, *Traveltalk™* provides a comprehensive resource for every important context of your visit.

Dialogues give you a sense of how the language sounds in conversation.

Travel Tips and Cultural Highlights Interspersed throughout the chapters are brief narratives highlighting cultural attractions and offering insiders' tips for getting the most out of your visit.

General Information is given throughout. Essential facts are presented to ease your transition into a new setting:

- legal holidays
- metric conversion tables
- important signs
- clothing/shoe size conversion charts

Grammar Guide A concise and easy-to-follow grammar summary is included for those who would like to understand the grammatical structure of Japanese.

Two-way 1,600-word Dictionary All of the key words presented in this book are listed in the Japanese-English/English-Japanese dictionary, including phonetic transcriptions of all the Japanese words.

BEFORE YOU LEAVE

VISAS

As of this writing, visas are not required for U.S. citizens visiting Japan for leisure or business purposes, as long as the stay is within 90 days. If you are planning on working or studying in Japan, contact the Japanese Consulate in the major city nearest you to check their policies and obtain a proper visa. Below are the addresses and phone numbers of four consulates:

CHICAGO
625 North Michigan Avenue, Chicago, IL 60611
Tel. (312) 280-0400

LOS ANGELES
250 East First Street, Suite 1507, Los Angeles, CA 90012
Tel. (213) 624-8305

NEW YORK
299 Park Avenue, New York, NY 10171
Tel. (212) 371-8222

WASHINGTON, D.C.
Visa Department, Embassy of Japan, 600 New Hampshire Avenue, Suite 675, Washington, D.C. 20037
Tel. (202) 234-2266

WHERE TO GET INFORMATION ON JAPAN

Following is a list of Japan National Tourist Office (JNTO) locations in major cities in the United States, as well as Tourist Information Centers (TICs) in Japan. They will be able to assist you in answering questions you may have, or will refer you to other organizations who can give you more information.

U.S.A.

Chicago
401 North Michigan Avenue, Suite 770, Chicago, IL 60611
Tel. (312) 222-0874

Dallas
2121 San Jacinto Street, Suite 980, Dallas, TX 75201
Tel. (214) 754-1820

Los Angeles
One Wilshire Building, 624 South Grand Avenue, Suite 2640, Los Angeles, CA 90017
Tel. (213) 623-1952

New York
Rockefeller Plaza, 630 Fifth Avenue, New York, NY 10111
Tel. (212) 757-5640

San Francisco
360 Post Street, Suite 401, San Francisco, CA 94108
Tel. (415) 989-7140

Japan

Kyoto
Kyoto Tower Building, Higashi-Shiokojicho, Shimogyo-ku, Kyoto 600
Tel. (075) 371-5649

Narita (New Tokyo International) Airport
Airport Terminal Building, Narita, Chiba-ken, 282
Tel. (0476) 32-8711

Tokyo
1-6-6 Chiyoda-ku, Tokyo 100
Tel. (03) 3502-1461

ABOUT THE JAPANESE LANGUAGE

The sounds of the Japanese language are produced by various combinations of fourteen consonants and five vowels. The pronunciation guide and charts that follow will help you with these sounds.

Written Japanese is represented by three different systems. The first is called *hiragana*, the standard Japanese "alphabet,"of which there are fifty "letters." The *katakana* system also has fifty "letters," and these are used most frequently in representing *gairaigo*, or "imported words" from foreign languages, in order to distinguish them from Japanese words. The third system is *kanji*, which consists of thousands of Chinese characters. Typically, a Japanese sentence may contain words written in all three of these systems.

There are two important factors to note concerning the Japanese language. First is the degree of variation in the language according to particular social situations, status, and gender. A Japanese speaker constantly makes adjustments in his or her language according to the audience. This concept is similar to the French differentiation between *vous* and *tu*, but in Japanese, there are more than a dozen ways to say "you," and one must choose the correct way by keeping in mind all of the factors mentioned above. This book uses the most standard forms of the language, so that each phrase can be said by both men and women in most situations without sounding too casual or too formal. Second, regional dialects are still very much alive in many parts of Japan. This book uses the Tokyo dialect, which is considered "standard" Japanese, but you may hear other pronunciations, intonations, or even different vocabulary depending on where you travel or with whom you speak.

PRONUNCIATION AND CHARACTER GUIDE

Every Japanese word or phrase in this book is presented along with its English equivalent and an easy-to-follow transcription (sound key) that shows correct pronunciation. Simply read the sound key as you would read English, and the result should be fairly comprehensible to most Japanese speakers.

Japanese sounds are often quite different from English sounds, so keep in mind that these transcriptions are only approximate guides. To improve your pronunciation, use the accompanying audiocassette. It follows this text closely and gives you the opportunity to listen to and imitate native speakers of Japanese. Try also to imitate the native speakers you encounter during your travels, and don't be afraid to practice your Japanese with them. Most people will be flattered by your attempts to learn their language and will gladly help you.

THE TRANSCRIPTION SYSTEM OF THIS BOOK

The most commonly used systems for transcribing Japanese sounds into English (Roman letters) are the *romaji* and the Hepburn systems. This book, however, uses a more directly phonetic method of representation, designed so that English speakers can approximate correct Japanese pronunciation more easily.

EXAMPLE: *romaji:* sayonara (good-bye)
Traveltalk™ phonetics: sah-Y<u>OH</u>-NAH-lah

Some English phrases in this book contain words in *romaji* since this system is often used in Japan. You are most likely to encounter *romaji* in the representation of names of people and places. However, in an effort to help

English-speaking tourists, key Japanese sentences or phrases (such as signs) are translated directly into English in major tourist sites or major train stations; they are almost never phoneticized into *romaji*.

Sounds that are higher in pitch than others are capitalized, as in *DOh-moh*. In this case, *DOh* starts higher in pitch, then lowers toward the end of the syllable (indicated by the lower case *h*); *moh* is pronounced at this lower pitch as well. The changes in pitch should be relatively subtle; standard Japanese is fairly monotone (although regional dialects may be much more colorful). The capitalized sounds should be regarded as slight ascensions in pitch rather than strong emphases. The letters that are underlined in the syllable DOh indicate a long vowel sound, as explained below.

STANDARD VOWELS

These are all short vowels.

Character	Approximate English Sound	Phonetic Symbol	Example of Phonetic Transcription
あ	shortened *ah*	ah	AH-meh (rain)
い	*i* as in Bali, only shorter and crisper	ih	IH-mah (now)
う	shortened *oo*	u	u-CHIH (house)
え	*e* in met	eh	EH-kih (station)
お	*o* in of	oh	oh-TOH (sound)

LONG VOWELS

Two consecutive identical vowels technically should be

pronounced separately. However, at normal conversational speed, they sound virtually the same as a simple extension of a vowel sound. This long vowel sound is indicated by underlining letters.

Characters	Approximate English Sound	Phonetic Symbol	Example of Phonetic Transcription
consonant+ ああ／あー	f*a*ther	ah	kah-doh (card)
consonant+ いい／いー	ch*ee*se	ee	ee-EH (no)
consonant+ うう／うー	*zoo*	u	Ku-kih (air)
consonant+ ええ／えー	extend *ea* in lead	eh	Eh (yes)
consonant+ おお／おー	*o*ld	oh	oh-KEe (big)

VOWEL COMBINATIONS

The sound keys for frequently used vowel combinations are as follows:

Characters	Approximate English Sound	Phonetic Symbol	Example of Phonetic Transcription
consonant + あい	d*i*ne	ahy	KAHy (shell)
consonant + えい	d*ay*	ay	ay-goh (English)
consonant + おい	t*oy*	oy	oY (nephew)

UNSTRESSED VOWELS

Certain vowels in a word, in combination with consonants, are sometimes pronounced so lightly that you virtually cannot hear them. This most often occurs with the vowels *i* and *u*. In these cases, the vowels are omitted from the transcription in this book. An apostrophe is used to respresent these unstressed vowels when one of them occurs in the middle of a word. For example: *Kohn-nih-ch'wah* (Hello/Good afternoon).

SIMPLE CONSONANT AND VOWEL COMBINATIONS

kah か	kih き	ku く	keh け	koh こ
gah が	gih ぎ	gu ぐ	geh げ	goh ご
sah さ	shih し	su す	seh せ	soh そ
zah ざ	jih じ	zu ず	zeh ぜ	zoh ぞ
tah た	chih ち	tsu つ	teh て	toh と
dah だ	zhih ぢ	zu づ	deh で	doh ど
nah な	nih に	nu ぬ	neh ね	noh の
hah は	hih ひ	hu ふ	heh へ	hoh ほ
pah ぱ	pih ぴ	pu ぷ	peh ぺ	poh ぽ
bah ば	bih び	bu ぶ	beh べ	boh ぼ

mah ま	mih み	mu む	meh め	moh も	
yah や		yu ゆ		yoh よ	
lah ら	lih り	lu る	leh れ	loh ろ	
wah わ				(w)oh を	n ん

COMPLEX CONSONANT AND VOWEL COMBINATIONS: consonant + *y* sound + vowel

kyah きゃ	kyu きゅ	kyoh きょ
gyah ぎゃ	gyu ぎゅ	gyoh ぎょ
shah しゃ	shu しゅ	shoh しょ
jah じゃ	ju じゅ	joh じょ
chah ちゃ	chu ちゅ	choh ちょ
nyah にゃ	nyu にゅ	nyoh にょ
hyah ひゃ	hyu ひゅ	hyoh ひょ
pyah ぴゃ	pyu ぴゅ	pyoh ぴょ
byah びゃ	byu びゅ	byoh びょ
myah みゃ	myu みゅ	myoh みょ
lyah りゃ	lyu りゅ	lyoh りょ

MISCELLANEOUS PRONUNCIATION NOTES

1) The use of *l*

Both the *romaji* and Hepburn systems of transcribing Japanese sounds use the letter *r* to represent the sounds ら(lah), り (lih), る (lu), れ (leh), and ろ (loh). However, there is absolutely no *r* sound in Japanese as it is pronounced in English, and since *l* is much closer to the actual sound, *l* is used throughout this book. Keep in mind, though, that an *l* is still an approximation. The true *lah* sound in Japanese can be imitated by pretending that you are going to say *dah*, but bouncing your tongue off the roof of your mouth less emphatically.

2) The use of *h*

The vowels *ah*, *ih*, *eh*, and *oh* all use the letter *h* to indicate their sounds. However, when they are in the middle of a syllable, the *h* is omitted to avoid visual clutter for *eh* and *ih* sounds (as in sen, not sehn, and kin, not kihn). Note, though, that for the sounds *ghin* (as in gingham) and *ghee* (as in geese), there is an *h* after the *g* so that these sounds are not confused with *gin* (as in gin and tonic) and *gee* (as Oh, gee!).

1 / USEFUL EXPRESSIONS

COURTESY

Thank you.	ありがとう。	ah-LIH-gah-toh.[1]
You're welcome.	どういたしまして。	DOH ih-TAHSH-MAHSH-teh.
Excuse me (in the sense of "sorry").	失礼します。	Shih-TS'lay sh'mahss.
It doesn't matter.	かまいません。	kah-MAHY-MAH-SEn.
Please (in offering something to someone).	どうぞ。	DOh-zoh.

GREETINGS

Good morning.	お早うございます。	oh-HAH-YOH GOH-ZAHY-MAHss.
Hello/Good afternoon.	今日は。	kohn-nih-ch'wah.
Good evening.	今晩は。	kohn-bahn-wah.
Good night.	おやすみなさい。	oh-YAHSS-MIH-NAH-SAHy.
Hello (on the telephone).	もしもし。	MOHsh-mohsh.
How do you do?	始めまして。	hah-JIH-MEH-MAHSH-teh.

[1] Please keep in mind that although the *romaji* and Hepburn systems would use an *r* for this word (*arigato*), the actual sound in Japanese is closer to *l*.

Pleased to meet you.	（どうぞ）よろしく。	(DOh-zoh) yoh-LOHSH-KU.[1]
Good-bye.	さようなら。	sah-YOH-NAH-lah.
See you later.	では、また。	DEH-wah, mah-TAH.
See you tomorrow.	また明日。	mah-TAH AHSH-TAH.
Let's go!	行きましょう！	ih-KIH-MAH-SHOh!

APPROACHING SOMEONE FOR HELP

You'll find that many Japanese are very willing to help tourists. Some might be a bit shy if you speak English, since they might not understand you or be able to answer you in English. However, if you try speaking even a little bit of Japanese, most people will be very flattered that you're making the effort to speak their language, and they'll be quite eager to help you.

Excuse me....	すみません（が）…	s'MIH-MAH-SEn (gah)...
Do you speak English?	英語話せますか？	AY-GOH hah-NAH-SEH-MAHss kah?
Do you understand English?	英語わかりますか？	AY-GOH wah-KAH-LIH-MAHss kah?
Yes.	はい。／ええ。	HAHy. /Eh.
No.	いいえ。	ee-eh.
I'm sorry.	ごめんなさい。	goh-MEN-NAH-SAHy.
I don't speak Japanese.	日本語話せません。	nih-HOHN-GOH hah-NAH-SEH-MAH-SEn.

[1] よろしく (yoh-LOHSH-KU) is a very difficult phrase to translate, since there is no exact equivalent in English. In introductions, it can mean something close to "Pleased to meet you," but it has different meanings according to the context. (For example, on page 63 in chapter 5, this phrase means something very close to "Give my regards to...")

I don't understand.	わかりません。	wa-KAH-LIH-MAH-SEn.
I understand a little.	少しわかります。	s'KOHsh wah-KAH LIH-MAHss.
I'm a tourist.	観光客です。	KAHN-KOh-kyahk dess.
I speak very little Japanese.	日本語は少ししか話せません。	nih-HOHN-GOH WAH s'KOHsh sh'kah hah-NAH-SEH-MAH-SEn.
Please speak more slowly.	もっとゆっくり話して下さい。	MOHT-toh yut-KU-lih hah-NAHsh-teh k'DAH-SAHy.
Please repeat.	もう一度。	moh-ih-chih-doh.
May I ask a question?	聞いていいですか？	kEE-teh EE-dess KAH?
Please help me out (usually for asking directions).	ちょっと教えて下さい。	CHOHT-toh oh-SHIH-EH-TEH K'DAH-SAHy.
Please give me a hand.	ちょっと手伝って下さい。	CHOHT-toh teh-TS' DAHT-teh k'DAH-SAHy.
Of course.	もちろん。	moh-CHIH-lohn.
Where is [the bathroom]?	[お手洗]はどこですか？	[oh-TEH ah-LAHy] wah DOH-koh dess kah?
Thank you very much.	どうも有難うございます。	DOh-moh ah-LIH-gah-toh goh-zahy-mahss.

QUESTION WORDS

Who?	誰？	DAH-leh?
What?	何？	NAH-nih?
Why?	なぜ？	NAH-zeh?

When?	いつ?	IH-tsu?
Where?	どこ?	DOH-koh?
Where are you going?	どこへ行くんですか?	DOH-koh eh ih-KUn dess-KAH?
How?	どうやって?	DOh-yaht-TEH?
How much (is it)?	いくらですか?	IH-k'ah dess KAH?

NUMBERS FOR COUNTING

Numbers one to one hundred are simple once you've learned one through ten; you can add one through nine after the number of tens, just as in English. Tens are counted as "one ten," "two tens," etc. Some numbers have two different names, but both are appropriate most of the time.

0	ゼロ/零	ZEH-loh/LAy
1	一	ih-CHIH
2	二	NEe/nih
3	三	sahn
4	四	shih/YOHn
5	五	goh
6	六	loh-KU
7	七	NAH-nah/shih-CHIH
8	八	hah-CHIH
9	九	ku/KYu
10	十	ju
11	十一	ju-ih-chih
12	十二	ju-nih
13	十三	Ju-sahn

14	十四	ju-shi/ju-YOHn
15	十五	Ju-goh
16	十六	ju-loh-ku
17	十七	ju-NAH-nah/ju-shih-chih
18	十八	ju-hah-chih
19	十九	Ju-ku/JU-KYu
20	二十	NIH-ju
30	三十	SAHn-ju
40	四十	YOHn-ju
50	五十	goh-Ju
60	六十	loh-KU-Ju
70	七十	nah-NAH-ju
80	八十	hah-CHIH-Ju
90	九十	KYU-ju
100	百	hyah-KU

Numbers above one hundred are constructed in the same way as English numbers. For example, 1,234 would be the equivalent of "one thousand, two hundreds, three tens, four." Please note the pronunciation variation of the word *hundred (hyah-KU)* according to the number that precedes it. A similar change occurs in counting the thousands, but only once, for 3,000. Another important point is that the 10,000 unit is not called "ten thousands" but has its own name, *MAHn*. Therefore, 100,000 is "ten MAHn," 1,000,000 is "100 MAHn," and 10,000,000 is "1,000 MAHn." The 100,000,000 unit also has a separate name, *OH-ku*.

200	二百	nih-HYAH-KU
300	三百	SAHn-byah-ku
400	四百	YOHn-hyah-ku
500	五百	goh-HYAH-KU
600	六百	loht-PYAH-KU
700	七百	nah-NAH-hyah-ku
800	八百	haht-PYAH-KU
900	九百	KYu-hyah-ku
1,000	千	SEn
3,000	三千	SAHN-ZEn
10,000	一万	ih-CHIH-MAHn
100,000	十万	JU-MAHn
1,000,000	百万	hyah-KU-MAHn
10,000,000	一千万	(ihs-) SEn-mahn
100,000,000	一億	ih-CHIH-oh-ku

ORDINAL NUMBERS

To form ordinal numbers, simply add *bahn* after a number.

first	一番	ih-CHIH-bahn
second	二番	NIH-bahn
tenth	十番	Ju-bahn
hundredth	百番	hyah-KU-bahn

NUMBERS FOR QUANTITIES

There is a separate set of numbers for counting quantities from one to ten. For example, the "one" in "one apple" is not the same as the number "one" in Japanese. In simply counting "one, two, three…" or to express quantities over ten, use the numbers listed above under Counting. To express a quantity from one to ten, such as "one apple," use the numbers below.

one	ひとつ	hih-TOHts
two	ふたつ	hu-TAHTS
three	みっつ	mit-TSU
four	よっつ	yoht-TSU
five	いつつ	ih-TSUts
six	むっつ	mut-TSU
seven	ななつ	nah-NAHts
eight	やっつ	yaht-TSU
nine	ここのつ	koh-KOH-nohts
ten	とお	TOh

Counting quantities in Japanese is fairly complicated. The object to be counted determines the particular suffix that is to be attached to each number; for example, two cylindrical objects (such as pencils) must be counted as "two *hohn*," whereas two flat objects (such as sheets of paper) must be counted as "two *mahy*." The counting method above is a generic one that applies to most objects, and is understandable without involving the use of these complicated suffixes.[1]

COUNTING PEOPLE

Yet another method is used for counting people. The correct way is

one person	ひとり	hih-TOH-lih

[1] Please note: In Japanese, nouns have only one form, instead of singular and plural forms.

two people	ふたり	hu-TAH-LIH

For three or more people, add *nin* (人) after the standard number, such as *goh-NIn* for five people.

QUANTITIES

a half	半分	HAHN-BUn
a third[1]	三分の一	sahn-bun-noh-ih-chih
a quarter	四分の一	yohn-bun-noh-ih-chih
two-thirds	三分の二	sahn-bun-noh-nih
3 percent	三パーセント	SAHN-PAH-SEn-toh
a lot, many	たくさん	tahk-SAHn
a little (of)	少し	s'KOHsh
a dozen (of)	一ダース	ih-CHIH-DAhss
a few/somewhat	多少	tah-SHOH
too little	少なすぎる	s'KU-NAH S'GIH-lu
too much	多すぎる	OH-S'GIH-lu
a glass of _____	_____を一杯	_____oh IT-pahy
once	一度/一回	ih-CHIH-DOH/it-KAHY
twice	二度/二回	nih-DOH/nih-KAHy
first time	初めて	hah-JIH-meh-teh
last	最後	SAHy-goh
That's enough.	もういいです。	MOh EE-dess.

[1]In Japanese fractions are read bottom number first. For example, one-fourth (1/4) is read "of the four parts, one part" (*yohn-bun-noh-ih-chih*).

ABOUT THE CURRENCY

The basic Japanese monetary unit is the *yen*. The exchange rate between the yen and the dollar constantly fluctuates, of course, and these rates are posted daily in banks. The variety of coins and bank notes is as follows:

Coins 小銭 koh-zeh-nih	Bank Notes お札 oh-sah-tsu
1, 5, 10, 50, 100, 500 yen.	1,000, 5,000, 10,000 yen.

DIALOGUE: AT THE BANK 銀行で ghin-k<u>oh</u> deh

お客： oh-KYAHK	100ドルを円に替えたいんですが。	hyah-KU-doh-lu oh En nih kah-EH-TAHY-n-dess gah.
銀行員： GHIN-K<u>OH</u>-in	はい、かしこまりました。今日のレートは1ドル130円ですので、一万三千円になります。	HAHy, kahsh-KOH-MAH-LIH-MAHsh-tah. KY<u>Oh</u> noh L<u>Eh</u>-toh wah ih-CHIH-doh-lu hyah-KU SAHN-J<u>u</u>-en dess noh-deh, ih-CHIH-MAHn SAHN-ZEN-EN NIH nah-LIH-MAHss.
お客： oh-KYAHK	わかりました。トラベラーズチェックです。	wah-KAH-LIH-MAHsh-tah. toh-LAH-BEH-L<u>AH</u>-ZU CHEt-ku dess.
銀行員： GHIN-K<u>OH</u>-in	サインをお願い致します。	SAHy-n oh oh-NEH-GAHY ih-TAHSH-MAHss.
お客： oh-KYAHK	はい。	HAHy.
銀行員： GHIN-K<u>OH</u>-in	パスポートも見せていただけますか。	pahss-P<u>OH</u>-toh moh MIH-seh-teh ih-TAH-DAH-KEH MAHss KAH.

お客： oh-KYAHK	これです。	koh-LEH-DEss.

Customer:	I'd like to change $100.
Teller:	Certainly. Today's rate is 130 yen to the dollar, so it will be 13,000 yen total.
Customer:	Okay. Here are my traveler's checks.
Teller:	Would you please sign them?
Customer:	Sure.
Teller:	May I also see your passport?
Customer:	Here it is.

BANKS AND MONEY

Banks are open from 9:00 A.M. to 3:00 P.M. Monday through Friday. Usually the types of exchange rates are posted in English as well as Japanese.

sell	売	u-LIH
buy	買	kahY
traveler's checks	T/C	toh-LAH-BEH-LAH-ZU CHET-ku

There are no offices in any Japanese city that deal exclusively with currency exchange. You can find currency exchange offices in airports, and your hotel may have a designated counter (ask at the front desk). Your best bet is to go to the bigger local banks, because they won't charge an extraneous service fee and smaller branches may not be able to exchange foreign currency.

In Japan, major stores, restaurants, and hotels take credit cards, but most of the smaller establishments, especially outside of large cities, deal on a cash-only basis. Businesses that take credit cards will have signs displayed at entrances. It is wise to keep a reasonable amount of cash or traveler's checks on hand. Theft is usually not a big problem if you take commonsense precautions, so you need not be as worried about it as you might be in other countries.

Where is the nearest bank?	一番近い銀行はどこですか？	ih-CHIH-BAHN chih-KAHy GHIN-KOH WAH DOH-koh dess KAH?
I want to send a telex.	テレックスを送りたいんです。	TEH-let-k'ss oh oh-KU-LIH-TAHY-n dess.
I'd like to change some dollars.	ドルを円に替えたいんです。	DOH-lu oh En nih kah-EH-TAHY-n dess.
How much is the dollar worth?	今一ドル何円ですか？	IH-mah ih-CHIH-doh-lu NAHn-en dess KAH?
I'd like to buy some yen.	円を買いたいんです。	En oh kahY-TAHY-n dess.
I'd like to cash this check.	この小切手を現金に替えたいんです。	koh-NOH koh-GHIT-teh oh GEN-KIN nih kah-eh-TAHY-n dess.
Where do I sign?	どこへサインするんですか？	DOH-koh eh SAHY-n s'LUn-dess KAH?
Please give me …	_____下さい。	_____ k'DAH-SAHy.
• large bills.	• 大きいお金を	• OH-KEe oh-KAH-NEH OH
• small bills.	• こまかいお金を	• koh-MAH-KAHy oh-KAH-NEH OH
• five 1,000 notes.	• 千円札を５枚	• SEN-En sahts oh goh-MAHY
• some change.	• 小銭を	• koh-ZEH-NIH-OH

TIPPING

In general, tipping does not exist in Japan. Whatever service charge there may be will always be already included in your bill. However, if you happen to be so impressed by someone's services that you feel you want to tip, go ahead—the receiver will certainly not be offended, although he or she may be surprised. The exception is at Japanese inns (see page 47), where the chambermaid should receive around 10 percent.

PAYING THE BILL

The bill, please.	お勘定お願いします。	oh-KAHN-JOH oh-NEH-GAHY sh'MAHss.
How much is it?	おいくらですか？	oh-IH-K'LAH DEss KAH?

TELLING TIME

In general, punctuality is important in Japan, so make sure you're on time for meetings and other gatherings. In fact, transportation systems usually run on such a precise schedule that there's a joke about being able to set your watch by the arrival or departure time of trains!

What time is it?	今何時ですか？	IH-mah NAHn-jih dess KAH?
It's…	_____です。	_____ dess.
• three o'clock.	• 三時	• SAHn-jih
• three-fifteen.	• 三時十五分	• SAHn-jin Ju -goh fun
• three-thirty.	• 三時半	• SAHN-JIH HAHn
• two forty-five.	• 二時四十五分	• NIH-jih YOHN-ju-GOH-fun

• three-ten. • ten to three.	• 三時十分 • 三時十分前	• SAHn-jih JUT-pun • SAHN-jih jut-PUN mah-eh
• midnight. • noon. • three A.M. • three P.M. • six P.M.	• 真夜中 • 正午 • 午前三時 • 午後三時 • 夜の六時	• mah-YOH-nah-kah • SHOh-goh • GOH-zen SAHn-jih • GOH-goh SAHn-jih • YOH-lu noh loh-KU-jih
five minutes ago	五分前	goh-FUn-mah-eh
in a half hour	三十分後	sahn-jut-pun-goh
since seven P.M.	午後七時から	GOH-goh shih-CHIH-jih kah-lah
after eight P.M.	午後八時以後	GOH-goh hah-CHIH-JIH IH-goh
before nine A.M.	午前九時前	GOH-zen ku-JIH MAH-eh
When does it begin?	いつ始まりますか？	IH-ts hah-JIH-MAH-LIH-MAHss KAH?
[I/he/she] came on time.	時間通りに来ました。	jih-KAHN-DOh-lih nih kih-MAHsh-tah.

THE 24-HOUR CLOCK

The Japanese often use the 24-hour clock for official matters, especially in transportation schedules. This system is similar to military time in the United States; simply add 12 to all times beyond 12 P.M.

12 A.M.	0:00	零時	LAY-jih
1 A.M.	1:00	一時	ih-CHIH-jih
2 A.M.	2:00	二時	NIH-jih
3 A.M.	3:00	三時	SAHn-jih

4 A.M.	4:00	四時	YOH-jih
5 A.M.	5:00	五時	GOH-jih
6 A.M.	6:00	六時	loh-KU-jih
7 A.M.	7:00	七時	shih-CHIH-jih
8 A.M.	8:00	八時	hah-CHIH-jih
9 A.M.	9:00	九時	KU-jih
10 A.M.	10:00	十時	Ju-jih
11 A.M.	11:00	十一時	JU-IH-CHIH-jih
12 P.M.	12:00	十二時	JU-NIH-jih
1 P.M.	13:00	十三時	JU-SAHn-jih
2 P.M.	14:00	十四時	JU-YOH-jih
3 P.M.	15:00	十五時	JU-GOH-jih
4 P.M.	16:00	十六時	JU-LOH-KU-jih
5 P.M.	17:00	十七時	JU-SHIH-CHIH-jih
6 P.M.	18:00	十八時	JU-HAH-CHIH-jih
7 P.M.	19:00	十九時	JU-KU-jih
8 P.M.	20:00	二十時	NIH-Ju-jih
9 P.M.	21:00	二十一時	NIH-ju ih-CHIH-jih
10 P.M.	22:00	二十二時	NIH-ju NIH-jih
11 P.M.	23:00	二十三時	NIH-ju SAHN-jih

2 / AT THE AIRPORT

ようこそ日本へ (YOH-koh-soh nih-HOHn eh!)
Welcome to Japan!

Customs formalities at Japanese airports should proceed smoothly. Nonresidents of Japan may bring 400 cigarettes or 100 cigars or 500 grams of tobacco, 3 bottles of alcohol, 2 ounces of perfume, or other items up to ¥200,000 in value duty-free. Customs officials at major airports will understand English to some degree. However, the dialogue and vocabulary below may help you to get through passport control.

DIALOGUE: IMMIGRATION AND CUSTOMS
入国審査／税関 NYU-KOHK SHin-sah/ZEH-KAHN

係官：kah-KAH-LIH kahn	パスポートを見せて下さい。	pahss-POH-toh oh MIH-seh-teh k'dah-sahy.
観光客：KAHN-KOh-kyahk	はい。	HAHy.
係官：kah-KAH-LIH kahn	アメリカ人ですか？	ah-MEH-LIH-KAH-JIN dess KAH?
観光客：KAHN-KOh-kyahk	はい、そうです。	HAHY, SOh-dess.
係官：kah-KAH-LIH-kahn	日本には何日滞在しますか？	nih-HOHn nih wah NAHn-nih-chih tahY-ZAHY SH'MAHss kah?
観光客：KAHN-KOh-kyahk	一週間です。	iss-SHU-kan dess.

Officer:	Please show me your passport.
Tourist:	Sure.
Officer:	Are you an American?
Tourist:	Yes, that's right.
Officer:	How long will you stay in Japan?
Tourist:	For a week.

AIRPORT ARRIVAL

What is your nationality?	あなたの国籍は？	ah-NAH-tah noh kohk-SEH-KIH WAH?
I'm an American.	アメリカ人です。	ah-MEH-LIH-KAH JIn dess.
What's your name?	お名前は？	oh-NAH-MAH-EH WAH?
(My name) is_____.	_____です。	_____ dess.
Where are you staying?	滞在先はどちらですか？	tahy-zahy sah-kih wah DOH-ch'lah dess KAH?
(I'm staying) at the _____Hotel.	_____ホテルです。	_____ HOH-teh-lu dess.
Are you here on vacation(i.e., a tourist)?	観光ですか？	KAHN-K<u>OH</u> DEss KAH?
Yes, I'm on vacation.	はい、観光です。	HAHy, KAHN-K<u>OH</u> DEss.
I'm just passing through.	乗り継ぎです。	noh-LIH-TS'GIH DEss.
I'm here on a business trip.	仕事で来ました。	shih-GOH-TOH DEH KIH-MAHsh-tah.

AT THE AIRPORT

I plan to be here for… • a week. • several weeks. • a few days.	_____いる予定です。 • 一週間 • 数週間 • 数日間	_____ ih-LU YOH-TEH DEss. • iss-SHU-kahn • SU-SHU-kahn • SU-JITS-kahn
Please open this bag.	荷物を開けて下さい。	NIH-mohts oh ah-KEH-TEH K'DAH-SAHy.
You have to pay duty on these items.	これらには関税がかかります。	koh-LEH-lah nih wah KAHN-ZEH GAH kah-KAH-LIH-MAHss.
It's for my own personal use.	自分で使うものです。	jih-BUN DEH TS'KAH-U MOH-noh dess.
These are gifts.	お土産です。	oh-MIH-YAH-GEH DEss.
I have nothing to declare.	申告する物は何もありません。	SHIN-KOHK s'LU MOH-NOH wah nah-NIH-MOH ah-LIH-MAH-SEn.
Nothing to Declare/Duty Free	免税	meN-ZEH
Goods to Declare	税関申告	ZEH-KAHN SHIn koh-ku

LUGGAGE AND PORTERS

Baggage carts are available at most airports (sometimes for a fee). Porters are less common, but they may be available at some airports for a set fee per piece of luggage.

Where can I find a porter?	ポーターはどこですか？	POH-TAH WAH DOH-koh dess KAH?

I need a baggage cart.	カートを借りたいんですが。	KAh-toh oh kah-LIH-TAHy-n dess gah.
This is mine.	これは私のです。	koh-LEH WAH wah-TAHSH NOH dess.
Take my bags to ...	荷物を_____まで運んで下さい。	NIH-mohts oh _____ mah-deh hah-KOHN-DEH K'DAH-SAHy.
• the taxi • the bus stop • the coin lockers	• タクシー • バス停 • コインロッカー	• TAHK-shee • bahss-TEH • koh-IN LOHT-kah
Be careful, please!	気をつけて下さい！	kih-OH-TS'KEH-teh k'dah-sahy!
How much is that?	おいくらですか？	oh-IH-K'LAH DEHss KAH?

AIRPORT TRANSPORTATION AND SERVICES

The New Tokyo International Airport (Narita Airport) is about a two-hour drive from Tokyo, so it's very expensive to travel from the airport to Tokyo by taxi. It's better to take the Airport Limousine Bus that goes to many major hotels in Tokyo, or the new train system called the Narita Express, which can get you from the airport to Tokyo Station in under an hour (call JNTO for more specific information about both).

Which bus goes to _____ hotel in Tokyo?	東京の_____ホテル行きのバスはどれですか？	TOH-KYOH NOH _____HOH-TEH-LU IH-KIH NOH BAHss wah DOH-leh dess KAH?
Could you let me know when we're there?	着いたら教えてくれますか？	TSU-ih-tah-lah oh-SHIH-EH-TEH K'LEH-MAHss KAH?

Where is/are...	_____はどこですか？	_____ wah DOH-koh dess KAH?
• the car rental agencies?	• レンタカーのカウンター	• LEN-TAH KAh noh kah-UN-TAH
• the taxis?	• タクシー	• TAHK-shee
• the duty-free shops?	• 免税品店	• MEN-ZEH-HIn ten
• the bus stop?	• バス停	• bahss-TEH
• the bus to Tokyo?	• 東京行きのバス	• TOH-KYOH-YU-KIH NOH BAHss
• the train to Tokyo?	• 東京行きの電車	• TOH-KYOH-YU-KIH NOH DEn-shah
• an information booth?	• 案内所	• ahn-nahy-joh
• the ticket counter?	• チケットカウンター	• chih-KET-TOH KAH-un-tah
• the luggage check-in?	• チェックインカウンター	• chet-KU-IN KAH-un-tah
• the bank?	• 銀行	• ghin-koh
• the bathroom?	• お手洗	• oh-TEH-AH-LAHy
• the exit?	• 出口	• DEH-g'chih
• a phone?	• 電話	• den-wah

FLIGHT ARRANGEMENTS

Is there a direct flight to Okinawa?	沖縄へ直行便はありますか？	oh-KIH-NAH-WAH EH choht-KOH-BIN WAH ah-LIH-MAHss KAH?
What time does it leave?	何時に出ますか？	NAHn-jih nih deh-MAHss KAH?
I'd like...	_____をお願いします。	_____ oh oh-NEH-GAHY sh'MAHss.
• a one-way ticket.	• 片道切符	• kah-TAH-MICH KIT-pu
• a round-trip ticket.	• 往復切符	• OH-HU-KU KIT-pu
• a seat in first class.	• ファーストクラスの席	• FAH-S'TOH KU-lahss noh SEH-kih

• a seat in coach class.	• エコノミークラスの席	• eh-KOH-NOH-MEE KU-lahss noh SEH-kih
• a seat in the non-smoking section.	• 禁煙席	• KIN En seh-kih
• a window seat.	• 窓際の席	• mah-DOH-GIH-WAH NOH SEH-kih
• an aisle seat.	• 通路側の席	• TSU-LOH-GAH-WAH NOH SEH-kih
What is the arrival time?	何時に着きますか？	NAHn-jih nih ts'KIH-MAHss KAH?
Do I need to change planes?	乗り継ぎの必要がありますか？	noh-LIH-TS'GIH NOH hih-TSU-YOH GAH ah-LIH-MAHss KAH?
When is check-in?	チェックインは何時からですか？	chet-KU-In wah NAHn-jih kah-lah dess KAH?
What is the flight number?	何便ですか？	nahN-BIN DEss KAH?
What is the gate number?	何番ゲートですか？	nahN-BAHN GEh-toh dess KAH?
I'd like to _____ my reservation for flight number [43].	[43]便の予約を_____したいんですが。	[YOHn-ju-SAHn] bin noh yoh-YAH-KU oh _____ shih-TAHY-n dess gah.
• confirm	• 確認	• kah-KU-NIN
• cancel	• キャンセル	• KYAHn-seh-lu
• change	• 変更	• heN-KOH
I'd like to check these bags.	この荷物をチェックしたいんですが。	koh-NOH NIH-mohts oh CHET-ku shih-TAHy-n dess gah.
I have only these carry-ons.	持込手荷物はこれしかありません。	mohch-KOH-MIH TEH-NIH-mohts

		wah koh-LEH shih-kah ah-LIH-MAH-SEn.
I would like my boarding pass.	搭乗券を下さい。	TOH-JOh-ken oh k'DAH-SAHy.
Will they be serving a meal?	機内食は出ますか？	kih-NAHy-shohk wah deh-MAHss KAH?
I missed my plane.	乗り遅れました。	noh-LIH-OH-K'LEH MAHsh tah.
Will my ticket be good for the next flight?	このチケットは次の便に使えますか？	koh-NOH-CHIH-KET-toh wah ts'GIH-noh bin nih ts'KAH-EH MAHss KAH?

HELPFUL SIGNS

Below is a list of the various signs you may encounter in Japan. Some may be in English, especially in areas with heavy tourist traffic. Unfortunately, the English translations are often inaccurate (and sometimes humorous), so it is safer to refer to this list. Words on road signs, as well as pictures of the signs, are included in chapter 9 (page 124 – 25).

貸します	kah-SHIH-MAHss	For Rent
エレベーター	eh-LEH-BEh-tah	Elevator
エスカレーター	ess-KAH-LEh-tah	Escalator
注意	CHu-ih	Caution
熱湯注意	net-TOH CHU-ih	Caution: Boiling Water
売物	u-LIH-MOH-NOH	For Sale
私道	shih-DOH	Private Road
猛犬注意	MOH-KEN CHu-ih	Beware of Dog

危険	kih-KEN	Danger
立入禁止	tah-CHEE-LIH KIN-SHIH	Keep Out
禁煙	kin-en	No Smoking
学校	gaht-KOH	School
お勘定	oh-KAHN-JOH	Cashier
ペットお断り	PEt-toh oh-KOH-TOH-WAH-LIH	No Pets
女	ohn-nah	Woman/Women
男	oh-TOH-KOH	Man/Men
飲料水	iN-LYoh-su-ih	Drinking Water
入口	ih-LIH-G'CHIH	Entrance
この水飲めません	koh-NOH MIH-ZU noh-MEH-MAH-SEn	Do Not Drink This Water
故障	koh-SHOH	Out of Order
閉店	heh-ten	Closed (for stores)
切符売場	kit-PU U-lih-bah	Ticket Window
高圧危険	KOH-AHTS kih-KEN	Danger: High Voltage
営業時間	AY-GYOH JIH-kahn	Business Hours
病院	byoh-in	Hospital
______禁止	_____ kiN-SHIH	Do Not ...
祝祭日	shu-KU-SAHy-jits	Holidays
空き	ah-KIH	Vacant
起こさないで下さい	oh-KOH-SAH-nahy-deh k'DAH-SAHy	Do Not Disturb (lit., Do Not Wake)
触らないで下さい	sah-WAH-LAH-NAHy deh k'DAH-SAHy	Do Not Touch
使用中	shih-YOH-CHU	Occupied

営業中	eh-gyoh-chu	Open
_____時より_____時まで営業	_____jih yoh-lih _____jih mah-deh EH-GYOH	Open from_____ to _____
地下道	chih-KAH-doh	Underground Passage
地下街	chih-KAH-gahy	Underground Shopping Mall
ペンキぬりたて	peN-KIH nu-LIH TAH-TEH	Wet Paint
押す	oh-SU	Push
引く	hih-KU	Pull
従業員室	JU-GYOH-In shih-tsu	Staff Only
案内所	ahN-NAHY-JOH	Information
_____番線	_____bahn-sen	Track No._____
予約席	yoh-YAHK seh-kih	Reserved Seats
待合室	mah-CHIH-AHy-shih-tsu	Waiting Room
大売出し／セール	OH-U-lih-dah-shih/SEh-lu	Sales, Discounts
ブザー	BU-zah	Bell, Buzzer
出口	DEH-g'chih	Exit
非常口	hih-JOh-g'chih	Emergency Exit
予約制	yoh-YAHK-SEH	By Appointment
駐車禁止	chu-shah kin-shih	No Parking
お手洗	oh-TEH-AH-lahy	Rest room(s)
_____番ホーム	_____BAHN HOH-mu	Platform No._____
時刻表	jih-KOH-KU HYOH	Time Schedule

3 / FINDING YOUR WAY

DIALOGUE: ON THE STREET 街中で mah-CHIH-NAH-KAH DEH

観光客： KAHN-KOh-kyahk	すみません、秋葉原へはどう行けばいいですか？	s'MIH-MAH-SEn, ah-KIH-HAH-bah-lah[1] eh wah DOh ih-keh-bah EE-dess KAH?
日本人： nih-HOHN-JIn	ここからそう遠くないですよ。真っ直ぐ行けば左側にあります。	koh-KOH-KAH-LAH SOH TOH-KU NAHy dess YOH. Mahss-SU-gu ih-KEH-bah hih-DAH-LIH-GAH-WAH NIH ah-LIH-MAHss.
観光客： KAHN-KOh-kyahk	そうですか、どうも。じゃあ、歩いて行けますね。	SOH-dess kah, DOh-moh. JYAh, ah-LU-ih-teh ih-KEH-MAHss NEH.
日本人： nih-HOHN-JIn	はい、もちろん。	HAHy, moh-CHIH-lohn.

Tourist:	Excuse me, how can I get to Akihabara?
Japanese:	It's not far from here. Continue straight ahead and it will be on your left.
Tourist:	I see. Thank you. So I can walk there?
Japanese:	Yes, of course.

[1] ah-KIH-HAH-bah-lah (秋葉原 *romaji*: Akihabara) is a famous district in Tokyo that is filled with electronics stores. It is near the Akihabara station on the Yamanote and Sobu train lines.

FINDING YOUR WAY IN TOKYO

Tokyo is an old city that became the booming capital of Japan about 400 years ago. A great majority of its streets, some of them quite old and narrow, sprawl about in a seemingly random fashion. The city is divided into twenty-three "wards"(区 ku), and each ward is divided into many districts. Addresses are sometimes difficult to locate, even for a native of Tokyo; sometimes taxi drivers cannot find their way to a specific address unless you show them where it is on a map. It is best to carry a good map of Tokyo showing the major train lines and their stops. Most tourist attractions will be listed on these maps. Also, many buildings are known by their names (e.g.,The Shinjuku Sumitomo Building) rather than their addresses, so it's easier to ask for directions if you know the name beforehand. You can call an establishment ahead of time to get directions as well, and if you are staying at a hotel, your concierge will be able to help you with an address.

WALKING AROUND

Since Tokyo is quite big and its streets do not follow a comprehensive grid, it would be easiest to take advantage of the extensive train system to get you to the general neighborhood you want to explore, then walk around the area with a map in hand. In the city center, street names are displayed(in Japanese), but be aware that in some older areas and in the outskirts, some streets do not have names.

In providing street directions, the Japanese usually refer to the distance in meters, since street patterns are often irregular. They may also point out landmarks such as traffic lights and tall buildings.

Excuse me ...	すみません(が)...	s'MIH-MAH-SEn (gah)...
Where is _____?	_____はどこですか？	_____ wah DOH-koh dess KAH?
Do you have a map of Tokyo?	東京の地図はありますか？	TOH-KYOH NOH CHIH-zu wah ah-LIH-MAHss KAH?
Where is that on my map?	それはこの地図ではどこですか？	soh-LEH-WAH koh-NOH CHIH-zu deh-wahDOH-koh dess KAH?
Can I walk there?	歩いて行けますか？	ah-LU-ih-teh ih-KEH-MAHss KAH?
How far is it?	どれぐらいかかりますか？	DOH-leh g'lahy kah-KAH-LIH-MAHss KAH?
I'm lost.	道に迷ったんですが。	mih-CHIH NIH mah-YOHT-tahn dess gah.
Where can I find this address?	この住所はどの辺でしょうか？	koh-NOH Ju-shoh wah doh-NOH HEN deh-SHOh kah?
How long does it take on foot?	歩いて何分ですか？	ah-LU-ih-teh NAHn-pun dess KAH?

Here are a few possible responses to your questions:

_____です。	_____ dess.	It's ...
• 真っ直ぐ	• mahss-SU-gu	• straight ahead.
• 真正面	• mah-SHOh-men	• directly in front.
• つきあたり	• ts'KIH-AH-TAH-LIH	• at the end of the street.
• 左	• hi-DAH-LIH	• left.
• 右	• mih-GIH	• right.
• あちら／あっち	• ah-CHIH-LAH/aht-CHIH	• over there/that way.
• こちら／こっち	• koh-CHIH-LAH/koht-CHIH	• over here/this way.

• [ホテル]の後ろ	• [HOH-teh-lu] noh u-SHIH-LOH	• behind [the hotel].
• [ホテル]の前	• [HOH-teh-lu] noh MAH-eh	• in front of [the hotel].
• [ホテル]の隣	• [HOH-teh-lu] noh toh-NAH-LIH	• next to [the hotel].
• [ホテル]の近く	• [HOH-teh-lu] noh CHIH-KAHk	• near [the hotel].
• [ホテル]の向う	• [HOH-teh-lu] noh mu-KOH	• beyond [the hotel].
交差点	koh-sah-ten	intersection
信号	shin-goh	traffic light
交差点で右に曲がって下さい。	KOH-SAH-TEN DEH mih-GIH NIH mah-GAHT-TEH k'DAH-SAHy.	Turn right at the intersection.
歩いては行けません。	ah-LU-ih-teh wah ih-KEH-MAH-SEn.	You can't walk there.

PUBLIC TRANSPORTATION

Tokyo has an extensive and convenient system of trains and subways that run throughout the metropolitan area. The trains are generally clean and very safe, and the fares are reasonable, considering the prices of everything else in Japan. The trains are run by Japan Railways(JR), which operates four lines: Yamanote, Chuo, Sobu, and Keihin Tohoku. You can use your Japan Rail Pass on these trains (for information on the Rail Pass, see page 42). There are ten subway lines, which are run by two different authorities, Eidan and Toei. All of the cars in both the train and the subway systems are color coded for easy identification. Tickets may be purchased at the station from two different sources: from the automatic ticket machines, or from the manned ticket booth. There is often a map of the train lines above the machines, with the station names written in *romaji* and the appropriate fare underneath. Some machines take ¥1,000 bills, but others only take change. If you are planning to use trains and subways extensively, you can purchase an "Orange Card" for the JR lines and a "Metrocard" for the subways at any ticket booth. You pay a flat fee in advance to buy these cards, and you insert them into designated vending machines that will deduct the price of the ticket you want to purchase. One way to make sure that you don't overpay is to buy the cheapest ticket (i.e., for the shortest trip), and the person who takes your ticket when you reach your destination will charge you the difference. Always remember to keep the ticket you purchased, because you will have to turn it in at the end of your trip. Neither the JR lines nor the subways run all night; though the last-train and first-train times vary, the lines close soon after midnight, and resume operation at approximately 5:00 A.M.

Bus routes are rather complicated and much less suited for non-Japanese speakers than trains and subways because of fewer English signs. Thus it is best to avoid them if you can, unless you have detailed directions at hand. Buses usually stop running earlier than trains and subways.

USING THE SUBWAY AND JR LINES

subway	地下鉄	chih-KAH-TETS
train	電車	DEn-shah
JR line	JR線	jay-ah-lu sen
ticket	切符	kit-PU
station	駅	EH-kih
Where's the nearest station?	一番近い駅はどこですか？	ih-CHIH-BAHN chih-KAHy eh-kih wah DOH-koh dess KAH?

What line goes to _____?	_____へ行くのは何線ですか？	_____ eh ih-KU noh wah nah-NIH SEN dess KAH?
Does this train stop at _____?	この電車は_____に止まりますか？	koh-NOH DEn-shah wah _____nih toh-MAH-LIH-MAHss KAH?
Is this the train to _____?	この電車は_____行ですか？	koh-NOH DEn-shah wah _____ YU-KIH DEss KAH?
Where do I change to go to _____?	_____へ行くにはどこで乗り換えたらいいですか。	_____eh ih-KU nih wah DOH-koh deh noh-LIH-KAH-eh tah-lah EE dess KAH?
Do I get off here to go to _____?	_____へ行くにはここで降りるんですか？	_____ eh ih-KU nih wah koh-KOH DEH oh-LIH-lun-dess KAH?

Subway/JR Line Signs

きっぷうりば	kit-PU U-lih bah	Tickets (both manned booths and vending machines)
改札口	KAHY-SAHTS-g'chih	Ticket Check (equivalent to turnstiles)
出口／入口	DEH-g'chih/ih-LIH-G'CHIH	exit/entrance

ON THE BUS

What bus do I take to go to _____?	_____へ行くにはどのバスに乗ればいいですか？	_____ EH ih-KU nih wah DOH-noh bahss nih noh-LEH-bah ee dess KAH?

Where is the nearest bus stop?	一番近いバス停はどこですか？	ih-CHIH-BAHN ch'KAHy bahss teh wah DOH-koh dess KAH?
Does this bus go to _____?	このバスは_____へ行きますか？	koh-NOH BAHss wah _____eh ih-KIH MAHss KAH?
When is the next bus to _____?	_____への次のバスはいつ出ますか？	_____eh noh ts' GIH noh bahss wah IH-ts deh-MAHss KAH?
What is the fare to _____?	_____までいくらですか？	_____MAH-deh IH-k'lah dess KAH?
I want to get off at _____.	_____で降りたいんです。	_____deh oh-LIH-TAHy-n-dess.
Please tell me when I should get off.	着いたら教えて下さい。	TSU-ih-tah-lah oh-SHIH-EH-TEH K'DAH-SAHy.
Do I need to change buses?	乗り換えが必要ですか？	noh-LIH-KAH-EH GAH hih-TSU-YOH DEss KAH?

Bus Signs

バス停	bahss TEH	Bus Stop
時刻表	jih-KOHK HYOH	Time Schedule

TAKING A TAXI

Taxis are clean, safe, and very convenient, and they are the only method of transportation during the hours past midnight after the trains stop running. They operate like taxis in the United States. You can identify an available taxi by a lighted sign located inside the front windshield that says empty (空車 ku-shah). At most places, you can hail a taxi anywhere you see one, but the downtown areas of certain cities may have designated taxi stands. Also, in the suburbs, you may have to call a taxi company to come pick you up since it's harder to catch one off the main roads. Meters are always used, and you almost never have to worry about getting swindled by a taxi driver, except for very rare occasions (e. g., in a bar district during very late hours, there may be "gypsy cabs" that overcharge you; make sure the meter is turned on when you get into the car). Night rates are expensive (as much as 30 percent more than the normal fare), so make sure you have an ample supply of cash, especially if you're traveling far. The time that these rates go into effect varies, so ask your driver.

Where is the nearest taxi stand?	一番近いタクシー乗り場はどこですか？	ih-CHIH-BAHN CHIH-KAHy tahk-SHEE noh-lih-bah wah DOH-koh dess KAH?
Can I get a taxi around here?	この辺でタクシーは拾えますか？	koh-NOH-HEN DEH TAHK-shee wah hih-LOH-EH MAHss KAH?
Taxi!	タクシー！	TAHK-shee!
What time do night rates begin?	夜間料金は何時からですか？	yah-KAHN LYOh-kin wah NAHn-jih kah-lah dess KAH?
How much is your night rate?	夜間料金はいくらですか？	yah-KAHN LYOh-kin wah IH-k'lah dehss KAH?
Please take me to …	_____までお願いします。	_____MAH-deh oh-NEH-GAHY SH'MAHss.
• the airport.	• 空港	• ku-koh
• Tokyo Station.	• 東京駅	• TOH-KYOh eh-kih
• the bus station.	• バスターミナル	• bahss TAh-mih-nah-lu

• Shinjuku.	• 新宿	• shin-juk
• the Hotel _____.	• _____ホテル	• _____ HOH-teh-lu
• this address.	• この住所	• koh-NOH Ju-shoh
• this restaurant.	• このレストラン	• koh-NOH LEII-s'toh-lahn
• this store.	• この店	• koh-NOH MIH-SEH
How much is it to _____?	_____までいくらですか？	_____MAH-deh IH-K'LAH DEss KAH?
I'm in a hurry.	急いでるんです。	ih-SOy-deh-lun-dess.
Stop here, please.	ここで止めて下さい。	koh-KOH DEH toh-MEH-TEH K'DAH-SAHy.
Please wait here; I'll be right back.	ここで待っていて下さい。すぐ戻ります。	koh-koh deh MAHT-teh-ih-teh k'dah-sahy. S'gu moh-DOH-LIH-MAHss.
How much is it?	おいくらですか？	oh-IH-K'LAH DEss KAH?

GOING LONG DISTANCES BY TRAIN

Intercity trains are operated either by Japan Rail (JR)or by private companies. JR is the most extensive train system that runs throughout the country. The famous "bullet train" (新幹線 SHIN-KAHn-sen) is run by JR, and it is the most convenient method of travel between major cities, though a bit expensive. For example, it takes two hours to travel from Tokyo to Nagoya by the bullet train, whereas it would take five to six hours by car. Service is very reliable. Other long-distance trains are slower, but equally convenient. As mentioned before, train schedules are very precise; this means that you can expect to leave on time, and that if you're late, plan to catch the next train instead.

To purchase a ticket, go to the designated long-distance train ticket booths, called "Green Ticket Windows" (みどりの窓口 MIH-doh-lih noh mah-DOH-g'chih). You can buy unreserved seats (自由席 jih-Yu-seh-kih) or reserved seats (指定席 sh'TEh-seh-kih); the latter are slightly more expensive. For the bullet trains, there is a first-class section called "Green Cars" (グリーンカー g'LEEn kah), which is significantly more expensive than regular class seats but offers no exceptional benefits; therefore first class is not recommended. If you are on a long-distance express train other than the bullet train, make sure you purchase an express ticket (特急券 toht-KYu-ken) besides the regular ticket at the ticket booth or from the conductor on the train, since the regular ticket by itself is good for a local train only.

Private train systems vary, and some can be rather complicated. When in doubt, ask someone at the ticket booth.

Japan Rail Pass

If you are planning to travel by JR train throughout Japan, the Japan Rail Pass is a very good deal. There are one-, two-, or three-week passes that give you unlimited access to JR trains across the country for that time period. They are available to non-Japanese citizens with tourist visas. You must purchase a pass in the United States before leaving on your trip, and you can buy one from bigger Japanese travel agencies located in major U.S. cities; the Japan National Tourist Office nearest you will be able to refer you to one of these agencies.

Sleeping Arrangements

There are long-distance trains that travel overnight. These tickets can also be purchased at the Green Windows. There are usually two classes of seats available, but service varies, so ask the person at the ticket booth for details.

Meals

Most long-distance trains have dining cars, though the meals are expensive for what they are. Vendors will come to your seat selling various snacks and drinks. You can also buy boxed lunches (お弁当 oh-BEN-TOH) from these vendors or from kiosks on the platform when your train stops briefly at a station. However, be aware of two things: some of the contents of these boxed lunches may be for the adventurous, and make sure you don't linger too long on the platform, for stops may be very short.

English	Japanese	Pronunciation
Where is/are the...	_____はどこですか？	_____ wah DOH-koh dess KAH?
• train station?	• 駅	• EH-kih
• ticket window (Green Window)?	• みどりの窓口	• MIH-doh-lih noh mah-DOH-g'chih
• platform?	• ホーム	• HOh-mu
• lost and found?	• 遺失物取り扱い所	• ih-SH'TS-buts toh-LIH-AHTS-KAHY JOH
• coin lockers?	• コインロッカー	• koh-IN LOHT-kah
Where is/are the _____car (s)?	_____は何号車ですか？	_____ wah NAHN-GOh-shah dess KAH?
• reserved-seat	• 指定席	• sh'TEh-seh-kih
• unreserved-seat	• 自由席	• jih-YU-seh-kih
• sleeping	• 寝台車	• SHIN-DAHy shah
• non-smoking	• 禁煙車	• KIN-En shah
I'd like a (n) _____ ticket to Kyoto.	京都まで_____一枚下さい。	KYOh-toh mah-deh _____ ih-CHIH-mahy k'DAH-SAHy.
• reserved	• 指定席券	• sh'TEH-SEH-KIH KEN
• unreserved	• 自由席券	• jih-YU-SEH-KIH KEN
• express	• 特急券	• toht-KYu ken
• one-way	• 片道	• kah-TAH-MIH -CHIH
• round-trip	• 往復	• oh-hu-ku

When does the next train leave?	次の電車はいつ出ますか？	ts'GIH-noh DEn-shah wah IH-ts deh-mahss KAH?
Does this train stop in _____?	______に止まりますか？	_____ nih toh-MAH-LIH-MAHss KAH?
From which platform does it leave?	何番ホームから出ますか？	NAHN-BAHN HOh-mu kah-lah deh-MAHss KAH?
Where does the non-smoking car stop?	禁煙車はどこに止まりますか？	KIN-En-shah wah DOH-koh nih toh-MAH-LIH-MAHss KAH?
Is the train on time?	時間通り出ますか？	jih-KAHN DOh-lih deh-MAHss KAH?
Do I need to change trains in _____?	_____で乗り換えが必要ですか？	_____ deh noh-LIH-KAH-EH GAH hih-TS'YOH DEss KAH?
I'm going to Osaka. Do I need to change trains?	大阪へ行くんですが、乗り換えは必要ですか？	OH-SAH-KAH EH ih-KUn-dess gah, noh-LIH-KAH-EH WAH hih-TS'YOH DEss KAH?
Is this seat free?	この席空いてますか？	koh-NOH SEH-kih ahY-TEH MAHss KAH?
This seat is occupied.	空いていません。	AHY-TEH-MAH-SEn.
Please tell me when we get to [Sendai].	[仙台]へ着いたら教えて下さい。	[SEn-dahy] eh TS'ih-tah-lah oh-SHIH-EH-TEH K'DAH-SAHy.
I forgot something on the train.	電車の中に忘れ物をしました。	DEn-shah noh nah-kah nih wah-S'LEH-MOH-NOH OH sh'MAHsh-tah.

Train Signs

みどりの窓口	MIH-doh-lih noh mah-DOH-g'chih	Long Distance Train Ticket Window
_____番ホーム	_____BAHN HOh-mu	Platform No._____
_____方面	_____HOh-men	(Train)Toward _____
上り	noh-BOH-LIH	(Train)Toward Tokyo
下り	ku-DAH-LIH	(Train)Away From Tokyo
禁煙席	KIN-En seh-kih	No Smoking Seats

Types of Train Services

特急	toht-KYU	Super Express
急行	kyu-koh	Express
準急	jun-kyu	Semi-Express
普通	hu-TSU	Local

TRAVELING BY BOAT

Most of your boat trips in Japan will be fairly short. In general, you will encounter either ferry boats or small tour boats, and a trip usually lasts less than half a day. There are some ferry lines along the Japan Sea and along northern Japan that run overnight trips. For more information, inquire at your local Japan National Tourist Organization or your travel agency.

When is the next boat for _____?	_____行の次の船はいつ出ますか？	_____yu-kih noh ts'GIH noh hu-neh wah IH-ts deh-MAHss KAH?

From where does the boat leave?	船はどこから出ますか？	HU-neh wah DOH-koh kah-lah deh-MAHss KAH?
How long is the crossing?	何時間かかりますか？	NAHN-JIH-kahn kah-KAH-LIH-MAHss KAH?
Where does the boat stop?	船はどこに止まりますか？	HU-neh wah DOH-koh nih toh-MAH-LIH-MAHss KAH?
How much is it per person for …	_____は一人いくらですか？	_____ wah hih-TOH-lih IH-k'lah dess KAH?
• first class?	• 一等室	• it-TOh-shih-tsu
• second class?	• 二等室	• nih-TOh-shih-tsu
• cabin class?	• 三等室	• SAHN-TOh-shih-tsu

4 / ACCOMMODATIONS

TYPES OF HOTELS AND INNS

There are several types of accommodations available within a wide range of prices in Japan. You can stay in anything from luxury Western-style hotels to Japanese inns, to minuscule "capsule hotels" that give you only space to sleep.

Keep in mind that during certain times of the year, lodgings near famous tourist attractions will be very crowded. Peak seasons are during summer vacations (mid-July to end of August), around New Year's Day (end of December to the beginning of January), spring vacation (end of March), and the "Golden Week" holidays (April 29 to May 5). If you are planning to travel during these times, make sure you have hotel reservations before you leave. It is best to make reservations at all of your lodgings as a general rule, as some of the more popular establishments will sell out quickly regardless of the time of year.

In most of the major cities, there are expensive Western-style hotels (ホテル HOH-teh-lu), some of them belonging to international chains. You can enjoy the conveniences you expect from the same kind of hotel in the United States.

A recommended alternative is to stay in a traditional Japanese inn (旅館 lyoh-KAHN). These are found throughout the country, and are sometimes the only available form of lodging in smaller towns. Prices normally include breakfast and dinner, which are often brought to your room. At these inns, you will have a chance to sleep on genuine futons on *tatami* mats, enjoy a hot bath or hot springs in a large tub, lounge in robe-style *yukatas* after your bath, try fish and rice for breakfast, and otherwise become exposed to some traditional aspects of life in

Japan.[1] Service is impeccable at the more expensive inns; there is a maid who is assigned to your room, and this is one of the rare occasions when you should tip. Give her around 10 percent of the price for one night's stay in advance, when she comes to greet you as soon as you arrive in your room. Make sure you are giving the right person the tip, since several employees may enter your room. Ask her, "Are you in charge of this room?" (係の方ですか？ KAH-kah-lih noh kah-TAH dess KAH?) to confirm. (It is not absolutely vital to tip, and since you are a tourist from abroad, the maid will not be too offended if you don't. The worst mistake is to tip too little; if you don't want to give her 10 percent, then it's better not to tip at all, for giving her small change is considered offensive.) You can also contact the Japan Ryokan Association for more information about these types of inns (1-8-3 Marunouchi, Chiyoda-ku, Tokyo, tel.[03]3231-5310).

Country inns (民宿 miN-SHU-KU) are similar to American bed-and-breakfasts. These are small, family-operated inns that are less expensive than traditional inns (rates vary according to region) where you can get lodging with breakfast and dinner. Of course, service is much less than at traditional inns, and you should remember to bring your own towels. There is a Japan Minshuku Association, which will have more specific information

[1] A note about baths in Japan: There are two types of baths you may encounter in a lodging. The first type is the family bath (家族風呂 kah-ZOHK-BU-loh), which is relatively small in size and is used by one family (or, if you prefer, one person) at a time. When you go to a family bath room and find that others are already using it, wait until they are done. The second type is the large bath (大浴場 dahY-YOHk-joh), which is a public bath. Baths are separated into the "women's bath" (女湯 ohN-NAH-YU) and "men's bath" (男湯 oh-TOH-KOH-YU). You may feel unaccustomed to the fact that others may be taking a bath at the same time. In any bath, remember to scrub up first, always wash off all your soap before entering the tub, and never unplug the drain of the bathtub.

(1-29-5 Takada no baba, Shinjuku-ku, Tokyo, tel.[03]3232-6561).

Business hotels are Western-style hotels, but the rooms are very small and cramped. Rates are reasonable but no meals are included.

Capsule hotels are designed for those who only want space to sleep for the night and nothing else. You pay for a little cubicle with a mattress; your room is about the size of a twin bed and about three feet tall.

Youth hostels are also an alternative. Some require a membership card, which you purchase for a fee from a youth hostel association. The price range is quite reasonable, including two meals, but the service is no-frills and most have curfews at night. For information, contact the Japan Youth Hostel Association (Hoken Kaikan, 1-1 Ichigaya Sadohara-cho, Shinjuku-ku, Tokyo, tel. [03] 3269-5831).

Finally, there are establishments called love hotels, which do not exist for lodging purposes in the usual sense. These hotels are very popular with Japanese couples who want to enjoy some private time in an unusual setting. The rooms are designed for maximum entertainment, and there are some that sport seriously outrageous decor and gimmicks.

DIALOGUE: ARRIVING AT THE INN 宿に着いて YAH-doh nih TSU-ih-teh

フロント： hu-LOHN-TOH	いらっしゃいませ。御予約はございますか？	ih-LAHSS-SHAHY-MAH-seh. Goh-YOH-YAHK WAH goh-ZAHY MAHss KAH?
お客： oh-KYAHK	ええ。名前は[ジャクソン]です。	<u>Eh</u>. nah-MAH-EH WAH [JAHK-sohn] dess.

フロント： hu-LOHN-TOH	ようこそいらっしゃいました。こちらの者がご案内いたします。	YOh-koh-soh ih-LAHSS-SHAHY MAHsh-tah. koh-CHIH-LAH NOH MOH-NOH gah goh-AHN-NAHY IH-TAHSH MAHss.

(You are escorted to your room.)

部屋係： heh-YAH GAH-kah-lih	いらっしゃいませ。私がお世話をさせていただきます田中と申します。どうぞよろしく。お食事は何時にいたしましょうか。	ih-LAHSS-SHAHY MAH-seh. wah-TAHK-SHIH GAH oh-SEH-wah oh sah-SEH-TEH IH-TAH-DAH-KIH-MAHss tah-NAH-KAH toh MOH-SHIH MAHss. DOh-zoh yoh-LOHSH-KU. oh-SHOHK-JIH WAH NAHn-jih nih ih-tahsh-mah-shoh KAH.
お客： oh-KYAHK	七時にお願いします。	shih-CHIH-jih nih oh-NEH-GAHY SH'MAHss.
部屋係： heh-YAH-GAH-kah-lih	かしこまりました。お食事の前にお風呂はいかがですか。ご案内致します。	kahsh-KOH-MAH-LIH MAHsh-tah. oh-SHOHK-JIH NOH MAH-eh nih oh-HU-loh wah ih-KAH-gah dess KAH. goh AHN-NAHY IH-TAHSH-MAHss.
お客： oh-KYAHK	有難う。これ少ないですが…	ah-LIH-gah-toh. koh-leh s'KU-NAHy dess gah…

Clerk:	Welcome. Do you have a reservation?
Guest:	Yes. The name is [Jackson].
Clerk:	We are delighted to have you stay with us. She will escort you to your room.

(You are escorted to your room.)

Maid: (brings tea and sweets)	Welcome. My name is Tanaka and I will be in charge of your room. When would you like to have your meal?
Guest:	I'd like to eat at seven.
Maid:	Certainly. Would you like to take a bath before your meal? I will escort you there.
Guest:	Thank you. (Handing over her tip) This is for you... (lit, This isn't much, but...)

HOTEL ARRANGEMENTS AND SERVICES

I'd like to make a reservation.	予約をしたいんですが。	yoh-YAHK OH sh-TAHy-n dess gah.
I'd like a room for ...	_____部屋をお願いします。	_____ BEH-YAH OH oh-NEH-GAHY SH'MAHss.
• one person. • two people. • three people.	• 一人 • 二人 • 三人	• hih-TOH-lih • hu-TAH-LIH • SAHN-NIn
I'd like a room with ...	_____のある部屋をお願いします。	_____ noh AH-lu heh-YAH oh oh-NEH-GAHY SH' MAHss.
• a private toilet. • a Western-style toilet. • an air conditioner.	• トイレ • 洋式トイレ • エアコン	• TOH-ih-leh • YOH-SHIH-KIH-TOH-ih-leh • eh-AH-KOHN
I'd like a good view from the room.	眺めのいい部屋をお願いします。	nah-GAH-MEH noh Ee heh-yah oh oh-NEH-GAHY SH'MAHss.
Is there hot water?	お湯は出ますか？	oh-YU WAH deh-MAHss KAH?

English	Japanese	Pronunciation
Does the room have a TV?	部屋にテレビはありますか？	heh-YAH nih TEH-leh-bih wah ah-LIH-MAHss KAH?
We'd like to stay for … • one night. • two nights. • three nights. • a week.	_____泊りたいんです。 • 一晩 • 二晩 • 三晩 • 一週間	_____ toh-MAH-LIH TAHy-n-dess. • hih-TOH-bahn • hu-TAH-bahn • mih-BAHN • iss-SHu-kahn
I'd like to change rooms.	部屋を変わりたいんです。	heh-YAH oh kah-WAH-LIH-TAHY-n-dess.
Do you have a room that's a little … • bigger? • quieter? • less expensive?	もう少し_____部屋はありますか？ • 大きい • 静かな • 安い	MOH-S'KOH-shih _____ heh-YAH wah ah-LIH-MAHssKAH? • OH-KEe • SHIH-zu-kah nah • yah-SU-ih
How much is it … • per night? • per week?	_____おいくらですか？ • 一晩 • 一週間	_____ oh-IH-K'LAH DEss KAH? • hih-TOH-bahn • iss-SHu-kahn
Does the price include … • taxes? • service?	値段には_____が入ってますか？ • 税金 • サービス料	neh-DAHN NIH wah _____ gah HAH-it-teh mahss KAH? • zay-kin • SAH-BISS lyoh
Where can I park?	車はどこに止めたらいいでしょうか？	k'LU-MAH WAH DOH-koh nih toh-MEH-TAH-lah Ee-deh-shoh kah?
Please have my bags sent up to my room.	荷物を部屋までお願いします。	NIH-mohts woh heh-YAH mah-deh oh-NEH-GAHY SH'MAHss.

I'd like to put this in your safe.	これを金庫に入れたいんです。	koh-LEH OH KIn-koh nih ih-LEH-TAHy-n dess.
I'd like to speak with …	＿＿をお願いします。	＿＿ oh oh-NEH GAHY SH'MAHss.
• the manager.	• マネージャー	• mah-NEH-jah
• the porter.	• ポーター	• POH-tah
• the maid (at a Western hotel).	• メードさん	• mEH-DOH SAHN
• the maid (at a Japanese inn).	• 部屋の係の人	• heh-YAH NOH KAH-kah-lih noh hih-toh
• the bellboy.	• ベルボーイ	• beh-LU BOhy
I'd like to have …	＿＿をお願いします。	＿＿ oh oh-NEH-GAHY SH'MAHss.
• a blanket.	• 毛布	• MOh-hu
• some hangers.	• ハンガー	• HAHn-gah
• some ice.	• 氷	• koh-lih
• a pillow.	• 枕	• MAH-k'lah
• some stationery.	• 便箋	• bin-sen
• some soap.	• 石鹸	• set-KEN
• a towel.	• タオル	• TAH-oh-lu
• toilet paper.	• トイレットペーパー	• TOY-LET-TOH PEh-pah
Where is the …	＿＿はどこですか？	＿＿ wah DOH-koh dess KAH?
• elevator?	• エレベーター	• eh-LEH-BEh-tah
• garage?	• 駐車場	• chu-shah-joh
• dining room?	• 食堂	• shoh-KU-DOH
• hotel restaurant?	• レストラン	• LEH-s'toh-lahn
• laundry?	• ランドリー	• LAHn-doh-lee
• beauty salon?	• 美容室	• bih-YOh-shih-tsu
The door won't open.	ドアが開かないんです。	DOH-ah gah ah-KAH-NAHy-n-dess.
There is a problem with …	＿＿がおかしいんです。	＿＿ gah oh-KAH-SHEe-n-dess.
• the heater.	• ヒーター	• HEE-tah
• the air conditioner.	• エアコン	• eh-AH-KOHN

There is no hot water.	お湯が出ないんです。	oh-YU GAH DEH-nahy-n-dess.
Please make up my room.	部屋を掃除して下さい。	heh-YAH oh SOH-JIH SH' TEH K'DAH-SAHy.
I'm in room _____ (lit., This is room _____).	_____号室です。	_____ GOh shih-tsu dess.
I'd like to get a baby-sitter.	ベビーシッターを頼みたいんです。	beh-BIH SHIT-tah oh tah-NOH-MIH TAHy-n-dess.
We're leaving tomorrow.	明日発ちます。	ahsh-TAH tah-CHIH MAHss.
We're leaving at 10 A.M.	朝十時に発ちます。	AH-sah Ju-jih nih tah-CHIH-MAHss.
Please prepare the bill.	お勘定をお願いします。	oh-KAHN-JOH oh oh-NEH-GAHY SH'MAHss.
Please call us a taxi.	タクシーを呼んで下さい。	TAHK-shee oh YOHN-DEH K'DAH-SAHy.
Please have my luggage brought downstairs.	荷物を下までお願いします。	NIH-mohts oh sh' TAH MAH-deh oh-NEH-GAHY SH'MAHss.

5 / SOCIALIZING

Meeting new people in Japan may be the most interesting part of your trip. You will probably encounter a wide variety of situations that reflect the differences and the similarities between American and Japanese cultures.

You may find that while some Japanese who don't speak English shy away from talking to you (especially in areas other than Tokyo), others are quite eager to strike up a conversation with you. The majority of Japanese people will make efforts to be extremely polite and will go out of their way to help you if you need it. In starting a conversation, you might think that the Japanese are vague and evasive in some ways, but you might also encounter some personal questions that you might not expect to be asked. If you keep an open mind and make an effort to respect cultural differences, you will have an enriching experience.

If you are traveling on business, remember the following points:

1) Always mention your company or organization name along with your own when you introduce yourself. English equivalent: "My name is _____, and I'm with [company name]."
2) Remember to bring an ample supply of business cards; they are a vital part of introductions. Often, people will just say the equivalent of "This is who I am"(私はこういう者です wah-TAHK-SHIH WAH KOH-YU MOH-noh dess) and hand you their business cards without more of a verbal introduction. (Some Japanese even have "personal cards" with their name, address, and phone number to give to others in purely informal social situations.)

DIALOGUE: INTRODUCING YOURSELF 自己紹介 jih-KOH-SHOh-kahy

ワトソン ジェームズ: WAH-toh-sohn JEh-mu-zu	今日は､始めまして。私はワトソン ジェームズと申します。	KOHN-NIH-CH-WAH, hah-JIH-MEH-MAHSH-teh. wah-TAHK-SHIH WAH WAH-toh-sohn JEh-muzu toh MOH-SHIH MAHss.
加藤文子: KAH-toh HU-mih-koh	どうも､始めまして。加藤文子です。どうぞよろしく。	DOh-moh, hah-JIH-MEH-MAHSH-teh KAH-toh Hu-mih-koh DEss. DOh-zoh yoh-LOHSH-KU.
ワトソン ジェームズ: WAH-toh-sohn JEh-mu-zu	こちらこそ、よろしく。	koh-CHIH-LAH KOH-soh, yoh-LOHSH-KU.
加藤文子: KAH-toh HU-mih-koh	日本には観光でいらしたんですか?	nih-HOHn nih wah KAHN-KOH DEH ih-LAHsh-tahn-dess KAH?
ワトソン ジェームズ: WAH-toh-sohn JEh-mu-zu	ええ、あと一週間いる予定です。	Eh, AH-toh iss-SHu-kahn ih-LU YOH-TEHy DEss.
加藤文子: KAH-toh HU-mih-koh	そうですか。どうぞよいご旅行を。	SOh-dess kah. DOh-zoh YOy goh-LYOH-KOH OH.
ワトソン ジェームズ: WAH-toh-sohn JEh-mu-zu	どうも有難うございます。	DOh-moh ah-LIH-gah-toh goh-ZAHY MAHss.

James Watson:	Hello, how do you do. My name is James Watson.

Humiko Kato:	How do you do, I'm Humiko Kato. Pleased to meet you.
James Watson:	Pleased to meet you, too.
Humiko Kato:	Are you here in Japan to see the sights?
James Watson:	Yes, I plan to be here for another week.
Humiko Kato:	I see. I hope you have a pleasant trip.
James Watson:	Thank you very much.

INTRODUCTIONS

This is _____ [Stein].[1]	こちらは_____の[スタイン]です。	koh-CHIH-LAH WAH _____ noh [s'TAHy-n] dess.
• President _____	• _____社長	• _____ shah-CHOH
• Vice-President _____	• _____副社長	• _____ hu-KU SHAH-choh
• Division Chief _____	• _____部長	• _____ bu-CHOH
• Section Chief _____	• _____課長	• _____ kah-CHOH
Pleased to meet you.	どうぞよろしく。	DOh-zoh yoh-LOHSH-KU.
My name is _____ , I work for [company name].(formal)	私は [company name]の_____と申します。	wah-TAHK-SHIH WAH [company name] noh _____ TOH MOH-SHIH MAHss.

[1] Keep in mind that Japan's society is very conscious of each individual's social status. In introducing someone from your firm, mention the person's position in the firm together with his or her name if that person is in management level or above. Introduce him or her by the last name without adding *sahn* (equivalent to Mr./Ms.). However, if you are being introduced to someone from another firm, use *sahn* after the name to be polite.

My name is _____ . (less formal)	私の名前は______です。	wah-TAHK-SHIH NOH nah-MAH-EH WAH _____ DEss.
What is your name?	お名前は？	oh-NAH-mah-eh WAH?
I am [James Watson] .[1]	[ワトソン　ジェームズ]です。	[WAH-toh-sohn JEh-mu-zu] dess.
This is ...	こちらは_____です。	koh-CHIH-LAH WAH _____ dess.
• my husband.	• 主人	• SHU-jin
• my wife.	• ワイフ/家内	• WAHy-hu/KAH-nahy
• my colleague.	• 同僚	• doh-lyoh
• my friend.	• 友達	• toh-MOH-DAHCH

FIRST CONTACT

Where do you live?	どこにお住いですか？	DOH-koh nih oh-SU-MAHY DEss KAH?
I live in New York.	ニューヨークに住んでいます。	NYU-YOh-ku nih SUn-deh ih-MAHss.
How do you like Japan?	どうですか、日本は…	DOh-dess kah, nih-HOHn wah?
I like Japan very much.	日本は大変気に入りました。	nih-HOHn wah TAHY- HEN kih-NEE-LIH MAHSH-tah.
The people are very kind.	皆さんとても親切です。	mih-NAH-sahn toh-TEH-MOH SHIn-sets dess.

[1] In Japanese, the first name comes after the last name; the Japanese order of James Watson is Watson James. It is acceptable to use the Western order for a foreign name; but you can reverse the order to suit the Japanese way for clarity's sake.

I like the countryside.	田舎が気に入りました。	ih-NAH-KAH GAH kih-NEE-LIH MAHsh-tah.
I find Japan very interesting.	日本はとても興味深い国です。	nih-HOHn wah toh-TEH-MOH KYOH-MIH B'KAHy ku-NIH DEss
What's your profession?[1]	お仕事は何ですか？	oh-SHIH-goh-toh wah NAH-n dess KAH?
I work for a company.	会社に勤めています。	KAHY-SHAH NIH ts'TOH-meh-teh ih-mahss.
I'm ...	_____です。	_____ DEss.
• a student.	• 学生	• gahk-SEH
• a doctor.	• 医者	• ih-SHAH
• a lawyer.	• 弁護士	• BEN-GOH-shih
I'm retired.	定年退職しました。	TEH-NEN TAHy-shohk shih-MAHsh-tah.

TALKING WITH PEOPLE YOU ALREADY KNOW

The phrases below are polite enough to use in most business settings, but not for those occasions that require an extreme degree of formality.

How are you?	お元気ですか？	oh-GHEn-kih dess kah?
I'm fine, thanks.	ええ、元気です。	Eh, GHEn-kih dess.
How's your family?	ご家族はお元気ですか？	goh-KAH-zohk wah oh-GHEn-kih dess KAH?

[1]See chapter 15 for a complete list of occupations.

Very well, thank you.	はい、おかげさまで。	HAHy, oh-KAH-GEH-SAH-MAH DEH.
How's business?	どうですか、仕事の方は。	DOh dess kah, shih-GOH-TOH-NOH HOh wah.
It's going pretty well.	ええ、まあまあですね。	Eh, MAh-MAh dess neh.

MAKING FRIENDS

The phrases below are appropriate for most informal gatherings among people of similar social positions who still don't know each other well enough to be casual.

May I offer you a drink?	一杯いかがですか？	IT-pahy ih-KAH-gah dess KAH?
Would you like to go have a drink?	飲みに行きませんか？	NOH-mih nih ih-KIH-MAH-SEn KAH?
Sure.	ええ。	Eh.
No, thanks.	いえ、結構です。	IH-eh, KET-koh dess.
I don't drink.	お酒は飲まないんです。	oh-SAH-KEH WAH noh-MAH-NAHy-n-dess.
Would you like to come with us to have a meal?	一緒にお食事しませんか？	iss-SHOH NIH oh-SHOHK-JIH shih-MAH-SEn KAH?
Yes, thank you.	ええ、有難うございます。	Eh, ah-LIH-gah-toh goh-ZAHY MAHss.
May I bring a friend?	友達を連れて来てもいいですか？	toh-MOH-DAHCH OH ts'LEH-TEH KIH-teh-moh Ee-dess KAH?

Do you mind if I smoke?	タバコを吸ってもいいですか？	tah-BAH-KOH OH sut-TEH-moh Ee-dess KAH?
Go ahead/Not at all.	どうぞ。	DOh-zoh.
I'm sorry, but I'm allergic to smoke.[1]	すみませんが、タバコアレルギーです。	s'MIH-MAH-SEn gah, tah-BAH-KOH ah-LEH LU-ghee dess.
May I telephone you?	お電話してもいいですか？	oh-DEn-wah shih-TEH-moh Ee-dess KAH?
What's your phone number?	お電話番号は？	oh-DEN-WAH BAHn-goh wah?
What is your address?	ご住所は？	goh-Ju-shoh wah?
Can I give you a ride?	車で送りましょうか？	k'LU-MAH DEH oh-KU-LIH-MAH-SHOh KAH?
Are you married?	ご結婚なさっているんですか？	goh-KEK-KOHN nah-SAHT-teh ih-LUn dess KAH?
I have a girlfriend/ boyfriend.	つき合っている人はいます。	ts'KIH-AHT-teh ih-lu hih-TOH-wah ih-MAHss.
I'm single.	独身です。	dohk-SHIN DEss.
I'm a widower/[widow].	家内[主人]は亡くなりました。	KAH-nahy/[SHU-jin] wah nah-KU-NAH-LIH-MAHsh-tah.

[1] A great number of Japanese smoke, and most people will not say that they mind others smoking. If you don't want others to smoke, the simplest way to handle the situation might be to tell a person that you're allergic. This way you still remain polite, but you'll get your point across.

I'm divorced.	別れました。	wah-KAH-LEH MAHsh-tah.
I'm traveling with a friend.	友達と一緒に旅行しているんです。	toh-MOH-DAHCH TOH iss-SHOH NIH lyoh-KOH SHIH-TEH-LUn-dess.
I'm traveling alone.	一人旅です。	hih-TOH-LIH tah-bih dess.
Why don't you come visit us at our house?	家へ遊びにいらっしゃいませんか？	u-CHIH NIH ah-SOH-BIH NIH ih-LAHSS-SHAHY-MAH-SEn KAH?
Is it all right?	よろしいんですか？	yoh-LOH-SHEEn-dess KAH?
I'd love to.	よろこんで。	yoh-LOH-KOHn deh.
Are you free …	_____お暇ですか？	_____ oh-HIH-MAH DEss KAH?
• this evening? • tomorrow?	• 今晩 • 明日	• KOHn-bahn • ah-SU/ahsh-TAH
I'll wait for you here.	ここで待ってます。	koh-KOH DEH MAHT-teh mahss.
I'll pick you up in the hotel lobby.	ホテルのロビーまで迎えに行きます。	HOH-teh-lu noh LOH-bee mah deh mu-KAH-EH NIH ih-KIH-MAHss.
It's getting late.	もうおそいですので。	MOh oh-SOY DEss noh deh.
It's time to get back.	もうおいとまいたします。	MOh oY-TOH-MAH ih-TAHSH-MAHss.
We're leaving tomorrow.	明日発ちます。	ahsh-TAH TAH-CHIH-MAHss.
Thank you for everything.	色々と有難うございました。	ih-LOH IH-LOH TOH ah-LIH-gah-toh goh-ZAHY-MAHsh-tah.

I had a very good time.	とても楽しかったです。	toh-TEH-MOH tah-NOH-sh'kaht-tah dess.
Give my best to Mr./ Ms. [Ogawa].	[小川] さんによろしく。	[oh-GAH-WAH] sahn nih yoh-LOHSH-KU.

TALKING ABOUT LANGUAGE

Do you speak ...[1]	______話せますか？	______ hah-NAH-SEH MAHss KAH?
• English?	• 英語	• AY-GOH
• Japanese?	• 日本語	• nih-HOHN-GOH
I only speak English.	英語しか話せません。	AY-GOH SH'KAH hah-NAH-SEH-MAH-SEn.
I speak a little Japanese.	日本語は少し話せます。	nih-HOHN-GOH WAH s' KOHsh hah-NAH-SEH-MAHss.
I'd like to learn Japanese.	日本語を習いたいんです。	nih-HOHN-GOH OH nah-LAHY TAHy-n-dess.
Please speak slowly.	ゆっくり言って下さい。	yut-KU-lih it-TEH K' DAH-SAHy.
Please repeat that one more time.	もう一度言って下さい。	MOH-ICH-DOH it-TEH K'DAH-SAHy.
I don't understand.	わかりません。	wah-KAH-LIH-MAH-SEn.
How do you write that in ...	それは______でどう書くんですか？	soh-LEH-WAH______ DEH DOh KAH-kun-dess KAH?
• Japanese?	• 日本語	• nih-HOHN-GOH
• *romaji*?	• ローマ字	• LOH-MAH-JIH

[1] For a list of languages, see page 210.

How do you say [beer] in Japanese?	[ビール] は日本語では何ですか？	[BEe-lu] wah nih-HOHN-GOH DEH-wah NAHn-dess KAH?
Is there anyone here who speaks English?	英語の出来る人はいますか？	AY-GOH NOH deh-KIH-lu hih-toh wah ih-MAHss KAH?
Please translate this for me.	これを訳して下さい。	koh-LEH OH yah-KU-sh'teh k'dah-sahy.
Can you understand me?	わかりますか？	wah-KAH-LIH-MAHss KAH?

THE FAMILY

I'm traveling with my family.	家族と一緒に旅行しています。	KAH-zohk toh iss-SHO'H NIH lyoh-KOH-SHIH-TEH-IH-MAHss.
I have …	_____がおります。	_____ gah oh-LIH-MAHss.
• a husband.	• 主人	• SHU-jin
• a wife.	• ワイフ／家内	• WAHy-hu/KAH-nahy
• a daughter.	• 娘一人	• mu-SU-MEH hih-TOH-lih
• a son.	• 息子一人	• muss-KOH hih-TOH-lih
• two daughters.	• 娘二人	• mu-SU-MEH hu-TAH-LIH
• two sons.	• 息子二人	• muss-KOH hu-TAH-LIH
• a father.	• 父	• CHIH-chih
• a mother.	• 母	• HAH-hah
• a grandfather.	• 祖父	• SOH-hu
• a grandmother.	• 祖母	• SOH-boh
• a grandson.	• 孫息子	• mah-GOH-MUss-koh

• a granddaughter.	• 孫娘	• mah-GOH-MUss-meh
• an older brother.	• 兄	• AH-nih
• a younger brother.	• 弟	• oh-TOH-TOH
• an older sister.	• 姉	• ah-NEH
• a younger sister.	• 妹	• ih-MOH-TOH
• a cousin.	• いとこ	• ih-TOH-koh
• an aunt.	• 叔母	• oh-BAH
• an uncle.	• 叔父	• oh-JIH
• a father-in-law.	• しゅうと	• shu-toh
• a mother-in-law.	• 姑	• shu-toh-meh
• relatives.	• 親戚	• shin-seh-kih
My eldest daughter	私の長女	wah-TAHSH NOH CHOh-joh
My eldest son	私の長男	wah-TAHSH NOH CHOH-NAHn
My second daughter	私の次女	wah-TAHSH NOH JIH-joh
My second son	私の次男	wah-TAHSH NOH JIH-nahn
My youngest daughter	私の末の娘	wah-TAHSH NOH su-EH NOH mu-SU-MEH
My youngest son	私の末の息子	wah-TAHSH NOH su-EH NOH muss-KOH
My children are still young.	私の子供はまだ小さいんです。	wah-TAHSH NOH koh-DOH-MOH WAH MAH-dah CHEE-SAHy-n-dess.
I have a girlfriend/boyfriend.	つき合っている人はいます。	ts'KIH-AHT-teh ih-lu hih-TOH-wah ih-MAHss.

IN THE HOME

When visiting a Japanese home, always remember to take your shoes off at the entrance hallway, before you step onto the raised floor.

Make yourself at home.	どうぞお楽に。	DOh-zoh oh-LAHK-NIH.
Please sit here.	こちらへおかけ下さい。	koh-CH'LAH EH oh-KAH-KEH K'DAH-SAHy.
What a great house!	素晴らしいお宅ですねえ！	s'BAH-LAH-SHEe oh-TAHK DEss NEh!
You live in such a nice neighborhood.	よい所にお住いですね。	YOy toh-koh-loh nih oh-S'MAHY DEss neh.
This is the …	ここが＿＿＿です。	koh-KOH GAH ＿＿＿dess.
• kitchen.	• キッチン	• KIT-chin
• living room.	• 居間	• ih-MAH
• dining room.	• ダイニング	• DAHy-nin-gu
• bedroom.	• 寝室	• shin-sh'tsu
• Western-style room.	• 洋間	• yoh-mah
• Japanese-style room.	• 和室	• wah-SHIH-TSU
This is a …[1]	これは＿＿＿です。	koh-LEH WAH ＿＿＿DEss.
• tatami[2] mat.	• 畳	• tah-TAH-MIH
• thick paper sliding door[3]	• 襖	• hu-SU-MAH

[1] For names of other furniture, please see the dictionary.
[2] A tatami mat is traditional flooring made of bound straw.
[3] Traditional Japanese rooms do not have Western-style doors; instead, rooms have sliding doors that also function as removable walls.

• paper-and-wood sliding door.	• 障子	• shoh-jih
I live in a(n) …	____に住んでいます。	____NIH SUn-deh ih-MAHss.
• house.	• 一戸建の家	• it-KOH-DAHCH noh ih-EH
• apartment.	• アパート	• ah-PAH-toh
• condominium.	• マンション	• MAHn-shohn
Would you like something to drink?	何かお飲みになりますか？	NAH-nih-kah oh-NOH-MIH-NIH nah-LIH-MAHss KAH?
Thanks for having invited us.	お招きいただいて有難うございました。	oh-MAH-NEH-KIH ih-TAH-DAHy-teh ah-LIH-gah-toh goh-ZAHY MAHsh-tah.
You must come and visit us at our home.	是非家にも遊びに来て下さい。	ZEH-hih u-CHIH NIH-moh ah-SOH-BIH-NIH KIH-teh k'DAH-SAHy.

6 / DINING OUT

Though the most well-known Japanese dishes in the United States may be sushi and tempura, there's much more to Japanese cuisine! In Tokyo, you will be able to find virtually any food from any part of the world, as well as standard Japanese fare and traditional dishes of Tokyo. Other areas of Japan are rich with wide varieties of regional dishes.

Types of food and price range vary greatly; you can get a burger from McDonald's or a steaming bowl of noodle soup, both for under $4 or so, or you can indulge in a full-course gourmet meal for over $100 per person. At most of the less expensive places, there will be a prominent display of dish "samples" at the entrance. These are made of wax, and they look remarkably like real food so you can get a good idea of what will be in a dish. Prices are also displayed alongside these samples.

One fact to note is that you might find the single-serving portion of any dish smaller than what you are used to seeing in the U.S. Do not expect to be full on one sandwich platter at an ordinary cafe. However, you can find meals that are filling if you look in the right places.

The following is a list of the basic types of eating establishments:

自動販売機 jih-DOH HAHN-BAHy-kih	You might be surprised by the number of vending machines that are located in a city. Usually they dispense various drinks and sodas, and some offer hot coffee and tea. Beer and whiskey are available from machines as well.
Fast Food (referred to by the name of the chain)	These establishments are found throughout Japan, and the menus are generally the same as in the U.S.

喫茶店 kiss-SAH-TEN スナック s'NAHT-ku	Equivalent to a cafe or a snack bar; generally light meals and non-alcoholic drinks are served here (though some might have alcoholic drinks in stock). Be aware that drink prices tend to be high, for you are basically paying to sit and relax. Typical menu: spaghetti, sandwiches, omelets, coffee, tea, soda, ice cream.
そば屋 SOH-bah yah ラーメン屋 LAH-MEN YAH うどん屋 u-DOHN YAH	Three types of noodle shops that serve a wide variety of noodles and soup. そば SOH-bah are buckwheat noodles, うどん u-DOHN are thick white noodles, and ラーメン LAh-men are thinner "Chinese-style" noodles. They make a quick, filling, and inexpensive meal, and are popular among the Japanese. Typical menu: u-DOHN noodles in hot broth with tempura(天ぷらうどん TEN-PU-LAH U-dohn), SOH-bah noodles to dip in cold sauce (ざるそば zah-LU-SOH-BAH), LAH-men noodles in soy-sauce soup with roast pork(チャーシューめん CHAH-SHU-MEN).
ファミリーレストラン fah-MIH-LEE LEH-s'toh-lahn	Family restaurants, similar to the American restaurant/diner chains (Denny's and others have branches in Japan). You can expect a variety of standard Japanese and Japanese-style Western meals at reasonable prices; found in department stores as well. Typical menu: hamburger steaks, rice with curry, fried shrimp, stir-fried rice, beef steak, soups, noodles, "box lunch"– style dishes (see below), various soft drinks, plus the fare found normally at cafes.
お好み焼き屋 oh-KOH-NOH-MIH-YAH-KIH YAH	Eateries that sell pancakes with vegetables and meat or seafood (do not expect a breakfast pancake and syrup; these pancakes are not sweet and are generally bigger and thicker). A bowl of pre-mixed ingredients is

brought to your table, which has a built-in hot plate. You can either make the pancakes yourself, or you can ask the waitress/waiter to cook it for you. These pancakes make a cheap, fun, and filling meal.

Typical menu: pancakes with cabbage and scallions plus choice of beef, pork, or squid, with brown sauce.

お弁当屋
oh-BEN-T OH-YAH

Establishments that make boxed lunches for takeout (though you can certainly eat them for dinner). A typical box will have rice, vegetables, and meat and/or seafood. These are also inexpensive and convenient.

寿し屋
su-SHIH-yah

Sushi-only restaurants that serve various types of sushi (寿し su-SHIH, raw fish over a serving of rice). Such places are popular in the U.S., and you can expect similar fare in Japan; however, be aware that there is a wide range in terms of price.

ケーキハウス
KEH-KIH HAH-u-su

Cake houses with various Western desserts as well as tea and coffee. They are good places to take a rest during a sight-seeing tour.

レストラン
LEH-s'toh-lahn

These restaurants charge midrange prices, and you can find a wide variety of cuisines, such as Japanese, Thai, Italian, Chinese, and American, at these establishments. Some Japanese restaurants have "set course" meals (定食 teh-shohk), which may include a main dish, rice, soup, salad, and dessert. The upper range of these restaurants may require reservations.

料亭
lyoh-teh

Consider these only if you want to experience traditional Japanese cuisine at astronomical prices. Reservations are a must and difficult to obtain (some places have waiting lists for days or even weeks, and others prefer that you have an introduction from one of their regular clients). Since you can get very good traditional Japanese meals at restaurants in the mid range category, these superexpensive establishments are not recommended unless you really feel like spending exorbitant amounts of money on a meal.

バー
Bah
クラブ
KU-lah-bu

Some bars are similar to American ones, where you can enjoy drinks with your friends or make new ones. However, others, called bars or clubs, are less wholesome establishments that provide not only drinks but women (or men) who entertain you by pouring your drinks and making conversation. Beware: drink prices at the clubs are extremely high.

飲み屋
noh-MIH-yah

Down-to-earth Japanese-style bars, identifiable by a characteristic red lantern at the door, serving mainly sake (Japanese rice wine) and beer. Many businesspeople frequent these establishments after work. They also have "finger foods" that you can eat with your drinks.

Typical menu: vagetables and fish cakes simmered until tender (おでん oh-DEn), chicken barbecued on skewers (焼鳥 yah-KIH-TOH-LIH), and numerous other vegetable, meat, and seafood dishes.

MEALS AND MEALTIMES

Breakfast (朝食 choh-shohk) is generally served until around 10 A.M. If you are staying at a Western-style hotel, you can expect a Continental breakfast. Some neighborhood cafes may offer American-style breakfasts. If you are staying at a Japanese-style inn, you will be served a traditional breakfast:

rice, soybean soup, grilled fish, and raw egg to mix into your rice with soy sauce.

Lunch (昼食　chu-shohk／ランチ　LAHn-chih) is about the same as it is in the United States in terms of time it is served and its size. Many people grab a noodle dish or bring lunch from home. If you are staying at any sort of Japanese-style inn, the only meal not included is your lunch, so this is a good opportunity to explore local cuisines. Keep in mind that restaurants in the business districts will be very busy from around noon until 2 P.M.

Dinner (夕食　yu-shohk) is the main meal of the day, and is usually served between 6 and 9 P.M. A typical Japanese dinner may consist of rice, pickles, some sort of soup, and a main dish (meat/seafood and vegetables). Traditionally, dessert is not eaten very often, if at all; the Japanese tend to eat sweets as afternoon snacks rather than after dinner. If you plan to drink a lot at a Japanese-style bar, you will usually find yourself eating several orders of finger food in place of dinner.

There is no strict order of courses in a typical Japanese meal. At home, food is usually served all at once. Soups are eaten with the main dish, as are salads. At a restaurant, you might start off with some appetizers, which are sometimes simply smaller portions of main dishes, then move on to your main dish. Dessert is often just a cup of green tea, but is sometimes accompanied by some sweets or possibly some fruit.

There are two popular expressions associated with eating: いただきます　ih-TAH-DAH-KIH-MAHss (lit., I'm going to have [the meal]) is said before you start your meal to show appreciation for the food. After you've finished, ごちそうさま　goh-CHIH-SOH SAH-MAH (lit., It was a treat) shows your gratitude.

DIALOGUE: AT THE RESTAURANT レストランで LEH-s'toh-lahn deh

ウェイター： waY-TAH	お決まりですか？	oh-KIH-MAH-LIH DEss KAH?
お客： oh-KYAHK	はい、すき焼きをお願いします。	HAHy, su-KIH-YAH-KIH OH oh-NEH GAHY SH'MAHss.
ウェイター： waY-TAH	お飲物は？	oh-NOH-MIH-moh-noh-WAH?
お客： oh-KYAHK	お茶を下さい。	oh-CHAH OH K'DAH-SAHy.
ウェイター： waY-TAH	かしこまりました。	kah-sh'KOH-MAH-LIH-MAH-sh'tah.

Waiter:	Have you decided what you'd like?
Customer:	Yes, I'd like Sukiyaki.
Waiter:	Something to drink?
Customer:	Green tea, please.
Waiter:	Certainly.

EATING OUT

A few words on mealtime etiquette; generally adhere to common sense, but also note the following:

Chopsticks

1) Don't point with them.
2) Don't pass food from your chopsticks directly to someone else's without putting the food down on a plate first (this is only done at funerals).
3) When you're sharing a dish with others, try not to pick from the communal plate with your chopsticks. Either

use the other end of your chopsticks, which haven't been in your mouth, or use the separate serving chopsticks if they are provided.

Acceptable Manners

1) It is fine to slurp your noodle soup (in fact, some insist that it's the only correct way to eat it!).
2) Pick up your rice and soup bowls and bring them to your mouth when you're eating from them.

Do you know any good restaurants nearby?	この辺にいいレストランはありますか？	koh-NOH-HEN NIH Ee LEH-s'toh-lahn wah ah-LIH MAHss KAH?
Is it expensive?	高いですか？	tah-KAHy dess KAH?
What's the name of the restaurant?	何というレストランですか？	NAHn toh yu LEH-s'toh-lahn dess KAH?
It's called _____.	_____です。	_____ dess.
Do I need to make reservations?	予約はいりますか？	yoh-YAHK WAH ih-LIH-MAHss KAH?
I'd like to make a reservation.	予約をしたいんですが。	yoh-YAHK OH shih-TAHy-n-dess gah.
For when?	いつでしょうか。	IH-ts deh-shoh kah.
For how many?	何人様ですか。	NAHn-nin-sah-mah dess KAH?
For …	_____です。	_____ dess.
• two people.	• 二人	• hu-TAH-LIH
• four people.	• 四人	• yoh-NIn
• tomorrow evening.	• 明日の晩	• ahsh-TAH NOH BAHN
• 8 P.M.	• 八時	• hah-CHIH-jih
I'd like to reserve …	_____をお願いします。	_____ oh oh-NEH-GAHY SH'MAHss.

• a tatami room.[1]	• 畳の部屋	• tah-TAH-MIH-NOH HEH-YAH
• a table by the window.	• のテーブル	• mah-DOH-GIH-WΛH NOH TEH-BU-LU
• a table in the no-smoking section.[2]	• 禁煙席	• KIN-En seh-kih
waiter waitress	ウェイター ウェイトレス	waY-TAH WAy-toh-less
Excuse me,…	すみません…	s'MIH-MAH-SEn,…
The menu, please.	メニューを下さい。	MEH-nyu oh k'DAH-SAHy.
Do you have any special local dishes?	郷土料理はありますか？	KYOH-DOH LYOh-lih wah ah-LIH-MAHss KAH?
Do you have a children's menu?	子供のメニューはありますか？	koh-DOH-MOH NOH MEH-nyu wah ah-LIH-MAHss KAH?
I'm ready to order.	オーダーしたいんですが。	Oh-dah sh'TAHy-n-dess gah.
To begin …	まずは	MAHz wah
Next …	つぎに	ts'GIH nih
Finally …	最後に	SAHy-goh nih
That's all.	それだけです。	soh-LEH-DAH-KEH dess.
Have you finished?	お済ですか？	oh-SU-MIH DEss KAH?

[1] Some Japanese restaurants have private rooms for each party, usually at no extra cost. These usually have tatami floors (bound straw mats), and you sit on a cushion on these mats and eat from a low table. These rooms offer privacy in a restaurant that might otherwise be crowded, and it's an excellent opportunity to experience how meals are traditionally eaten in Japan.

[2] A great number of Japanese smoke, and very few restaurants have no-smoking sections.

Please bring me some/a(n) ...	_____を下さい。	_____ OH k'DAH-SAHy.
• water.	• 水	• mih-ZU
• bread.	• パン	• PAHn
• butter.	• バター	• BAH-tah
• soy sauce.	• お醤油	• oh-SHOH-YU
• salt.	• お塩	• oh-SHIH-oh
• pepper.	• こしょう	• koh-SHOh
• mustard.	• からし	• kah-LAH-SHIH
• lemon.	• レモン	• LEH-mohn
• sugar.	• お砂糖	• o-sah-TOh
• ketchup.	• ケチャップ	• keh-CHAHT-pu
• Japanese horseradish.	• わさび	• WAH-sah-bih
• mayonnaise.	• マヨネーズ	• mah-YOH-NEh-zu
• Worcestershire sauce.	• ウースターソース	• U-S'TAH SOh-su
• chopsticks.	• お箸	• oh-HAH-shih
• fork.	• フォーク	• FOh-ku
• spoon.	• スプーン	• s'PU-n
• knife.	• ナイフ	• NAHy-hu
• napkin.[1]	• ナプキン	• nahp-KIn
• cup/glass.	• コップ	• koht-PU
• mug.	• コーヒーカップ	• KOH-HEE-KAHT-pu
• ashtray.	• 灰皿	• HAHY-ZAH-lah
• plate.	• お皿	• oh-SAH-LAH
I'd like a little more _____.	_____をもう少し下さい。	_____ oh MOH-S'KOHsh k'DAH-SAHy.
Please bring me _____.	_____をお願いします。	_____ OH oh-NEH-GAHY SH'MAHss.
Where is the bathroom?	お手洗いはどこですか？	oh-TEH-AH-lahy wah DOH-koh dess KAH?

[1] You will find that a lot of eating establishments do not have napkins (especially Japanese restaurants). If you are accustomed to eating with a napkin handy, you might want to carry along a handkerchief or small package of tissues.

NOODLE DISHES 麺類 MEn lu-ih

うどん u-DOHN	thick white noodles usually served in a hot soy sauce－based soup, but sometimes served cold
そば SOH-bah	buckwheat noodles served in a hot soy sauce－based soup, or served cold to dip in soy-based sauce (see below: "Noodles Served Cold Only")

u-DOHN and SOH-ba Noodle Dishes in Hot Soup

月見 ts'KIH-MIH	with poached egg and vegetables
きつね kih-TSU-NEH	with fried bean curd and scallions
たぬき TAH-nu-kih	with fried batter and vegetables
おかめ oh-KAH-meh	with fish cake, soy-bean product, mushroom, and spinach
あんかけ ahN-KAH-KEH	with slightly sweet thick cornstarched soup
天ぷら ten-pu-lah	with deep-fried seafood (usually shrimp) and vegetables
山菜 sahn-sahy	with herbs and vegetables
カレー kah-LEH	with curry soup; u-DOHN noodles only
鍋焼き nah-BEH-YAH-KIH	a winter favorite, in boiling hot broth with poached egg, scallions, fried bean curd, and fish cake; u-DOHN only
ラーメン LAh-men	thin noodles served in hot broth with meats and/or vegetable

Noodles Served Cold Only

ひやむぎ hih-YAH-MU-gih	spaghetti-size white noodles served with soy sauce—based sauce for dipping
そうめん SOH-MEn	angel-hair-size white noodles served with soy sauce—based sauce for dipping
冷やし中華 hih-YAHSH CHu-kah	cold LAh-men noodles topped with vegetables and meat (often cucumbers, egg, and ham) with soy sauce and mustard-based sauce; a summer favorite
ざるそば zah-LU-SOH-BAH	cold SOH-bah noodles to dip in soy sauce—based sauce

Miscellaneous Noodle Dishes

スパゲティー s'PAH-GHEH-tee	spaghetti, usually in tomato sauce, sometimes with meatballs
焼きそば yah-KIH-SOH-BAH	stir-fried noodles with soy sauce—based sauce, with optional vegetables and meat

RICE DISHES ご飯物 goh-HAHN MOH-NOH

ご飯 GOH-hahn	cooked white rice
おかゆ oh-KAH-YU	gruel
どんぶり dohn-bu-lih	cooked white rice with various toppings

Other Rice Dishes

親子どんぶり oh-YAH-KOH DOHn-bu-lih	dohn-bu-lih with chicken, scrambled eggs, and vegetables

チャーハン CHAh-hahn	stir-fried rice with egg, vegetables, meat, and/or seafood
色ご飯 ih-LOH-GOH-hahn	rice boiled with soy sauce-based seasonings, vegetables, and sometimes chicken
釜飯 kah-MAH-MEH-SHIH	cooked and served hot in individual rice cookers; rice topped with seafood, vegetables, and/or meat
お餅 oh-MOH-CHIHSHIH	rice cakes: white sticky dough made of grains, served baked and seasoned with soy sauce and wrapped in seaweed; also found in sweet red-bean soup (see below) and clear soup (a must for New Year's celebration)

SANDWICHES[1] サンドイッチ SAHN-DOH-IHT-chih
BURGERS ハンバーガー HAHN-BAh-gah

ミックスサンド mit-KU-SU SAHn-doh	usually a combination of ham, egg salad, and vegetable sandwiches on white bread
野菜サンド yah-SAHY SAHn-doh	vegetable sandwich; usually slices of cucumber
カツサンド kah-TSU SAHn-doh	deep-fried pork cutlet sandwich; normally the most substantial meal of the sandwich group
ハンバーガー HAHN-BAh-gah	hamburger on a bun
チーズバーガー CHEE-ZU BAH-gah	cheeseburger on a bun

[1] Beware: at most places, sandwich portions are quite small!

SOUPS スープ SU-pu

味噌汁 mih-SOH-SHIH-lu	soybean-paste soup (light or dark, according to region) with possibly vegetables, seaweed, bean curd, or seafood (especially clams)
お吸物 oh-SU-IH-MOH-NOH	a clear soup (stock taken from bonito or seaweed) with vegetables and/or varieties of soybean products
かき卵汁 kah-KIH TAH-MAH-GOH JIH-lu	basically an egg-drop soup

BEEF DISHES 牛肉料理 GYU-NIK LYOh-lih

すき焼き su-KIH-YAH-KIH	ingredients and a hot plate are brought right to your table so you can cook thinly sliced beef, bean curd, noodles, and vegetables yourself in soy sauce–based sauce, then dip them in raw egg before you eat (optional)
しゃぶしゃぶ shah-BU SHAH-BU	a pot of boiling water and a hot plate are brought to your table, and you quickly boil very thinly sliced beef, vegetables, bean curd, mushrooms, and clear noodles and dip them in either vinegar–soy sauce mix or sesame sauce
ステーキ s'TEh-kih	a basic steak; keep in mind that beef in general is very expensive in Japan (but it can be of excellent quality)
焼肉 yah-KIH-NIK	beef grilled either by you or a chef right before you eat it; accompanied by vegetables grilled in the same way
ビーフシチュー BEE-HU SH'chu	beef stew

カレーライス kah-LEH LAHy-su	a stew-type curry with vegetables, meats, or seafood, served over rice; generally not as spicy as Indian curry

PORK DISHES 豚肉料理 bu-TAH-NIK LYOh-lih

とんカツ tohN-KAHTS	pork cutlet coated with bread crumbs and deep fried; served with special sauce and raw cabbage salad on the side
しょうが焼き shoh-gah yah-kih	pork cutlet sautéed in ginger sauce
けんちん汁 keN-CHIN JIH-lu	a soybean-paste soup with pork and vegetables (often carrots, white daikon radish, and scallions)
焼き豚 yah-KIH BU-TAH	Chinese-style seasoned roast pork, served in thin slices
ギョーザ gyoh-zah	steamed or fried crescent-shaped Chinese-style dumplings with pork and vegetables

POULTRY DISHES 鶏肉料理 KEH-NIK LYOh-lih

チキンカツ chih-KIN KAHTS	chicken cutlet coated with bread crumbs and deep fried
みずたき mih-ZU-TAH-KIH	chicken (or pork), carrots, radishes, Chinese cabbage, bean curd, mushrooms, and clear noodles boiled in water at your table, served with soy sauce and vinegar sauce for dipping
照り焼き teh-LIH-YAH-KIH	chicken teriyaki: boneless chicken marinated in teriyaki sauce and fried
から揚げ kah-LAH AH-GEH	crisp, deep-fried pieces of chicken (without batter)

焼鳥 yah-KIH-TOH-LIH	marinated chicken barbecued on skewers; various parts of chicken are available for the more adventurous, and you can specify what you want

SEAFOOD DISHES 魚料理 sah-KAH-NAH LYOh-lih 貝料理 kahY LYOh-lih

にぎり寿し nih-GIH-LIH z'shih	regular sushi (raw fish on a serving of rice)
ちらし寿し chih-LAH-SHIH z'shih	sushi ingredients (raw fish, seaweed, vegetables, etc.) on a bed of rice (as opposed to individual balls of rice)
刺身 sah-SHIH-MIH	sashimi: slices of raw fish
エビフライ eh-BIH HU-lahy	shrimp coated with bread crumbs and deep fried
カキフライ kah-KIH HU-lahy	oysters coated with bread crumbs and deep fried

EGG DISHES 卵料理 tah-MAH-GOH LYOh-lih

茶碗蒸し chah-WAHN MU-shih	a mixture of eggs, mushrooms, vegetables, and possibly chicken, steamed in individual bowls
蟹たま kah-NIH TAH-MAH	an omelet with crabmeat and green peas, served with a thick soy sauce–based sauce
オムレツ oh-MU-LEH-TSU	a basic omelet
オムライス oh-MU LAHy-su	an omelet filled with stir-fried rice seasoned with ketchup

CHEESE DISHES チーズ料理 CHEE-ZU LYOh-lih

グラタン gu-LAH-TAHN	macaroni au gratin

VEGETABLE DISHES 野菜料理 yah-SAHY LYOh-lih

おにつけ oh-NIH-ts'keh	vegetables simmered in soy sauce and sugar until tender
コロッケ koh-LOHT-keh	mashed potatoes, vegetables, and meat shaped into a ball, coated with bread crumbs, and deep fried
サラダ SAH-lah-dah	a basic salad with lettuce and greens
おひたし oh-HIH-TAH-shih	leafy greens (such as Chinese cabbage or spinach), quickly boiled then left unseasoned or mixed with various types of sauces
酢のもの SU noh moh-noh	a cold dish; vegetables, seaweed, and/or seafood tossed with vinegar

PICKLES つけもの ts'KEH-MOH-NOH

たくあん tah-KU-AHn	pickled daikon radish, usually yellow in color
福神漬 hu-KU-JIN-Z'KEH	pickled minced daikon radish, eggplant, and other vegetables; red in color, and often served with curry and rice
らっきょう laht-KYOH	pickled shallotlike vegetable; very sour
うめぼし u-MEH-BOH-SHIH	very sour pickled plums, often served with plain rice in beN-TOH lunch boxes
塩づけ shih-OH Z'KEH	vegetables pickled in salt

SNACKS AND SWEETS スナック／お菓子 s'NAHK-ku／oh-KAH-shih

アイスクリーム ahY-S'KU-LEE-mu	ice cream; various flavors, including green tea and red bean
ケーキ KEh-kih	cakes; some popular ones include strawberry shortcake, chocolate cake, and chestnut-cream cake; they usually have less sugar than Western cakes
シュークリーム SHU-K'LEe-mu	cream puffs with custard filling
クッキー KUT-kee	cookies
チョコレート choh-KOH-LEh-toh	chocolates
ようかん YOh-kahn	sweet red-bean-based dessert, sometimes with chestnuts
まんじゅう MAHN-Ju	flour-based cakes with sweet red-bean filling
たいやき tahY-YAH-KIH	cakes (similar to Western pancake mix) with sweet red-bean filling (shaped like a fish, but there's no fish in it!)
おしるこ oh-SHIH-LU-KOH	sweet red-bean soup served hot with rice cakes; a winter favorite
せんべい SEn-bay	flat, round rice crackers, traditionally flavored with soy sauce
あられ ah-LAH-LEH	small SEn-bay crackers
ミント MIn-toh	mints

MISCELLANEOUS PRODUCTS

はるさめ hah-LU-SAH-MEH	clear cellophane noodles made from potato starch

かんぴょう KAHN-PYOh	gourd shaped into long ribbonlike strips, cooked until tender
ふ hu	flour and water molded into shapes; used often in clear soups
こんにゃく kohn-nyahk	paste made from yamlike vegetable molded into a rectangle or into noodlelike filaments often in sukiyaki(すきやき su-KIH-YAH-KIH)

PREPARATION METHODS 調理方法 CHOH-LIH HOh-hoh

いためる ih-TAH-MEH-lu	stir-fry
焼く yah-KU	basically pan-fry, but also means to grill, bake, roast, and broil
煮る nih-LU	boil/simmer
揚げる ah-GEH-LU	deep-fry
蒸す MU-su	steam
生 NAH-mah	raw; served uncooked

HERBS, SPICES, AND SEASONINGS 調味料／やくみ CHOH-MIH-lyoh／yah-KU-MIH

さんしょう	SAHN-SHOh	Japanese pepper
みょうが	myoh-gah	Japanese ginger
わさび	WAH-sah-bih	Japanese horseradish
ごま	goh-MAH	sesame

しそ	shih-SOH	aromatic leaves
ゆず	YU-zu	Chinese lemon
しょうが	shoh-gah	ginger
にんにく	nin-nik	garlic
酢	su	vinegar
みりん	mih-LIN	sweet rice wine
だし	dah-SHIH	soup stock; usually bonito or seaweed base

VEGETABLES 野菜 yah-SAHY

アスパラガス	ahss-PAH-LAH-gahss	asparagus
なす	NAH-su	eggplant
かぶ	kah-BU	beet
にんじん	nin-jin	carrot
セロリ	SEH-loh-lih	celery
キャベツ	KYAH-bets	cabbage
白菜	hahk-SAHy	Chinese cabbage
大根	DAHY-KOHn	Japanese white radish
カリフラワー	kah-LIH-HU-LAH-wah	caulifower
きゅうり	KYu-lih	cucumber
ほうれん草	hoh-len-soh	spinach
五月豆	goh-GAHTS mah-meh	green beans
さやいんげん	sah-YAH In-gen	snow peas
枝豆	eh-DAH-MAH-MEH	soybeans

グリーンピース	g'LEEN PEE-su	pea
レタス	LEH-tah-su	lettuce
唐もろこし／コーン	TOH-MOH-loh-kohsh/KOHn	corn
玉葱	tah-MAH-NEH-gih	onion
ねぎ	NEH-gih	Japanese scallion
三つ葉	mih-TSU-BAH	three-leaved herb
ししとう	shih-SHIH-TOH	hot green pepper
ピーマン	PEE-mahn	green pepper
じゃがいも	jah-GAHY-MOH	potato
トマト	TOH-mah-toh	tomato
里芋	sah-TOY-MOH	Japanese taro
ごぼう	goh-BOH	burdock
さつまいも	sah-TSU-MAHY-MOH	sweet potato
蓮／れんこん	hah-SU/LEn-kohn	lotus root
山芋	yah-MAHY-MOH	Japanese yam
もやし	moh-YAH-SHIH	bean sprout
かぼちゃ	kah-BOH-CHAH	squash
ブロッコリ	b'LOHT-koh-lih	broccoli
せり	seh-LIH	watercress
たけのこ	tah-KEH-NOH-KOH	bamboo shoot

MUSHROOMS　きのこ　KIH-noh-koh

しい茸	SHEe-tah-keh	black shiitake mushroom

えのき茸	eh-NOH-KIH-dah-keh	small white mushroom
松茸	mahts-TAH-KEH	very aromatic mushroom (very expensive)

FRUITS 果物 K'DAH-moh-noh

柿	kah-KIH	persimmon
すもも	su-MOH-MOH	plum
みかん	MIH-kahn	mandarin orange
夏みかん	nah-TSU MIH-kahn	Japanese grapefruit
グレープフルーツ	g'LEH-PU HU-LUts	grapefruit
ネクター	NEK-tah	nectarine
梨	nah-SHIH	pear
りんご	lin-goh	apple
バナナ	BAH-nah-nah	banana
キーウィー	KEE-wee	kiwi fruit
すいか	su-IH-KAH	watermelon
メロン	MEH-lohn	melon
ぶどう	bu-DOH	grape
さくらんぼ	sah-K'LAHN-BOH	cherry
レモン	LEH-mohn	lemon
ライム	LAHy-mu	lime
いちじく	ih-CHIH-jik	fig
びわ	BIH-wah	loquat
いちご	ih-CHIH-GOH	strawberry
ブルーベリー	bu-LU BEH-lee	blueberry
桃	moh-MOH	peach

栗	ku-LIH	chestnut
ざくろ	ZAHK-loh	pomegranate
パイナップル	pahY-NAHT-pu-lu	pineapple
ほしぶどう	hoh-SHIH BU-doh	raisin

MEATS AND POULTRY 肉類 nih-KU-lu-ih

牛肉	gyu-nik	beef
豚肉	bu-TAH-NIK	pork
チキン	CHIH-kin	chicken
マトン	MAH-tohn	lamb
レバー	LEH-bah	liver
あひる	ah-HEE-lu	duck
ソーセージ	SOh-seh-jih	sausage
ハム	HAH-mu	ham
ベーコン	BEh-kohn	bacon

SEAFOOD, SEAWEED, AND SEAFOOD PRODUCTS
魚介類 gyoh-KAHy-lu-ih
海苔 noh-LIH
練り物 neh-LIH-MOH-noh
(Includes sushi ingredients)

赤貝	ah-KAH-gahy	ark shell
あさり	ah-SAH-LIH	short-necked clam
あわび	AH-wah-bih	abalone
ぶり	BU-lih	yellowtail (grown)
えび	eh-BIH	shrimp
はまち	hah-MAH-CHIH	yellowtail (young)
はまぐり	hah-MAH-g'lih	clam

ひらめ	hih-LAH-MEH	flounder
いか	ih-KAH	squid
いくら	ih-KU-LAH	salmon roe
いわし	ih-WAH-SHIH	sardine
かれい	KAH-lay	turbot (similar to flounder)
蟹	kah-NIH	crab
かつお	kah-TSU-OH	bonito
貝柱	KAHY-BAHsh-lah	scallop
ロブスター	LOH-buss-tah	lobster
まぐろ	mah-GU-LOH	tuna
めんたいこ	MEN-TAHy-koh	spicy cod roe
さば	sah-BAH	mackerel
鮭	SAH-keh	salmon
さんま	sahN-MAH	mackerel pike
ししゃも	shih-SHAH-MOH	smelt
たこ	TAH-koh	octopus
たら	TAH-lah	cod
たらこ	tah-LAH-KOH	cod roe
鯛	TAHy	sea bream
うなぎ	u-NAH-GIH	eel
うに	U-nih	sea urchin
のり	noh-LIH	seaweed
わかめ	wah-KAH-meh	wakame seaweed
こんぶ	KOHn-bu	konbu seaweed
かまぼこ	kah-MAH-BOH-KOH	fish cake (shaped into a half circle)
ちくわ	chih-KU-WAH	fish cake (cylindrical with a center hole)

はんぺん	HAHN-PEn	fish cake (flat and white)

SOYBEAN-RELATED PRODUCTS

大豆	DAHy-zu	soybean
豆腐	toh-hu	tofu (bean curd)
油揚げ	ah-BU-LAH-ah-geh	fried soybean product
厚揚げ	ah-TSU AH-GEH	fried bean curd
凍り豆腐	KOH-LIH DOh-hu	processed bean curd
味噌	MIH-soh	soybean paste
納豆	naht-TOh	fermented soybeans

NON-ALCOHOLIC BEVERAGES 飲物 noh-MIH-moh-noh

コーヒー	KOH-HEe	coffee
ミルク	MIH-lu-ku	milk
クリーム	k'LEE-mu	cream
砂糖	sah-TOh	sugar
紅茶	koh-chah	Western tea
ミルクティー	mih-LU-KU TEe	tea with milk
レモンティー	leh-MOHN TEe	tea with lemon
水	mih-ZU	water
氷水	KOH-LIH mih-zu	ice water
コカコーラ	koh-KAH KOh-lah	Coca-Cola
スプライト	su-PU-LAHy-toh	Sprite
ソーダ	SOh-dah	soda

____ジュース	____ Ju-su	____ juice
• オレンジ	• oh-LEN-JIH	• orange
• トマト	• toh-MAH-TOH	• tomato
• グレープフルーツ	• g'LEH-PU HU-LUTS	• grapefruit
• アップ.ル	• aht-PU-LU	• apple
アイスティー	ahY-SU TEe	iced tea
アイスコーヒー	ahY-SU KOh-hee	iced coffee
お茶	oh-CHAH	generic green tea
麦茶	mu-GIH-chah	buckwheat tea, served cold

ALCOHOLIC BEVERAGES アルコール類 ah-LU-KOH-LU lu-ih

Many Japanese have beer or sake with their meals. Wine is available at many Western-cuisine restaurants, but not at regular Japanese establishments. If you are dining with a Japanese who drinks, he or she will most likely ask you to have something to drink also, and if you don't want to drink, be polite but firm. Japanese usually decline an offer at the beginning to show modesty and be polite, so they may think that you're merely being shy by refusing their offer for a drink. If you are going to join others for a drink, it's customary to pour the beer or sake for the other person.

カクテル	KAHK-teh-lu	cocktail
ウィスキー	WISS-KEe	whiskey
コニャック	koh-NYAHT-ku	cognac
ウォッカ	WOHT-kah	vodka
• オンザロック	• OHN-ZAH-LOHT-ku	• on the rocks
• 水割り	• mih-ZU-WAH-LIH	• with water
• ストレート	• s'TOH-L Eh-toh	• straight up

酒	sah-KEH	rice wine
焼酎	shoh-chu	white potato liquor
梅酒	u-MEH-SHU	plum wine
ビール • 生 • ライト	BEe-lu • NAH-mah • LAHy-toh	beer • draft • light
ワイン • 赤 • 白	WAHy-n • AH-kah • SHIH-loh	wine • red • white

SPECIAL DIETS

I'm on a diet.	ダイエットしているんです。	DAHy-et-toh shih-TEH IH-LUn dess.
I'm on a special diet.	決った食べ物しか食べません。	kih-MAHT-TAH TAH-BEH-MOH-noh sh'kah tah-BEH-MAH-SEn.
Do you have vegetarian dishes?	ベジタリアンの料理は出来ますか。	beh-JIH-TAH-lih-ahn noh LYOh-lih wah deh-KIH-MAHss KAH?
I'm allergic to _____.	_____にアレルギーです。	_____ NIH ah-LEH-LU-ghee dess.
I can't eat …	_____はだめなんです。	_____ WAH dah-MEH nahn-dess.
• salt. • fat. • greasy food. • sugar. • flour.	• 塩 • 脂肪 • 油っこいもの • 砂糖 • メリケン粉	• shih-OH • shih-BOH • ah-B'LAHT-KOy moh-noh • sah-TOh • meh-LIH-KEN-KOH
I'm diabetic.	糖尿病です。	TOH-NY OH-BYOH DEss.

I don't eat pork.	豚肉は食べません。	bu-TAH-NIK WAH tah-BEH-MAH-SEn.

THE BILL

The wax samples so prevalent in restaurants and the price of dishes displayed prominently next to them mean that you'll know what your bill will be beforehand. Even in places without these displays, the menu should have the price of each dish clearly indicated. However, sometimes the numbers are in Japanese, so if you're not sure, ask your server. The only exception is the superexclusive Japanese cuisine establishment. Meal tax is 3 percent and is normally not included in the price of a dish given on the menu. There is no need to tip; service is always included.

Excuse me, the check, please.	すみません、お勘定お願いします。	s'MIH-MAH-SEn, oh-KAHN-JOH oh-NEH-GAHY SH'MAHss.
What is this amount for?	これはどの分ですか。	koh-LEH WAH DOH-noh-bun dess KAH?
Do you accept …	______でいいですか？	_____ deh Ee-dess KAH?
• credit cards?	• クレジットカード	• k'LEH-JIT-TOH KAh-doh
• traveler's checks?	• トラベラーズチェック	• toh-LAH-BEH-LAH-ZU CHET-ku
The meal was excellent.	とてもおいしかったです。	toh-TEH-MOH OY-SHIH-kaht-tah dess.

COMPLAINTS

I'm sorry, but I think there is a mistake.	すみませんが、間違いがあるようですが。	s'MIH-MAH-SEn, gah mah-CHIH-GAHy gah ah-lu-yoh dess gah.

This isn't what I ordered.	これは頼んでいません。	koh-LEH WAH TAH-NOHn-deh ih-MAH-SEn.
I just can't eat this.	これ、食べられないんです。	koh-LEH, tah-BEH-LAH-LEH-NAHy-n dess.
Could I get something else instead?	他のものととり変えてくれますか？	hoh-KAH NOH MOH-NOH toh toh-LIH-KAH-eh-teh k'LEH MAHss KAH?
This is too …	これは______過ぎです。	koh-LEH WAH _____ S'GIH DEss.
• well done.	• 焼き	• yah-KIH
• salty.	• しょっぱ	• shoht-PAH
• bitter.	• にが	• nih-GAH
• sweet.	• 甘	• ah-MAH
This isn't cooked enough.	これはよく焼けてません。	koh-LEH WAH YOHK yah-KEH-TEH-MAH-SEn.
This is dirty.	汚れています。	yoh-GOH-LEH-TEH IH-MAHss.
I'm missing a _____.	______が無いんですが。	_____ gah NAHy-n dess gah.
This is cold.	これ、冷めてます。	koh-LEH, SAH-meh-teh mahss.
I'd like to see the manager.	マネージャーを　呼んで下さい。	mah-N<u>EH</u>-<u>jah</u> oh YOHN-DEH k'DAH-SAHy.

7 / PERSONAL CARE

DIALOGUE: AT THE BEAUTY PARLOR 美容室で bih-YOH-shih-tsu deh

お客： oh-KYAHK	カットをお願いします。	KAHT-TOH oh oh-NEH-GAHY SH'MAHss.
美容師： bih-YOh-shih	どんなスタイルになさいますか？	DOHn-nah s'tahy-lu nih nah-SAHY-MAHss KAH?
お客： oh-KYAHK	揃えるだけでいいです。	soh-LOH-EH-lu dah-keh deh Ee dess.
美容師： bih-YOh-shih	パーマをおかけになりますか？	PAh-mah oh oh-KAH-KEH NIH NAH-LIH-MAHss KAH?
お客： oh-KYAHK	いいえ、シャンプーとセットだけでいいです。	ee-EH, SHAhn-pu toh SET-toh DAH-KEH deh Ee dess.

Customer:	I'd like a haircut, please.
Beautician:	How would you like your hair done?
Customer:	I just need a trim.
Beautician:	Would you like a perm?
Customer:	No, shampoo and set are enough.

AT THE BARBERSHOP/BEAUTY PARLOR

Is there a _____ nearby?	_____はこの近くにありますか？	_____ wah koh-noh CHIH-KAHk nih ah-LIH-MAHss KAH?
• barbershop	• 床屋	• toh-KOH-YAH
• beauty parlor	• 美容室	• bih-YOh-shih-tsu

• hair salon	• ヘアサロン	• heh-AH SAH-lohn
I'd like to make an appointment for today.	今日の予約をとりたいんですが。	KYOh noh yoh-YAHK OH toh-LIH-TAHy-n-dess gah.
I need a haircut.	カットをお願いします。	KAHT-toh oh oh-NEH-GAHY SH'MAHss
Please leave it long here.	ここは長いままにしておいて下さい。	koh-KOH WAH nah-GAHy mah-mah nih shih-TEH Oy-teh k'dah-sahy.
Please cut it short.	短く切って下さい。	mih-JIH-KAHk KIT-teh k'dah-sahy.
Not too short!	短く切りすぎないで！	mih-JIH-KAHk kih-LIH-S'GIH-nahy deh!
Cut a bit more off …	_____をもう少し切って下さい。	_____ oh MOH-S'KOHSH KIT-teh k'dah-sahy.
• here.	• ここ	• koh-KOH
• in front.	• 前	• MAH-eh
• on the side.	• 横	• yoh-KOH
• at the neck.	• 首の所	• ku-BIH NOH TOH-koh-loh
• the back.	• 後ろ	• u-SHIH-LOH
• the top.	• 上の方	• u-EH NOH HOh
I'd like a …	_____お願いします。	_____ oh-NEH-GAHY SH'MAHss.
• razor cut.	• レザーカット	• leh-ZAH KAHT-toh
• shampoo.	• シャンプー	• SHAHn-pu
• set.	• セット	• SET-toh
• permanent.	• パーマ	• PAh-mah
• blow dry.	• ブロードライ	• b'LOH DOH-LAHy
• color rinse.	• 毛染め	• keh-ZOH-MEH
• manicure.	• マニキュア	• mah-NIH-KYU-AH
• facial.	• フェーシャル／美顔	• FEh-shah-lu/bih-GAHN

No hair spray, please.	ヘアースプレーはしないで下さい。	heh-<u>AH</u> S'PU-L<u>Eh</u> wah sh' NAHy-deh k'dah-sahy.
I'd like to see a color chart.	染める色のチャートを見せて下さい。	soh-MEH-LU IH-LOH noh CH<u>Ah</u>-toh oh MIH-seh-teh k'dah-sahy.
I prefer ...	_____にして下さい。	_____ nih sh'TEH K'DAH-SAHy.
• a lighter shade.	• もう少し明るい色	• M<u>OH</u>-S'KOHSH ah-KAH-LU-IH IH-LOH
• a darker shade.	• もう少し濃い色	• M<u>OH</u>-S'KOHSH KOy ih-loh
I'd like a shave.	髭を剃って下さい。	hih-GEH OH SOHT-teh k'dah-sahy.
Please trim my ...	_____を整えて下さい。	_____ oh toh-TOH-NOH-eh teh k'dah-sahy.
• mustache.	• 口髭	• k'CHIH-HIH-GEH
• beard.	• あご髭	• ah-GOH-HIH-GEH

LAUNDRY/DRY CLEANING

Where is the nearest ...	一番近い_____はどこですか？	ih-CHIH-BAHN CH'KAHy _____ wah DOH-koh dess KAH?
• laundry/dry cleaners?	• クリーニング屋	• k'LEE-NING YAH
• laundromat?	• コインランドリー	• koYN LAHn-doh-lee
• tailor?	• 洋服屋	• y<u>oh</u>-hu-ku yah
Please have these clothes ...	これを_____して下さい。	koh-LEH OH _____ SH'TEH K'DAH-SAHy.

• washed.	• 洗濯	• SEN-TAHK
• dry-cleaned.	• ドライクリーニング	• doh-LAHY K'LEe-nin-gu
• pressed.	• プレス	• PU-leh-su
Please iron these.	これにアイロンをかけて下さい。	koh-LEH NIH ahY-LOHN OH KAH-keh-teh k'dah-sahy.
Please mend these rips.	ほころびを直して下さい。	ho-KOH-LOH-BIH OH nah-OHsh-teh k'dah-sahy.
Please sew on this button.	このボタンをつけて下さい。	koh-noh BOH-tahn oh ts'KEH-teh k'dah-sahy.
Could you try to get this stain out?	このしみは落ちませんか?	koh-NOH SHIH-MIH WAH oh-CHIH-MAH-SEn KAH?
When will they be ready?	いつ出来ますか？	IH-ts deh-KIH-MAHss KAH?
I'm leaving tomorrow.	明日発つんです。	ahsh-TAH TAHts-n-dess.
This isn't/these aren't mine.	これは私のじゃありません。	koh-LEH WAH wah-TAHSH NOH jah ah-LIH-MAH-SEn.
There is a _____ missing.[1]	_____が一枚足りません。	_____ gah ih-CHIH-mahy tah-LIH-MAH-SEn.
• shirt (men's)	• ワイシャツ	• wahY-SHAHTS
• T-shirt	• ティーシャツ	• TEE-SHAHTS
• blouse	• ブラウス	• b'LAH-u-su
• skirt	• スカート	• s'KAH-TOH
• pair of pants	• ズボン	• ZU-bohn
• suit	• スーツ	• Su-tsu

[1]See "Western-Style Clothing" in chapter 12 for a complete list.

8 / HEALTH CARE

Before you leave, you should check with your health insurance company to find out whether or not your policy covers accident and illness expenses overseas, and to what extent.

In Tokyo, you can contact one of the foreign-affiliated hospitals (such as St. Luke's, tel. 03-3541-5151, or the International Catholic Hospital, tel. 03-3951-1111) that employ doctors who speak English. You might encounter some difficulty in finding an English-speaking private practitioner in rural areas of Japan. There are some private doctors who do speak English, however, and the American embassies or consulates can help you locate one. Also, the International Association for Medical Assistance to Travelers (IAMAT) offers a list of approved English-speaking doctors, and you can obtain this list by contacting IAMAT at 417 Center Street, Lewiston, NY 14092, tel. (716) 754-4883. In Kyoto, try the Japan Baptist Hospital (tel. 075-781-5191), and in Osaka, try the Tane General Hospital (tel. 06-581-1071).

One important note: medication is usually given to you at the doctor's office upon your visit, which means that you need not look for a pharmacy to have your prescription filled. Pharmacies sell mostly over-the-counter drugs, but you do not need a prescription to buy painkillers, tranquilizers, and sleeping pills.

DIALOGUE: AT THE DOCTOR'S 医院で IH-in deh

医者： ih-SHAH	どうしましたか？	DOh sh'mahsh-tah KAH?
観光客： KAHN-KOh-kyahk	よくわからないんですが…。 頭痛がして、気分が悪いんです。	YOH-ku wah-KAH-LAH-NAHy-n-dess gah … zu-TSU GAH SH'TEH, KIH-bun gah wah-LU-in dess.
医者： ih-SHAH	吐き気がしましたか？	hah-KIH-KEH gah sh' MAHsh-tah KAH?
観光客： KAHN-KOh-kyahk	ええ、今朝吐きました。	Eh, KEH-sah hah-KIH-MAHsh-tah.
医者： ih-SHAH	いつから具合が悪いんですか？	IH-ts kah-lah gu-AHY GAH wah-LU-in dess KAH?
観光客： KAHN-KOh-kyahk	日曜日からです。	nih-CHIH-YOh-bih kah-lah dess.

Doctor:	What's the matter?
Tourist:	I'm not quite sure…. I have a headache and I'm not feeling well.
Doctor:	Have you been nauseated?
Tourist:	Yes, I threw up this morning.
Doctor:	Since when have you been ill?
Tourist:	Since Sunday.

HEALTH CARE

PATIENT/DOCTOR EXPRESSIONS

Before the Visit

English	Japanese	Pronunciation
Please call me a doctor.	医者を呼んで下さい。	ih-SHAH OH YOHN-DEH K'DAH-SAHy.
It's an emergency.	急病なんです。	KYU-BYOH NAHn-dess.
Where is the doctor's office?	お医者さんはどこですか？	oY-SHAH-SAHN wah DOH-koh dess KAH?
I need a doctor who speaks English.	英語の出来るお医者さんをお願いします。	AY-GOH NOH DEH-KIH-lu oY-SHAH-SAHN OH oh-NEH-GAHY SH'MAHss.
When can the doctor see me?	いつ看ていただけるんですか？	IH-ts MIH-teh ih-TAH-DAH-KEH-LUn-dess KAH?
Could the doctor see me here?	ここで看てもらえますか？	koh-KOH DEH MIH-teh moh-LAH-EH MAHss KAH?
I'd like to make an appointment for	_____予約をとりたいんです。	_____ yoh-YAHK OH toh-LIH-TAHy-n-dess.
• today.	• 今日の	• KYOh noh
• tomorrow.	• 明日の	• ahsh-TAH NOH
• as soon as possible.	• なるべく早い	• nah-LU-BEK HAH-YAHy
What are the doctor's visiting hours?	診療時間はいつですか？	SHIN-LYOH JIH-kahn wah IH-ts dess KAH?
I need	_____の先生をお願いします。	_____ NOH SEN-SEh OH oh-NEH-GAHY SH'MAHss.
• a general practitioner.	• 内科	• NAHY-KAH

HEALTH CARE

• a pediatrician.	• 小児科	• SHOH-NIH-KAH
• a gynecologist.	• 産婦人科	• SAHN-HU-JIN-KAH
• an eye doctor.	• 眼科	• GAHN-KAH

Talking to the Doctor

I don't feel well.	具合が悪いんです。	gu-AHY GAH WAH-LU-in dess.
I'm sick.	病気なんです。	BYOH-KIH NAHn-dess.
I don't know what I've got.	何の病気かわかりません。	NAHn noh BYOH-KIH KAH wah-KAH-LIH-MAH-SEn.
I have a fever.	熱があります。	neh-TSU gah ah-lih-mahss.
I don't have a fever.	熱はありません。	neh-TSU wah ah-LIH-MAH-SEn.
I'm nauseated.	吐き気がします。	hah-KIH-KEH gah sh'mahss.
I'm feeling dizzy.	めまいがします。	meh-MAHy gah sh'mahss.
I can't sleep.	眠れないんです。	neh-MU-LEH-NAHy-n-dess.
I threw up.	吐きました。	hah-KIH-MAHsh-tah.
I'm constipated.	便秘です。	BEN-PIH DEss.
I have ...	_____なんです。	_____ NAHn-dess.
• asthma.	• ぜんそく	• ZEN-SOHK
• menstrual cramps.	• 生理痛	• SEH-LIH-TSU
• rheumatism.	• リュウマチ	• LYU-MAHCH
• sunstroke.	• 日射病	• niss-SHAH-BYOH
I've developed...	_____が出来たんです。	_____ gah DEH-kih tahn-dess.

• bruises. • a lump. • a swelling.	• うちみ • しこり • はれもの	• u-CHIH-MIH • shih-KOH-LIH • hah-LEH-MOH-NOH
I got an insect bite.	虫にさされました。	mu-SHIH NIH sah-SAH-LEH-MAHsh-tah.
I burned myself.	やけどをしました。	yah-KEH-DOH OH SH'MAHsh-tah.
I've caught a cold.	かぜをひきました。	kah-ZEH OH HIH-KIH-MAHsh-tah.
I have diarrhea.	下痢してるんです。	geh-LIH SHIH-TEH-lun-dess.
I've a stinging pain.	チクチク痛いんです。	CHIK-chik ih-TAHy-n-dess.
My stomach is upset.	お腹をこわしました。	oh-NAH-KAH OH koh-WAHSH MAHsh-tah.
There's something in my eye.	目に何か入ったんです。	MEH nih NAH-nih-kah HAH-it-tahn dess.
I have a cough.	咳が出ます。	seh-KIH gah deh-mahss.
I cut myself here.	ここを切ったんです。	koh-KOH OH KIT-tahn-dess.
My _____ hurts.	_____が痛いんです。	_____ gah ih-TAHy-n-dess.
• head (=headache) • throat (=sore throat) • stomach	• 頭 • のど • お腹	• ah-TAH-mah • NOH-doh • oh-NAH-KAH
I'm allergic to penicillin.	ペニシリンにアレルギーです。	peh-NIH-SHIH-LIN NIH ah-LEH-LU-ghee dess.

Here is the medicine I take.	これが今飲んでいる薬です。	koh-LEH GAH IH-mah NOHn-deh-ih-lu k'SU-LIH DEss.
I've had this pain for two days.	もう二日も痛いんです。	MOh huts-KAII MOH IH-TAHy-n-dess.
I had a heart attack four years ago.	四年前に心臓発作を起こしました。	yoh-NEN MAH-eh nih SHIN-ZOH HOHSS-sah OH oh-KOHSH-MAHsh-tah.
I'm four months pregnant.	妊娠四ヶ月です。	NIN-SHIN YOHN-KAH-gets dess.

PARTS OF THE BODY

right/left	右の／左の	mih-GIH NOH/hih-DAH- LIH NOH
ankle	くるぶし	ku-LU-bu-shih
appendix	盲腸	MOh-choh
arm	腕	u-DEH
artery	動脈	doh-myahk
back	背中	seh-NAH-KAH
bladder	膀胱	boh-koh
bone	骨	hoh-NEH
bowels	大腸	DAHy-choh
breast	乳房	CHIH-bu-sah
buttocks	お尻	oh-SHIH-LIH
calf	すね	su-NEH
chest	胸	mu-NEH
ear	耳	mih-MIH
eye(s)	目	meh

face	顔	kah-OH
finger	指	yu-BIH
foot	足	ah-SHIH
forehead	ひたい	hih-TAHY
gland	腺	SEn
hair	髪	kah-MIH
hand	手	teh
head	頭	ah-TAH-mah
heart	心臓	shin-zoh
hip	腰	koh-SHIH
jaw	あご	ah-GOH
joint	関節	kahn-sets
kidneys	腎臓	jin-zoh
knee	ひざ	hih-ZAH
leg	脚	ah-SHIH
lip	唇	k'CHIH-BIH-LU
liver	肝臓	kahn-zoh
lungs	肺	hahY
mouth	口	k'CHIH
muscle	筋肉	KIn-nik
nail	爪	tsu-MEH
neck	首	ku-BIH
nose	鼻	hah-NAH
penis	ペニス	PEH-nih-su
ribs	肋骨	loht-KOHTS
shoulder	肩	KAH-tah
skin	肌	HAH-dah

spine	背骨	seh-BOH-NEH
stomach (the organ)	胃	ih
stomach area	お腹	oh-NAH-KAH
teeth	歯	hah
thigh	腿	MOH-moh
throat	のど	NOH-doh
thumb	親指	oh-YAH-yu-bih
toe	足の指	ah-SHIH NOH YU-BIH
tongue	舌	shih-TAH
tonsils	へんとう腺	hen-t<u>oh</u>-sen
vagina	膣	CHIH-tsu
vein	静脈	j<u>oh</u>-myahk
wrist	手首	TEH-ku-bih

WHAT THE DOCTOR SAYS

服を脱いで下さい。	hu-KU OH NU-ih-deh k'dah-sahy.	Please take off your clothes.
横になって下さい。	yoh-KOH-NIH NAHT-teh k'dah-sahy.	Please lie down.
口を開けて。	k'CHIH OH ah-KEH-TEH.	Open your mouth.
せきをして。	seh-KIH oh sh'teh.	Cough.
深呼吸をして。	SHIN-KOH-ky<u>u</u> oh sh'teh.	Breathe deeply.
どこが痛いんですか。	DOH-koh gah ih-TAHy-n-dess KAH?	Where does it hurt?
舌を出して下さい。	shih-TAH oh DAHsh-teh k'dah-sahy.	Stick out your tongue.

HEALTH CARE

服を着て下さい。	hu-KU oh kih-TEH-K'DAH-SAHy.	Please get dressed.
いつから痛いんですか？	IH-ts kah-lah ih-TAHy-n-dess KAH?	How long have you had these pains?
_____いいます。	_____ ih-MAHss.	It's...
• はずれて	• hah-ZU-LEH-TEH	• dislocated.
• 折れて	• OH-leh-teh	• broken.
• 化膿して	• kah-NOH SH'TEH	• infected.
ねんざです。	NEN-ZAH DEss.	It's sprained.
重体です。	JU-TAHY DEss.	It's serious.
たいしたことはありません。	TAHy-sh'tah koh-toh wah ah-LIH-MAH-SEn.	It's not serious.
痛み止めを出しましょう。	ih-TAH-MIH-DOH-MEH OH dahSH-MAH-SHOh.	I'm going to give you a painkiller.
_____を紹介しましょう。	_____ OH SHOH-KAHY sh'MAH-SHOh.	I'll refer you to ...
• 病院	• BYOH-IN	• a hospital.
• 専門医	• SEN-MOHn-ih	• a specialist.
_____を計ります。	_____ OH hah-KAH-LIH-MAHss.	I'm going to take your ...
• 熱	• neh-TSU	• temperature.
• 血圧	• keh-TSU-AHTS	• blood pressure.
_____です。	_____ DEss.	You have ...
• 盲腸炎	• MOH-CHOh en	• appendicitis.
• 骨折	• kohss-SETS	• a broken bone.
• 胃炎	• ih-EN	• gastritis.
• 流感	• LYU-KAHN	• the flu.
• 食中毒	• shohk-CHu-dohk	• food poisoning.
_____の検査をします。	_____ noh KEn-sah oh sh'MAHss.	I need to examine your ...
• 血液	• keh-TSU-eh-kih	• blood.
• 便	• BEn	• stool.
• 尿	• NYOh	• urine.

PATIENT QUESTIONS

Is it serious?	かなり重いですか？	KAH-nah-lih oh-MOy dess KAH?
Is it contagious?	うつりますか？	u-TS'LIH MAHss KAH?
How long should I stay in bed?	どれ位安静にしていればいいですか？	doh LEH-G'LAHY AHN-SEH NIH SH'TEH ih-LEH bah Ee-dess KAH?
What exactly is wrong with me?	どこが悪いんでしょうか？	DOH-koh gah wah-LU-in-deh-shoh kah?
How frequently do I take this medication?	この薬は一日何回飲むんですか？	koh-NOH K'SU-lih wah ih-CHI-NICH NAHn-kahy noh-mun-dess KAH?
Do I need to see you again?	又来る必要がありますか？	mah-TAH KU-lu hih-TS'YOH GAH ah-LIH-MAHss KAH?
Are these pills or suppositories?	これは錠剤ですか、座薬ですか？	koh-LEH WAH JOH-ZAHY DEss kah, zah-YAHK DEss KAH?
Can I have a bill for my insurance?	保健のための請求書をもらえますか？	hoh-KEN NOH TAH-MEH noh SEH-KYU-SHOH oh moh-LAH-EH-MAHss KAH?
Could you fill out this medical form?	この書類に記入してもらえますか？	koh-NOH SHOH-LU-IH NIH kih-NYU SH'TEH MOH-LAH-EH-MAHss KAH?

AT THE HOSPITAL

Where is the nearest hospital?	一番近い病院はどこですか？	ih-CHIH-BAHN CH'KAHy BYOH-IN wah DOH-koh dess KAH?
Call an ambulance!	救急車を呼んで！	KYU-KYu-shah oh YOHN-DEH!
Help me![1]	助けて！	tahss-KEH-TEH!
Get me to a hospital!	病院へつれてって下さい！	BYOH-IN EH ts'LEH-TET-teh k'dah-sahy!
I need first aid fast!	すぐ応急手当を！	SU-gu OH-KYU-TEH-ah-teh OH!
I was in an accident.	事故に会ったんです。	JIH-koh nih AHT-tahn dess.
I cut	＿＿＿を切ったんです。	＿＿＿ oh KIT-tahn dess.
• my hand.	• 手	• TEH
• my leg.	• 脚	• ah-SHIH
I can't move [my neck].	[首]が動かないんです。	[ku-BIH]gah u-GOH-KAH-nahy-n-dess.
I hurt my head.	頭にけがをしたんです。	ah-TAH-MAH nih keh-GAH OH sh'tahn-dess.
I ＿＿＿ my ankle.	くるぶしを＿＿＿です。	ku-LU-bu-shih OH ＿＿＿ dess.
• twisted	• くじいたん	• k'JEE-tahn
• broke	• 折ったん	• OHT-tahn
It's swollen.	はれているんです。	hah-LEH-TEH IH-LUn dess.

[1]Note that although the examples say "me" or "I," they are interchangeable with "he/she," "her/him," "himself/herself," etc.

I'm bleeding heavily.	出血がとても多いんです。	SHUT-KETS GAH toh-TEH-MOH Oh-in dess.
She/he's unconscious.	気を失ったんです。	kih OH u-SHIH-NAHT-TAHn dess.
I burned myself.	火傷をしたんです。	yah-KEH-DOH OH SH' TAHn dess.
I have food poisoning.	食中毒です。	shohk-CHu-dohk dess.
When can I leave?	いつ帰れますか？	IH-ts kah-EH-LEH MAHss KAH?
When will the doctor come?	先生はいつ来て下さいますか？	SEN-SEh wah IH-ts kih-teh k'DAH-SAHY-MAHss KAH?
I can't sleep.	眠れないんです。	neh-MU-LEH-NAHy-n-dess.
Where's the nurse?	看護婦さんはどこですか？	KAHN-GOH-hu sahn wah DOH-koh dess KAH?
What are the visiting hours?	面会時間はいつですか？	MEN-KAHY JIH-kahn wah IH-ts dess KAH?

THE DENTIST

Please refer me to a dentist.	歯医者さんを紹介して下さい。	HAHy-shah sahn oh SHOH-KAHY SH'TEH-K'DAH-SAHy.
It's an emergency.	緊急なんです。	KIN-KYU NAHn-dess.
I'm in a lot of pain.	すごく痛いんです。	s'GOHk ih-TAHy-n-dess.
My gums are bleeding.	歯ぐきから血が出ているんです。	HAH-g'kih kah-lah chih GAH DEH-teh ih-lun dess.

I've lost a filling.	つめものがとれたんです。	ts'MEH-MOH-noh gah TOH-leh-tahn dess.
I broke a tooth.	歯がかけました。	HAH gah kah-KEH-MAHsh-tah.
This tooth hurts.	この歯が痛いんです。	koh-NOH HAH gah ih-TAHy-n-dess.
Please don't extract it.	抜かないで下さい。	nu-KAH-NAHy deh k'DAH-SAHy.
Please fill it with	_____でつめて下さい。	_____ deh TS'meh-teh k'DAH-SAHy.
• gold.	• 金	• KIn
• silver.	• 銀	• GHIn
Can you fill it temporarily?	仮につめてもらえますか？	kah-LIH NIH TS'meh-teh moh-LAH-EH-MAHss KAH?
I want a local anesthetic.	局部麻酔をお願いします。	kyohK-BU MAH-su-ih OH oh-NEH-GAHY SH'MAHss.
My _____ is broken.	_____がこわれました。	_____ gah koh-WAH-LEH-MAHsh-tah.
• denture	• 入れ歯	• ih-LEH-BAH
• bridge	• ブリッジ	• bu-LIT-jih
• crown	• 歯冠	• shih-KAHN

WHAT THE DENTIST SAYS

炎症を起こしています。	EN-SHOH OH oh-KOHsh-teh ih-mahss.	There's an infection.
虫歯があります。	mu-SHIH-BAH GAH ah-LIH-MAHss.	You have a rotten tooth.
化膿しています。	kah-NOH SH'TEH IH-MAHss.	You have an abscess.

痛いですか？	ih-TAHy dess KAH?	Does that hurt?
この歯は抜かなければなりません。	koh-NOH HAH wah nu KAH-NAH-keh-leh-bah nah-LIH-MAH-SEn.	This tooth must come out.
_____ 又来て下さい。	_____ mah-tah KIH-teh k'dah-sahy.	You'll need to come back ...
• 明日	• ahsh-TAH	• tomorrow.
• 三日後	• mit-KAH-GOH	• in three days.
• 来週	• lahY-SHU	• next week.

THE OPTICIAN

My _____ broke.	_____がこわれたんです。	_____ gah koh-WAH-leh-tahn dess.
• frame	• フレーム	• hu-LEh-mu
• lens	• レンズ	• LEn-zu
My contact lens ripped.	コンタクトレンズが破れたんです。	KOHN-TAHK-TOH LEn-zu gah yah-BU-leh-tahn-dess.
I lost ...	_____をなくしたんです。	_____ OH nah-KUsh-tahn-dess.
• my glasses.	• メガネ	• MEH-gah-neh
• my contact lens.	• コンタクトレンズ	• KOHN-TAHK-TOH LEn-zu
Can they be replaced right away?	替えはすぐ出来ますか？	kah-EH WAH SU-gu deh-KIH-MAHss KAH?
I'd like _____ contact lenses.	_____レンズをお願いします。	_____ LEn-zu OH oh-NEH-GAHY SH'MAHss.
• hard	• ハード	• HAh-doh
• soft	• ソフト	• soh-HU-TOH
Here's the prescription.	処方箋です。	shoh-HOH-SEN DEss.
When will they be ready?	いつ出来ますか？	IH-ts deh-kih-mahss KAH?

I need sunglasses.	サングラスがいるんです。	SAHN-G'lahss gah ih-LUn dess.

AT THE PHARMACY

Pharmacies operate during normal business hours (around 10 A.M. to around 6 P.M.). Twenty-four-hour convenience stores may have some basics such as aspirin, bandages, and cough drops. If you are taking prescription drugs, make sure you bring an ample supply on your trip since medication is usually given out at hospitals in Japan, and most pharmacies cannot fill prescriptions.

Where is the nearest pharmacy?	一番近い薬局はどこですか？	ih-CHIH-BAHN CH'KAHy yahk-KYOHK WAH DOH-koh-dess KAH?
I need something for …	_____に効く薬を下さい。	_____ NIH KIH-KU K'SU-lih oh k'DAH-SAHy.
• a cold.	• かぜ	• kah-ZEH
• constipation.	• 便秘	• BEN-PIH
• a cough.	• 咳	• seh-KIH
• diarrhea.	• 下痢	• geh-LIH
• fever.	• 熱	• neh-TSU
• hay fever.	• アレルギー性鼻炎	• ah-LEH-LU-GHEE-SEH BIH-en
• headache.	• 頭痛	• zu-TSU
• an insect bite.	• 虫さされ	• mu-SHIH-SAH-SAH-LEH
• sunburn.	• 日焼け	• hih-YAH-KEH
• motion sickness.	• 乗物酔い	• noh-LIH-MOH-NOH-YOY
• an upset stomach.	• 消化不良	• SHOH-KAH HU-lyoh
I'd like (some/a[n]) ….	_____を下さい。	_____ OH k'DAH-SAHy.
• alcohol.	• アルコール	• ah-LU-KOH-LU
• analgesic.	• 鎮痛剤	• CHIN-TSu-zahy

• aspirin.	• アスピリン	• ahss-PIH-LIN
• bandage.	• 包帯	• HOH-TAHY
• Band-Aids.	• バンドエード	• BAHN-DOH Eh-doh
• contact lens solution.	• コンタクトレンズ用の液	• KOHN-TAHK-TOH LEN-ZU YOH NOH EH-kih
• contraceptives.	• 避妊用具	• hih-NIN YOh-gu
• cotton.	• 脱脂綿	• dahss-SHIH-men
• cough drops.	• 咳止め	• seh-KIH-DOH-MEH
• disinfectant/ antiseptic.	• 消毒薬	• SHOH-DOHK-yahk
• eye drops.	• 目薬	• meh-GU-s'lih
• gauze.	• ガーゼ	• GAh-zeh
• insect spray.	• 虫よけスプレー	• mu-SHIH YOH-KEH S'PU-leh
• iodine.	• ヨードチンキ	• YOH-DOH-CHIN-kih
• laxative.	• 下剤	• geh-ZAHY
• nose drops.	• 点鼻薬	• TEN-BIH-yahk
• painkillers.	• 痛み止め	• ih-TAH-MIH-DOH-MEH
• pills.	• 丸薬	• GAHN-YAHK
• sanitary napkins.	• 生理用ナプキン	• SEH-LIH-YOH NAHP-kin
• sleeping pills.	• 睡眠薬	• SU-IH-MIn-yahk
• suppositories.	• 座薬	• zah-YAHK
• tablets.	• 錠剤	• JOH-ZAHY
• tampons.	• タンポン	• TAHn-pohn
• tranquilizers.	• 安定剤	• AHN-TEh-zahy
• thermometer.	• 体温計	• TAHY-OHN-KEH
• vitamins.	• ビタミン剤	• bih-TAH-MIn-zahy
It's urgent!	急いでるんです！	ih-SOy-deh-lun-dess!

9 / ON THE ROAD

Driving in Japan can be difficult, expensive, and often much slower than public transportation. It is not recommended that you rent a car unless you truly want to drive just for the experience. Road signs are seldom in English, except for major roads and highways in big cities, and few roads have names in the suburbs, let alone street signs. Streets tend to be narrow, and traffic can be extremely heavy during rush hour. Street parking in a city requires a lot of luck and skill; you should opt for a parking garage instead. Rental fees and tolls are expensive, and gas prices are astronomical. Your best bet is to rely on the very efficient public transportation system; bullet trains can cover the same distance as a car in less than half the time.

If you want to try driving despite these factors, here are some basic points to keep in mind:

1) You must have an international driver's license in order to drive. Your local AAA office will be able to help you obtain one. Also, bring your passport to the rental car agency when you pick up your car. The minimum age to rent is 18.
2) Drive on the left side of the road (as in the United Kingdom).
3) Rates vary, but expect to pay around $80 per day. The price includes insurance against accidents, and has no mileage limit.
4) It would be wise to arrange for car rentals before you leave for Japan. Hertz and Avis have offices in Tokyo.

DIALOGUE: AT THE RENTAL CAR AGENCY レンタカー会社で leN-TAH-KAH GAhy-shah deh

お客： oh-KYAHK	安い料金の車を借りたいんですが。	yah-SU-ih lyoh-kin noh k'lu-mah oh kah-LIH-TAHy-n-dess gah.
係： KAH-kah-lih	かしこまりました。小型車が一台残っております。	kahsh-KOH-MAH-LIH-MAHsh-tah. koh-GAH-TAH-shah gah ih-CHIH-dahy noh-KOHT-teh oh-lih-mahss.
お客： oh-KYAHK	三日間借りたいんですが。	mit-KAH-kahn kah-LIH-TAHy-n-dess gah.
係： KAH-kah-lih	結構です。キロ数に制限はありません。	KET-koh dess. kih-LOH Su nih SEH-GHEN wah ah-LIH-MAH-SEn.
お客： oh-KYAHK	じゃあ、それをお願いします。	JYAh, soh-LEH OH OH-NEH-GAHY SH'MAHss.

Customer:	I'd like to rent an inexpensive car.
Employee:	Certainly. We still have a small car left.
Customer:	I'd like to rent it for three days.
Employee:	That would be fine. There's no mileage limit on the car.
Customer:	I'll take it, then.

Is there a car rental agency in this town?	この町にレンタカー会社はありますか？	koh-NOH MAH-CHIH nih LEN-TAH-KAH GAHy-shah wah ah-LIH-MAHss KAH?

English	Japanese	Pronunciation
I'd like to rent…	_____を借りたいんです。	_____oh kah-LIH-TAHy-n-dess.
• a small car.	• 小型車	• koh-GAH-TAH-shah
• a midsize car.	• 中型車	• CHU-GAH-TAH-shah
• a large car.	• 大型車	• OH-GAH-TAH-shah
• the least expensive car.	• 一番安い車	• ih-CHIH-BAHN YAH-SU-ih k'lu-mah
• a car with automatic transmission.	• オートマティックの車	• OH-TOH-MAH-TIT-ku noh k'lu-mah
How much is the rate…	_____いくらですか？	_____IH-k'lah dess KAH?
• per day?	• 一日	• ih-CHIH-NICH
• per week?	• 一週間	• ss-SHU-kahn
Do you accept this credit card?	このカードは使えますか？	koh-NOH KAh-doh wah ts'KAH-EH MAHss KAH?
Do you need my driver's license?	免許証はいりますか？	MEN-KYOH-shoh wah ih-LIH-MAHss KAH?
Can I rent it here and return it in Tokyo?	ここで借りて 東京 で返せますか？	koh-KOH DEH KAH-LIH-TEH TOH-KYOH DEH kah-EH-SEH-MAHss KAH?

RENTING A BICYCLE

Bicycles are a common mode of transportation in Japan. People often use bikes to run errands as well as for recreation. If you want to enjoy a refreshing ride in the countryside, you might be able to rent a bicycle from your lodging or at a recreational park.

I'd like to rent a bicycle.	自転車を借りたいんです。	jih-TEN-SHAH OH KAH-LIH-TAHy-n-dess.
How much is it per hour?	一時間いくらですか？	ih-CHIH-jih-kahn IH k'lah dess KAH?
When do you close?	何時までですか？	NAHn-jih mah-deh dess KAH?

DRIVING

Purchase a good road map and study it well. Maps with romanized (i.e., English) place-names are available at some bookstores (try larger bookstores that have a foreign-language books section) and at some Japanese bookstores in the United States.

Is this the road to Tokyo?	この道は 東京 へ行きますか？	koh-NOH MIH-CHIH WAH TOH-KYOH eh ih-KIH-MAHss KAH?
How far is it to_____?	_____までどれ位ありますか？	_____MAH-deh DOH-leh-g'lahy ah-LIH-MAHss KAH?
Where can I get a road map of_____?	_____の地図はどこで売ってますか？	_____noh CHIH-zu wah DOH-koh deh ut-TEH MAHss kah?
Do I…	_____んですか？	_____n-dess KAH?
• go straight?	• まっすぐ行く	• mahss-SU-gu ih-KU
• turn right?	• 右へまがる	• mih-GIH EH MAH-GAH-LU
• turn left?	• 左へまがる	• hih-DAH-LIH EH MAH-GAH-LU
• make a U-turn?	• ユーターンをする	• YU-TAHn oh s'lu
Is there a parking lot nearby?	近くに駐車場はありますか？	chih-KAHK nih CHU-SHAH-JOH WAH ah-LIH-MAHss KAH?

DISTANCES AND LIQUID MEASURES

Japan uses the metric system as a standard. Below are basic conversion charts for your convenience.

MILES/KILOMETERS

1 kilometer (km) = .62 miles	1 mile =1.61 km (1.61 km)
Kilometers	**Miles**
1	0.62
5	3.1
8	5.0
10	6.2
15	9.3
20	12.4
50	31.0
75	46.5
100	62.0

GALLONS/LITERS

1 liter (l) =.26 gallon	1 gallon = 3.75 liters (3.75 l)
Liters	**Gallons**
10	2.6
15	3.9
20	5.2
30	7.8
40	10.4
50	13.0
60	15.6
70	18.2

THE SERVICE STATION

Where is the nearest service station?	一番近いガソリンスタンドはどこですか？	ih-CHIH-BAHN CH'KAHy gah-SOH-LIN S' TAHn-doh wah DOH-koh dess KAH?
Fill it with...	＿＿を満タンお願いします。	＿＿oh MAHN-TAHN oh-NEH-GAHY SH'MAHss.
• regular (unleaded).	• レギュラー	• LEH-gyu-lah
• super.	• ハイオク	• hahY-OH-KU
• diesel.	• 軽油	• KEH-YU
Give me 20 liters of regular.	レギュラーを20リッター下さい。	LEH-gyu-lah oh nih-JU LIT-tah k'dah-sahy.
Give me ¥5,000 of regular.	レギュラーを5,000円分下さい。	LEH-gyu-lah oh goh-SEN-EN BUN K'DAH-SAHy.
Please check...	＿＿をチェックして下さい。	＿＿oh CHET-ku sh'teh k'dah-sahy.
• the battery.	• バッテリー	• baht-TEH-LEE
• the brake fluid.	• ブレーキオイル	• bu-LEH-KIH OY-lu
• the carburetor.	• キャブレター	• kyah-BU-LEH-tah
• the oil.	• オイル	• Oy-lu
• the tire pressure.	• エアー	• EH-ah
• the water.	• 水	• mih-ZU
Please change...	＿＿を取り替えて下さい。	＿＿oh toh-LIH-KAH-eh teh k'dah-sahy.
• the oil.	• オイル	• Oy-lu
• the tire.	• タイヤ	• tahY-YAH
My car has broken down.	車が故障しました。	k'LU-MAH GAH koh-SHOH SH'MAHsh-tah.
Can you repair it?	直りますか？	nah-OH-LIH-MAHss KAH?

It won't start.	エンジンがかかりません。	En-jin gah kah-KAH-LIH-MAH-SEn.
I have a flat tire.	パンクしました。	PAHN-KU SH'MAHsh-tah.
The battery's dead.	バッテリーがあがりました。	baht-TEH-LEE GAH ah-GAH-LIH-MAHsh-tah.
It's overheated.	オーバーヒートしてるんです。	OH-BAH-HEE-toh sh'TEH-lun-dess.
Can you tow me?	牽引してもらえますか？	KEN-IN SH'TEH moh-LAH-EH-MAHss KAH?
I have a problem with…	_____がおかしいんです。	_____gah oh-KAH-SHEEn dess.
• the directional signal.	• ウィンカー	• wiN-KAH
• the gears.	• ギアー	• GIH-ah
• the brakes.	• ブレーキ	• bu-LEH-kih
• the ignition.	• イグニション	• ih-GU-NIH-shohn
• the radiator.	• ラジエーター	• lah-JIH-EH-tah
• the starter.	• スターター	• s'TAH-TAH
• the transmission.	• トランスミッション	• toh-LAHNSS-MISS-shohn
Do you have…	_____はありますか？	_____wah ah-LIH-MAHss KAH?
• a flashlight?	• 懐中電灯	• KAHY-CHU-DEn-toh
• a jack?	• ジャッキ	• JYAHT-kih
• jumper cables?	• バッテリーケーブル	• baht-TEH-LEE KEh-bu-lu
• a road map?	• 道路地図	• DOH-LOH CHIH-zu
How long will it take?	どれ位かかりますか？	doh-LEH G'LAHY KAH-KAH-LIH-MAHss KAH?
I need it today.	今日いるんです。	KYOh ih-LUn dess.

ROAD SIGNS

路肩弱し	loh-KAH-TAH YOH-wah-shih	Soft Shoulders
点灯せよ	TEN-TOH SEH-yoh	Headlights On
シートベルト着用	SHEE-TOH BEH-lu-toh chah-KU-YOH	Fasten Your Seat Belts
進入注意	SHIN-NYU CHu-ih	Merging Traffic
工事中	koh-jih-chu	Construction
スリップ注意	su-LIT-pu CHU-ih	Slippery Road
落石注意	lahk-SEH-KIH CHu-ih	Falling Rocks
片側駐車	kah-TAH-GAH-WAH CHu-shah	Parking on One Side Only
立入禁止	tah-CHIH-IH-LIH KIN-SHIH	No Trespassing/Do Not Enter
急坂	kyu-zah-kah	Steep Hill
ローギアー	LOH-GIH-ah	Steep Descent: Downshift Gear
回り道	mah-WAH-LIH MIH-CHIH	Detour
右車線	mih-GIH SHAH-sen	Right Lane
左車線	hih-DAH-LIH SHAH-sen	Left Lane
行き止まり	ih-KIH-DOH-MAH-LIH	Dead End
歩行者禁止	hoh-KOh-shah KIN-SHIH	No Pedestrians
駐車場	chu-shah-joh	Parking Lot
ふみきり一時停止	hu-MIH-KIH-LIH ih-CHIH-jih TEH-SHIH	Railroad Crossing: Stop Briefly

ROAD CLOSED

NO ENTRY FOR VEHICLES

LEFT TURN ONLY

NO PASSING

NO STOPPING

NO PARKING

NO U-TURN

HEIGHT LIMIT

WEIGHT LIMIT

SPEED LIMIT

MINIMUM SPEED

ONE WAY

PEDESTRIANS ONLY

BUS LANE

SLOW

STOP

PEDESTRIAN CROSSING

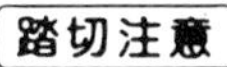

RAILWAY CROSSING

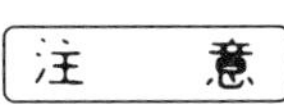

CAUTION

EMERGENCY PARKING ZONE

PARKING AREA / PARKING PERMITTED

TRAFFIC LIGHT AHEAD

ROTARY

SCHOOL ZONE

INTERSECTION

SLIPPERY ROAD

ROAD NARROWS

CONSTRUCTION

FALLING ROCK ZONE

横断歩道	OH-DAHN HOH-doh	Pedestrian Crossing
有料道路	YU-LYOH DOh-loh	Toll Road
料金所	lyoh-kin-joh	Toll Booth
左に寄れ	hih-DAH-LIH NIH YOH-LEH	Yield to the Left
私有地	shih-YU-chih	Private Property
徐行	joh-KOH	Slow
危険	kih-KEN	Danger
最高速度_____キロ	SAHY-KOH SOHk-doh_____kih-loh	Speed Limit: _____ km/hr
バスレーン	bah-SU LEHn	Bus Lane
一方通行	it-POH TSu-koh	One Way
左側通行	hih-DAH-LIH-GAH-WAH TSu-koh	Keep Left
高速道路	KOH-SOHK DOh-loh	Highway
出口	DEH-g'chih	Exit
入口	ih-LIH-'cCHIH	Entrance
駐車禁止	chu-shah kin-shih	No Parking
本線	HOHn-sen	Through Traffic
凍結注意	TOH-KETS CHu-ih	Icy Road
カーブ危険	KAh-bu kih-KEN	Caution: Curves Ahead
北	kih-TAH	North
南	mih-NAH-MIH	South
東	hih-GAH-SHIH	East
西	nih-SHIH	West

10 / COMMUNICATIONS

In order to sound polite over the phone, it is necessary to use a certain type of language. The dialogue may seem complicated, since it uses some words that are a bit too polite for everyday use; however, the phrases are used in phone conversations frequently, especially in a business setting. For example, the polite way to say "My name is _____" is "wah-TAHSH WAH _____ toh MOH-SHIH-MAHss." Also, "MOHsh mohsh" means "hello" in phone conversations only, and you should note the use of "shih-TS'lay sh'mahss" (normally translated as "Pardon me"): this phrase is often used in ending a phone conversation, instead of the standard "sah-YOH-NAH-lah" (Good-bye).

DIALOGUE: A PHONE CONVERSATION 電話の会話 den-wah noh kahy-wah

リサ ロバーツ： LIH-sah LOH-bah-tsu[1]	もしもし。	MOHsh mohsh.
加藤次郎： KAH-toh JIH-loh[1]	もしもし、加藤ですが。	MOHsh mohsh, KAH-toh dess gah.
リサ ロバーツ： LIH-sah LOH-bah-tsu	ブラウンさんはいらっしゃいますか？	bu-LAH un sahn wah ih-LAHSS-SHAHY MAHss KAH?
加藤次郎： KAH-toh JIH-loh	少々お待ち下さい…。すみません、席をはずしているようですが。	SHOH-shoh oh-MAHCH K'DAH-SAHy.... s'MIH-MAH-SEn, SEH-kih oh hah-ZU-SH'TEH IH-LU YOh dess gah.

[1]Note again the order of names: in Japanese, the first name comes after the last name. It is, however, acceptable to use the Western order for a foreign name.

リサ ロバーツ：LIH-sah LOH-bah-tsu	私はリサ　ロバーツと申しますが、ブラウンさんがおもどりになったらお電話をいただけますか？	wah-TAHSH WAH LIH-sah LOH-bah-tsu toh MOH-SHIH MAHss gah, bu-LAH-un sahn gah oh-MOH-DOH-LIH NIH NAHT-tah lah oh-DEn-wah oh ih-TAH-DAH-KEH-MAHss KAH?
加藤次郎：KAH-toh JIH-loh	わかりました、そう伝えます。	wah-KAH-LIH-MAHsh-tah, SOH TS'TAH-EH-MAHss.
リサ ロバーツ：LIH-sah LOH-bah-tsu	どうも。失礼します。	DOh-moh. shih-TS'lay sh'mahss.
加藤次郎：KAH-toh JIH-loh	失礼します。	shih-TS'lay sh'mahss.

Lisa Roberts:	Hello.
Jiro Kato:	Hello, this is Kato speaking.
Lisa Roberts:	Is Mr. Brown there?
Jiro Kato:	One moment, please.... I'm sorry, he's not at his desk right now.
Lisa Roberts:	My name is Lisa Roberts. Could you ask him to call me when he gets back?
Jiro Kato:	Sure, I'll give him the message.
Lisa Roberts:	Thank you. Good-bye.
Jiro Kato:	Good-bye.

TELEPHONES

In Japan, pay phones are conveniently located on streets, in restaurants, stores, train stations, on trains, and in other public areas. As of this writing, local calls are ¥10, and long-distance rates vary by city. Red, blue, pink, and yellow phones only accept coins (¥10 coins or sometimes ¥100 coins) and only allow you to make domestic calls, but you can make international calls from many of the green phones (look for a gold-colored sign plate saying so in English on the phone). These green phones also take telephone cards, which are quite handy when you don't have change. You can purchase these disposable cards at various places: vending machines, hotels, tourist gift shops, etc. They normally have pictures on them (anything from popular singers to a tourist site such as a temple or garden), and are avidly collected by some Japanese.

To make an overseas call by using an operator, dial 0051. You can also use the Home Country Direct service, which lets you get in touch with an operator from the United States. Dial 0039-111, and a U.S. operator will let you make collect calls or bill your calling card.

You can also obtain tourist information in English over the phone. Travel-Phone is a system run by JNTO that lets you talk to an English-speaking agent, and is available daily from 9:00 A.M. to 5:00 P.M. In Tokyo, dial 3502-1461, and in Kyoto, dial 371-5649. Outside those two cities, call 0210-222800 for eastern Japan and 0120-444800 for western Japan information. You can also call the Teletourist Service, a prerecorded guide to events in Tokyo (call [03] 3503-2911) and Kyoto (call [075] 361-2911).

Keep in mind that all Tokyo numbers now start with an extra "3" at the beginning, making them 8-digit numbers. For example, a number previously listed as 123-4567 is now 3123-4567.

Emergency numbers are 110 for police and 119 for emergency medical service.

I'd like to make a call.	電話をかけたいんです。	DEN-WAH OH kah-KEH-TAHy-n-dess.
Is there a pay phone nearby?	近くに公衆電話はありますか？	chih-KAHk nih KOH-SHU-DEn-wah wah ah-LIH-MAHss KAH?
Do you have a phone directory?	電話帳はありますか？	deN-WAH-CHOH WAH ah-LIH-MAHss KAH?
Can you find this name in the phone book for me?	この名前を電話帳で捜してもらえますか？	koh-NOH NAH-MAH-EH OH DEN-WAH-CHOH DEH sah-GAHSH-TEH MOH-LAH-EH-MAHss KAH?
What do I dial to get …	_____は何番ですか？	_____ wah NAHn-bahn dess KAH?
• an operator?	• オペレーター	• oh-PEH-L Eh-tah
• the international operator?	• 国際電話のオペレーター	• kohk-SAHY DEn-wah noh oh-PEH-LEh-tah
I'd like to call…	_____をかけたいんです。	_____ oh kah-KEH-TAHy-n-dess.
• overseas.	• 国際電話	• kohk-SAHY DEn-wah
• collect.[1]	• コレクトコール	• koh-LEK-TOH KOh-lu
My number is _____.	こちらは_____です。	koh-CHIH-LAH WAH _____ dess.

[1]Note that there is no domestic collect-calling system within Japan.

What is the area code for _____ ?	_____の市外局番は何番ですか？	_____ noh shih-GAHY KYOHK-bahn wah NAHn-bahn dess KAH?
I was cut off.	途中で切れたんですが。	toh-CHU DEH KIH-leh-tahn-dess gah.
To whom am I speaking?	どちら様ですか。	DOHch-lah sah mah dess KAH?
Please speak more slowly.	もっとゆっくり話して下さい。	MOHT-toh yut-KU-lih hah-NAHsh-teh k'dah-sahy.
Could you telephone for me?	代りに電話をかけてくれませんか？	kah-WAH-LIH NIH DEN-WAH OH KAH-keh-teh k'LEH-MAH-SEn KAH?
I'd like to speak to Mr./Ms. _____ (lit., Is _____ there?).	_____さんいらっしゃいますか？	_____ sahn ih-LAHSS-SHAHY-MAHss KAH?
Please leave the following message.	お言付けをお願いします。	oh-KOH-TOH-Z'KEH OH oh-NEH-GAHY SH'MAHss.

WHAT YOU MAY HEAR

どちら様ですか？	DOHch-lah sah-mah dess KAH?	Who's calling?
ちょっとお待ち下さい。	CHOHT-toh oh-MAHCH-K'DAH-SAHy.	One moment, please.
誰も出ません。	dah-LEH MOH deh-MAH-SEn.	There's no answer.
間違いですよ。	mah-CHIH-GAHy dess YOH.	You've got the wrong number.

只今外出中ですが。	tah-DAHy-mah GAHY-SHUTS-CHU DEss gah.	He/she is out right now.
席を外しておりますが。	SEH-kih oh hah-ZU-SHIH-TEH OH-LIH-MAHss gah.	She/he is away from her/his seat.
何かお言付けはございますか？	NAH-nih-kah oh-KOH-TOH-Z'KEH WAH GOH-ZAHY-MAHSS KAH?	Can I take a message?
こちらからおかけしましょうか？	kohch-LAH KAH-LAH oh-KAH-KEH SHIH-MAH SHOh KAH?	Can he/she/I call you back?
後で又かけていただけますか？	AH-toh deh mah-tah KAH-keh-teh ih-TAH-DAH-KEH-MAHss KAH?	Could you call again later?
お話中です。	oh-HAH-NAHSH-CHU DEss.	The line is busy.
お電話です。	oh-DEn-wah dess.	You have a call.
どの番号にかけたいんですか？	DOH-noh bahn-goh nih kah-KEH-TAHy-n-dess KAH?	What number do you want?

POST OFFICE AND MAIL

Generally, post offices are open 8 A.M. to 5 P.M. on weekdays, and 8 A.M. to noon on Saturdays. They are closed on Sundays. Some services (such as sending packages overseas) are not available at the smaller locations, so you might want to try going to a major post office of any given city, which usually has longer hours than those listed above. The central post office near Tokyo Station is open 24 hours a day throughout the year.

An easy way to receive your mail is to have it sent to an American Express office. There should be an office in all major cities; the address for the Tokyo office is American Express, the Halifax Building, 16-26 Roppongi, 3 cho-me, Minato-ku, Tokyo. You can also have mail sent to the International Post Office at 2-3-3 Otemachi, Chiyoda-ku, Tokyo (tel.03-3241-4891). Notify the post office that you expect mail so that it will be held there until you pick it up.

A very convenient method of sending packages within Japan and also to and from the United States is courier service (宅急便 taht-KYU-BIN). There are several ways you can use this system:

1) When you first arrive at the airport, look for a courier sevice counter. It is possible to send your luggage from there to an address in Japan, so that it will arrive on the next day. It costs only about $10 per piece of luggage, and this way, you can leave the airport with just a small overnight bag and not have to worry about lugging around large suitcases. On your way home, you can call two days ahead to ask for a pickup of your luggage, which will be waiting at the airport on the day of your departure.
2) These courier services also deliver regular packages within Japan.
3) It is possible to send packages overseas using this method, though it is a bit costly; however, compared to regular mail, service is speedier and more reliable. There are several major companies that operate this service. Some have offices in the United States, such as 日通 nit-TSU, also known as Nippon Express USA (212)683-4940 and クロネコヤマト k'LOH-NEH-KOH YAH-mah-toh, also known as Yamato Transport USA (718) 204-8800. Federal Express and DHL also have offices in Japan.

I'm looking for the post office.	郵便局を捜してるんです。	YU-BIn-kyohk oh sah-GAHSH-TEH-LUn-dess.

Where's the nearest mailbox?	一番近いポストはどこですか？	ih-CHIH-BAHN CH'KAHY POHss-toh wah DOh-koh dess KAH?
I'd like to mail a letter.	手紙を送りたいんです。	teh-GAH-MIH OH oh-K'LIH TAHY-n-dess
How much is it to mail…	_____はおいくらですか？	_____ wah oY-K'LAH DEss KAH?
• this letter?	• この手紙	• koh-NOH TEH-GAH-MIH
• a registered letter?	• 書き留め	• kah-KIH-TOH-MEH
• a special-delivery letter?	• 速達	• sohk-TAHTS
• this package?	• この小包	• koh-NOH koh-ZU-ts'mih
Which window is it for…	_____はどの窓口ですか？	_____ wah DOH-noh mah-DOH-g'chih dess KAH?
• general delivery?	• 普通便	• hu-TSU-BIN
• stamps?	• 切手	• kit-TEH
• money orders?	• 為替	• kah-WAH-SEH
Is there mail for me?	私宛の郵便はありますか？	wah-TAHSH AH-TEH NOH YU-BIN WAH ah-LIH-MAHss KAH?
I'd like…	_____を下さい。	_____ OH k'DAH-SAHy.
• ¥ _____ stamps.	• _____円切手	• _____ EN KIT-teh
• stamps for this letter.	• この手紙の分の切手	• koh-NOH teh-GAH-MIH NOH BUn noh kit-TEH

TELEGRAMS AND FACSIMILE

You can send telegrams and faxes at post offices. At larger branches, there will be a designated window for telegrams. Also, your hotel can assist you with sending facsimiles.

Which window is it for telegrams?	電報はどの窓口ですか？	DEN-POH WAH DOH-noh mah-DOH-g'chih dess KAH?
I'd like to send a telegram.	電報を送りたいんです。	DEN-POH OH oh-K'LIH-TAHy-n-dess.
How much is it per word?	一語いくらですか？	ih-CHIH-goh IH-k'lah dess KAH?
When will it get there?	いつ着きますか？	IH-ts ts'KIH-MAHss KAH?
I'd like a telegram form.	頼信紙を下さい。	lahY-SHIn-shih oh k'DAH-SAHy.
I'd like to send a fax.	ファックスを送りたいんです。	faht-KU-SU OH oh-KU-LIH-TAHy-n-dess.
How much is it per page?	一枚いくらですか？	ih-CHIH-mahy IH-k'lah DEss KAH?

WIRING CASH FROM THE UNITED STATES

You should go to Japan with an ample supply of traveler's checks, but if you run out of money, you can have some sent from your bank in the United States to its branch or agent in Japan, if there is one. American Express MoneyGrams are also another means of getting cash; call 1-800-543-4080 before you leave the United States to get locations in Japan where you can contact an American Express agent. A third way is to have money sent through Western Union.

THE MEDIA

You can obtain newspapers and magazines from various parts of the world in Tokyo. Some popular English-language newspapers are the *Japan Times*, the *Daily*

Yomiuri, Mainichi Daily, and the *Asahi Evening News.* The *International Herald Tribune* and the *Asian Wall Street Journal* are also available. As for magazines, there are several that keep you up-to-date with events in and around Tokyo, including the *Tokyo Journal.*

Books in foreign languages including English can be found in some large bookstores such as Kinokuniya (紀伊国屋 kih-NOHK-NIH-YAH) in Tokyo, and Maruzen (丸善 mah-LU-zen) branch stores in various cities.

On TV, the nightly news is available in both Japanese and English in many cities. There is also a telecast of CNN News on Satellite TV, which also periodically broadcasts English-language movies. Program listings can be found in English-language newspapers.

Books, Magazines, and Newspapers

Do you have...	_____はありますか？	_____ wah ah-LIH-MAHss KAH?
• newspapers in English?	• 英語の新聞	• AY-GOH NOH SHIN-BUN
• magazines in English?	• 英語の雑誌	• AY-GOH NOH ZAHSS-SHIH
• books in English?	• 英語の本	• AY-GOH NOH HOHn

Radio and Television

Which is the _____ channel?	どれが_____のチャンネルですか？	DOH-leh gah _____ NOH CHAHn-ne-lu dess KAH?
• English-speaking	• 英語	• AY-GOH
• news	• ニュース	• NYU-su
• weather	• 天気予報	• TEN-KIH-YOH-hoh
• Satellite	• 衛星放送	• EH-SEH HOh-soh

COMMUNICATIONS

What is the number on the dial?	これは何チャンネルですか？	koh-LEH WAH NAHN-CHAHn-neh-lu dess KAH?
What is this television station?	これはどの放送局ですか？	koh-LEH WAH DOH-noh HOH-SOh-kyohk dess KAH?
What is this program?	これは何の番組ですか？	koh-LEH WAH NAHn-noh bahn-g'mih dess KAH?
Do they have international news in English?	英語の国際ニュースはありますか？	AY-GOH NOH kohk-SAHY NYU-su wah ah-LIH-MAHss KAH?
When is the weather forecast?	天気予報はいつですか？	TEN-KIH-YOH-hoh wah IH-ts dess KAH?

11 / SEEING THE SIGHTS

PLACES OF INTEREST

It would be best to consult a guidebook and plan out what sights you want to see before you leave on your trip. Check the Japan National Tourist Office and your travel agent for tips and information (for locations in the United States and Japan, see "Before You Leave," and for phone numbers of tourist information in English, see chapter 10). There are information booths at many railway stations that offer help for tourists. Most lodgings will have information about local points of interest.

A note about safety: in general, Japan is considered a safe place to travel. Of course, there's always a certain degree of risk anywhere, especially in large cities, so use common sense in deciding where and when to go sightseeing, especially if you are traveling alone.

DIALOGUE: AT THE SHINTO SHRINE 神社で JIn-jah deh

由美： YU-mih	日本に神社はたくさんありますが、中でもこの伊勢神宮はとても有名です。	nih-HOHn nih JIn-jah wah tahk-SAHN AH-LIH-MAHss gah, NAH-kah deh-moh koh-NOH ih-SEH JIn-gu wah toh-TEH-MOH YU-MEH DEss.
トム： TOH-mu	ここには誰がまつってあるんですか？	koh-KOH NIH-wah DAH-leh gah mah-TSUT-TEH AH-lun-dess KAH?
由美： YU-mih	天照大神です。	AH-mah-teh-lahss OH-MIH-kah-mih dess.

トム： TOH-mu	いつ建てられたんですか？	IH-ts tah-TEH-LAH-leh-tahn-dess KAH?
由美： YU-mih	古代からあると言われますが、この建物は二十年毎に建て替えられるんですよ。	KOH-dahy kah-lah AH-lu toh ih-WAH-LEH-MAHss gah, koh-NOH TAH-TEH-moh-noh wah nih-J<u>U</u>-NEN GOH-toh nih tah-TEH-KAH-EH-LAH-LEH-lun-dess YOH.
トム： TOH-mu	そうなんですか。	S<u>Oh</u>-nahn-dess kah.

Yumi:	There are many shrines in Japan, but this one in Ise is very famous.
Tom:	Who is enshrined here?
Yumi:	The Sun goddess (Amaterasu Omikami).
Tom:	When was this built?
Yumi:	It's said that it's existed since the ancient times, but this building is rebuilt every twenty years.
Tom:	Is that so!

SIGHTSEEING

What are some places to see in this area?	この辺の名所はなんですか？	koh-NOH HEN NOH M<u>EH</u>-SHOH wah NAHn-dess KAH?
How far is it from here?	ここからどれ位ですか？	koh-KOH KAH-LAH DOH-leh-g'lahy dess KAH?
Where is the tourist office?	観光案内所はどこですか？	KAHN-K<u>OH</u> AHN-NAHY-JOH wah DOH-koh dess KAH?

Are there ...	_____はありますか？	_____wah ah-LIH-MAHss KAH?
• guided tours?	• ガイド付ツアー	• gahY-DOH TS'KIH TSU-ah
• excursions?	• ツアー	• TSU-ah
Are there English-speaking guides?	英語の出来るガイドさんはいますか？	AY-GOH NOH DEH-KIH-lu GAHy-doh-sahn wah ih-MAHss KAH?
We'd like a guide for...	ガイドさんを_____頼みたいんです。	GAHy-doh-sahn oh _____tah-NOH-MIH-TAHy-n-dess.
• a day.	• 一日	• ih-CHIH-NICH
• half a day.	• 半日	• HAHN-NICH
When does the excursion begin?	ツアーは何時からですか？	TSU-ah wah NAHn-jih kah-lah dess KAH?
Is breakfast (lunch, dinner) included?	朝食（昼食、夕食）付ですか？	CHOH-SHOHK (CHU-SHOHK, YU-SHOHK) TS'KIH DEss KAH?
How much is the excursion, everything included?	ツアーは全部でいくらですか？	TSU-ah wah ZEn-bu deh IH-k'lah dess KAH?
When do we return to the hotel?	何時にホテルにもどりますか？	NAHn-jih nih HOH-teh-lu nih moh-DOH-LIH-MAHss KAH?
From where do the tours start?	ツアーはどこから出発しますか？	TSU-ah wah DOH-koh kah-lah shut-PAHTS SHIH-MAHss KAH?

AROUND TOWN

Among the most popular tourist spots are temples, shrines, and gardens. A great number of them are centuries old, and they will give you a flavor of traditional architecture, art, and religion. Other popular structures include castles, which have massive moats and stone walls, and old houses that allow you a glimpse into the Japan of the past. There are many other things to see in each region, of course, and seasonal festivals are among them. Festivals range from religious ceremonies and historical parades to crafts fairs, and have very distinct local flavors.

I'd like to go to the …	＿＿へ行きたいんです。	＿＿eh ih-KIH-TAHy-n-dess.
• amusement park.	• 遊園地	• YU-En-chih
• aquarium.	• 水族館	• SU-IH-ZOHK-kahn
• art gallery.	• ギャラリー	• GYAH-lah-lee
• art museum.	• 美術館	• bih-JUTS-kahn
• Japanese gardens.	• 日本庭園	• nih-HOHN TEh-en
• business district.	• 繁華街	• HAHN-KAH-gahy
• castle.	• お城	• oh-SHIH-LOH
• factories.	• 工場	• KOH-BAH
• festival.	• お祭り	• oh-MAHTS-LIH
• flea market.	• のみの市	• noh-MIH NOH IH-chih
• harbor.	• 港	• mih-NAH-TOH
• historic sites.	• 史跡名所	• shih-SEH-KIH MEH-SHOH
• hot springs.	• 温泉	• ohN-SEN
• library.	• 図書館	• toh-SHOH-kahn
• market.	• 市場	• IH-chih-bah
• monument.	• 記念碑	• kih-NEn-hih
• museums.	• 博物館	• hah-KU-BUTS-kahn
• national treasure.[1]	• 国宝	• kohk-HOH
• the old parts of town.	• 古い街並み	• h'LU-ih mah-CHIH-NAH-MIH
• pagoda.	• 塔	• TOh
• palace.	• 御所	• GOH-shoh

[1] Certain artifacts are designated "national treasures" by the government.

• park.	• 公園	• KOH-EN
• planetarium.	• プラネタリウム	• pu-LAN-NEH-TAH-LYu-mu
• ruins of_____.	• _____の跡	•_____noh AH-toh
• shrine.	• 神社/神宮	• JIn-jah/jiN-Gu
• shopping district.	• 商店街	• SHOH-TEn-gahy
• stadium.	• 球場	• KYU-JOH
• stock exchange.	• 証券取り引き所	• SHOH-KEN TOH-LIH-HIH-KIH-JOH
• theater.	• 劇場	• geh-KIH-JOH
• torii[1] gates .	• 鳥居	• toh-LEE
• tower.	• タワー	• TAH-wah
• town hall.	• 市役所	• shih-YAHK-shoh
• university.	• 大学	• dahY-GAHK
• zoo.	• 動物園	• DOH-BUTS-en
I'd like to see…	_____を見たいんです。	_____oh mih-TAHY-n-dess.
• a historic house.	• 民家	• MIn-kah
•_____'s house.	• _____の家	•_____NOH ih-EH
•_____'s grave.	• _____の墓	•_____noh hah-kah
• the statue of_____.	• _____の像	•_____noh ZOh
Would you take our picture?	写真を撮ってもらえますか？	shah-SHIN OH TOHT-teh moh-LAH-EH-MAHss KAH?

TOKYO FOR FREE

Tokyo offers a variety of attractions that are free of charge. Some interesting cost-free things to see and do are listed below.

Pedestrian Heavens (歩行者天国 hon-KOH-SHAH TEn-gohk)**:** Certain streets are closed off from traffic on

[1]Torii gates (鳥居 toh-LEE) are characteristic gates normally associated with shrines.

Sundays in Ginza, Harajuku, and Shinjuku (these closed-off streets are referred to as "pedestrian heaven"). You can mingle with the crowds or people-watch.

Fireworks (花火 HAH-nah-bih): Every summer on July 27, you can enjoy a fireworks display over the Sumida River.

Festivals (祭り mah-TSU-LIH): At Tokyo's festivals, you can enjoy parades and browse for traditional festival foods and souvenir items at the various booths. Major ones include:

Sanja Festival (三社祭り SAHN-JAH MAH-tsu-lih) May 14-18 at Asakusa Shrine

Sanno Festival (山王祭り SAHN-NOH MAH-tsu-lih) June 10-16 at Akasaka Hie Shrine

Kanda Festival (神田祭り KAHN-DAH MAH-tsu-lih) May 12-15 at Kanda Shrine

Parks (公園 koh-en): Ueno Park (上野公園 u-EH-NOH KOh-en) and Hibiya Park (日比谷公園 hih-BIH-YAH KOh-en) are perhaps two of the most popular parks in Tokyo. They are good places to relax and people-watch.

KYOTO FOR FREE

Kyoto also has a number of recreational and cultural attractions that are free.

Festivals: Major ones are Aoi Festival (葵祭り ah-OY MAH-tsu-lih, May 15), Gion Festival (祇園祭り gih-OHN MAH-tsu-lih, July 17), and Jidai (時代祭り jih-DAHY MAH-tsu-lih, October 22). The Daimonji Gozan Okuribi, popularly called Daimonji-yaki (大文字焼き dahY-MOHN-JIH YAH-KIH, August 16) is a large-scale bonfire on one side of a mountain, believed to serve as a guide for departing ancestral spirits.

Imperial Palaces and Villas: The Kyoto Imperial Palace, Katsura, and Shugakuin Imperial Villas are imperial holdings of the past that are now open to visitors. You must make reservations to visit these sites.

AT THE TEMPLE/SHRINE/MUSEUM

When does the temple/shrine /museum …	お寺／神社／博物館は何時に_____ますか？	oh-TEH-LAH/JIn-jah/ hah-KU-BUTS-kahn wah NAHn-jih nih _____MAHss KAH?
• open? • close?	• 開き • 閉り	• hih-LAH-KIH • shih-MAH-LIH
Entrance fee (generic)	入場料	NYU-JOh-lyoh
Entrance fee (for temples and shrines)	拝観料	HAHY-KAHn-lyoh
How much is it for …	_____一人いくらですか？	_____hih-TOH-lih IH-k'lah dess KAH?
• an adult? • a child?	• 大人 • 子供	• oh-TOH-NAH • koh-DOH-MOH
Do you have a pamphlet in English?	英語のパンフレットはありますか？	AY-GOH NOH PAHN-HU-LET-toh wah ah-LIH-MAHss KAH?
Can I take pictures?	写真を撮ってもいいですか？	shah-SHIN OH TOHT-teh moh Ee-dess KAH?
I'm interested in …	_____に興味があるんです。	_____nih KYOH-MIH GAH AH-lun-dess.

• anthropology.	• 人類学	• JIN-LU-ih-gahk
• architecture.	• 建築	• KEN-CHIK
• art history.	• 美術史	• bih-JUTS-shih
• archaeology.	• 考古学	• KOH-KOH gahk
• ceramics/pottery.	• 陶器	• TOh-kih
• fine arts.	• 美術	• BIH-juts
• furniture.	• 家具	• KAH-gu
• geography.	• 地理	• CHIH-lih
• geology.	• 地質学	• chih-SHIH-TS'gahk
• handicrafts.	• 手工芸品	• shu-KOH-GEH-hin
• history.	• 歴史	• leh-KIH-SHIH
• natural history.	• 自然史	• shih-ZEn-shih
• sculpture.	• 彫刻	• CHOH-KOHK
• zoology.	• 動物学	• DOH-BUTS-gahk

IN THE OLD PART OF TOWN

Some major cities have historical parts of town that are different from the more modern parts in their flavor and atmosphere. These districts are charming alternatives to the busy city centers.

When was that___ built?	あの_____はいつ頃のものですか？	ah-NOH _____wah ih-TS-GOH-LOH NOH MOH-NOH dess KAH?
• structure	• 建物	• TAH-TEH-moh-noh
• house	• 家	• IH-EH
• statue	• 像	• ZOh
Has this part of town changed much?	この辺は昔と変っていますか？	koh-NOH HEN WAH mu-KAHSH TOH KAH-WAHT-TEH IH-MAHss KAH?
Has your family always lived here?	代々ここに住んでいるんですか？	DAHy-dahy koh-KOH NIH SUn-deh ih-lun-dess KAH?

IN THE COUNTRY

Japan's countryside offers an entirely different perspective from city life. For a country its size, Japan has a great variety of landscapes: there are numerous mountains, valleys, lakes, and waterfalls, and you will encounter many rice fields and traditional farmhouses, as well as such characteristic sights as rustic devotional figures and old-fashioned small stores.

Can you tell me how to get to_____?	_____へはどう行けばいいですか？	_____EH wah DOh ih-keh-bah Ee-dess KAH?
Where can I get the best view of the landscape?	一番眺めのいい所はどこですか？	ih-CHIH-BAHN NAH-GAH-MEH noh Ee toh-KOH-LOH wah DOH-koh dess KAH?
That's beautiful.	それは美しいですね。	soh-LEH-WAH u-TSUK-SHEe dess - neh.

WORD LIST

beach	浜辺／海岸	hah-MAH-BEH/ KAHY-GAHN
bridge	橋	hah-SHIH
cliff	崖	gah-KEH
farm	農場	NOH-JOH
field	野原	NOH-hah-lah
flowers	花	hah-NAH
foliage	緑	MIH-doh-lih
foliage (in autumn)	紅葉	KOH-YOH
forest	森	moh-LIH
garden	庭	nih-WAH

gorge	渓谷	KEH-KOHK
hill	岡	oh-KAH
inn	宿	YAH-doh
lake	湖	mih-ZU-mih
meadow	牧場	mah-KIH-BAH
mountain	山	yah-MAH
mountain pass	山道	yah-MAH-mich
national park	国立公園	koh-K'LITS KOh-en
peak	峰	mih-NEH
pond	池	ih-KEH
rice fields	田んぼ	tahN-BOH
river	川	kah-WAH
road/path	道	mih-CHIH
sea	海	U-mih
spring	泉	ih-ZU-MIH
stream	小川	oh-GAH-WAH
swamp	沼	nu-MAH
valley	谷	tah-NIH
vegetable fields	畑	hah-TAH-KEH
village	村	mu-LAH
waterfall	滝	tah-KIH

RELIGIOUS SERVICES

There are churches in Tokyo, as well as a mosque and a synagogue, but places of worship for Western religions may be harder to find in other cities (the notable exception is Kobe, which contains all three places of worship). You can obtain a list of religious groups and their locations from JNTO, and check the English-language newspapers for more information. Various Protestant sects are called by their own names, rather than by the larger category of Protestantism.

Is there a _____ in this town?	この町に_____はありますか？	koh-NOH MAH-CHIH nih_____wah ah-LIH-MAHss KAH?
• [Catholic] church	• [カトリックの]教会	• [kah-TOH-LIT-ku] noh kyoh-kahy
• mosque	• モスク（イスラム教会）	• MOHSS-ku (ih-SU-LAH-MU-KYOh-kahy)
• synagogue	• シナゴグ（ユダヤ教会）	• SHIH-nah-goh-gu (yu-DAH-YAH KYOh-kahy)
• Buddhist temple	• お寺	• oh-TEH-lah
I'm looking for an English-speaking…	英語の出来る_____を捜しているんです。	AY-GOH NOH DEH-KIH-lu _____woh sah-GAHSH-TEH-LUn-dess.
• minister/priest.	• 牧師	• bohk-shih
• rabbi.	• ラビ	• LAH-bih

12 / SHOPPING

Stores generally open at 10 A.M. and close between 6 P.M. and 8 P.M. They are usually closed on a designated weekday each week so that they can stay open on weekends. These days vary with each store, so you may want to check ahead to make sure a store is open.

Department stores and malls offer a wide variety of products, though prices tend to be high. However, you should be able to find some wonderful items at fair prices; see the specific store entries, below. Keep in mind that bargaining is not a custom in Japan.

DIALOGUE: AT THE CERAMICS STORE 陶器の店で TOh-kih noh mih-SEH deh

店員： TEN-IN	いらっしゃいませ。	ih-LAHSS-SHAHY-MAH-seh.[1]
お客： oh-KYAHK	すみません、花瓶を見せて下さい。	s'MIH-MAH-SEn, kah-BIN OH MIH-seh-teh k'dah-sahy.
店員： TEN-IN	かしこまりました。こちらにございます。この青いのはいかがでしょうか。	kahsh-KOH-MAH-LIH-MAHsh-tah. koh-CHIH-LAH NIH GOH-ZAHY-MAHss. koh-NOH ah-Oy-noh wah ih-KAH-gah deh-shoh kah.
お客： oh-KAYHK	ああ、それにします。	Ah, soh-LEH NIH SH'MAHss.
店員： TEN-IN	有難うございます。	ah-LIH-gah-toh goh-ZAHY-MAHss.

[1]Note: "ih-LAHSS-SHAHY-MAH-seh" basically means "Welcome" and you will be greeted by it at virtually every store and restaurant you enter.

お客： oh-KYAHK	おいくらですか？	oY-K'LAH DEss KAH?
店員： TEN-IN	二千八百円になります。	nih-SEn-haht-PYAHK-en nih nah-LIH-MAHss.

Salesperson:	Welcome.
Customer:	Excuse me, I'd like to see some vases.
Salesperson:	Certainly. They're over here. How about this blue one?
Customer:	Oh, I'll take that one.
Salesperson:	Thank you very much.
Customer:	How much is it?
Salesperson:	It'll be 2,800 yen.

TYPES OF STORES

Where is there a/an …	_____はどこにありますか？	_____ wah DOH-koh nih ah-LIH-MAHss KAH?
• antiques shop?	• 骨董品屋	• koht-TOH-HIN-YAH
• art gallery?	• 画廊	• gah-LOH
• art-supply store?	• 画材店	• gah-ZAHy-ten
• bakery?	• パン屋	• PAHn-yah
• bank?	• 銀行	• ghin-koh
• barber?	• 床屋	• toh-KOH-YAH
• beauty parlor?	• 美容室	• bih-YOh-sh'ts
• bookstore?	• 本屋	• HOHn-yah
• Buddhist-goods store?	• 仏具屋	• bu-TS'GU-YAH
• butcher shop?	• 肉屋	• nih-KU-yah
• camera store?	• カメラ屋	• kah-MEH-LAH-YAH
• ceramics store?	• 陶器の店	• TOh-kih noh mih-seh

• clothing store?	• 洋品店	• YOH-HIn-ten
• crafts/folk-art store?	• 民芸品店	• MIN-GEH-HIn-ten
• cutlery store?	• 刃物屋	• hah-MOH-NOH-YAH
• department store?	• デパート	• deh-PAh-toh
• drugstore/ pharmacy?	• 薬屋	• k'SU-LIH-YAH
• dry cleaners/ laundry?	• クリーニング屋	• k'LEE-NING-YAH
• electronics store?	• 電機屋	• deN-KIH-YAH
• fabric store?	• 布地屋	• nu-NOH-JIH-YAH
• festival booth?	• お祭りの屋台	• oh-MAH-TS'LIH NOH YAH-tahy
• fish store?	• 魚屋	• sah-KAH-NAH-YAH
• flower shop?	• 花屋	• hah-NAH-yah
• furniture store?	• 家具屋	• kah-GU-yah
• futon store?	• ふとん屋	• hu-TOHN-YAH
• grocery store?	• 八百屋	• yah-OH-YAH
• hardware store?	• 金物屋	• kah-NAH-MOH-NOH-YAH
• health food store?	• 健康食品店	• KEN-KOH-SHOHK-HIn-ten
• household goods store?	• 雑貨屋	• zaht-KAH-YAH
• imported foods store?	• 輸入食料品店	• yu-NYU-SHOHK-LYOH-HIn-ten
• Japanese sweets store?	• 和菓子屋	• wah-GAHSH-YAH
• jeweler?	• 宝石店	• HOH-SEH-KIH-ten
• kimono store?	• 呉服屋	• goh-HU-KU-YAH
• laundromat?	• コインランドリー	• koY-N LAHn-doh-lee
• library?	• 図書館	• toh-SHOH-kahn
• liquor store?	• 酒屋	• sah-KAH-YAH
• market?	• 市場	• IH-chih-bah
• newsstand?	• キオスク	• kih-OHss-ku
• optician?	• 眼鏡屋	• meh-GAH-NEH-YAH

• pastry shop?	• ケーキ屋	• keh-kih-yah
• pet store?	• ペットショップ	• pet-TOH SHOHT-pu
• photographer?	• カメラマン	• kah-MEH-LAH-mahn
• police station?	• 警察署	• keh-sahts-shoh
• post office?	• 郵便局	• YU-BIn-kyohk
• record store?	• レコード屋	• leh-KOH-DOH YAH
• shoe store?	• 靴屋	• k'TSU-yah
• shopping center?	• ショッピングセンター	• shoht-PING SEn-tah
• souvenir shop?	• 土産物屋	• mih-YAH-GEH-MOH-NOH-YAH
• sporting goods store?	• スポーツ用品店	• s'POHTS YOH-HIn-ten
• stationery store?	• 文房具屋	• BUN-BOH-G'YAH
• supermarket?	• スーパーマーケット	• SU-PAH-MAh-ket-toh
• tailor?	• 洋服屋	• YOH-HU-KU-yah
• tea store?	• お茶屋	• oh-CHAH-YAH
• toy store?	• 玩具屋	• oh-MOH-CHAH-YAH
• travel agency?	• 旅行社	• lyoh-KOh-shah
• used bookstore?	• 古本屋	• hu-LU-HOHN-YAH
• videotape store?	• ビデオショップ	• bih-DEH-OH SHOHT-pu
• watch store?	• 時計屋	• toh-KEH-YAH

GIFTS AND SOUVENIR SHOPPING

As for gifts and souvenirs, there are the typical ones, such as kimonos, lacquer ware, dolls, fans, and pearls. Some department stores have a souvenir section where you will be able to find a selection of these items, which is convenient if you are pressed for time. However, if you have time to explore, you may be able to find other interesting things to take home. Here are a few suggestions:

1) Japan is famous for its ceramics, and the prices vary greatly; you can purchase a signed masterpiece for a fortune, but you can also find some good bargains at local ceramic ware fairs.
2) Textiles are a lighter-weight option to carry home. Dyeing and weaving are traditional arts practiced differently in each region. High-quality everyday fabrics such as cottons and silks are also available for a good price at fabric stores.
3) Crafts and folk art are always good choices, and they can be found at local gift shops. They include cloisonnés, ironware, wooden crafts, paper crafts, and much more. They are full of regional flavor and make charming gifts.

Some less conventional finds include:

Practical Items: Examples are housewares, such as kitchen utensils and plastic ware, sold at supermarkets and department stores, and fine cutlery on sale at specialty stores. They are good-quality products and are sometimes rather innovative in design and function.

Stationery and Art Supplies: A great many Japanese stationery products are imported into the United States and sold for more than twice their price in Japan. In addition to writing paper, many stationery shops sell photo albums, notebooks, pens, and other desktop items, most of them uniquely functional and well designed. Also, you can find a large variety of Japanese blank cards decorated in traditional motifs, which make lightweight and charming gifts. Art-supply stores offer special brushes and inks rarely available in the United States.

You may think it's a good idea to purchase electronics in Japan, but keep two things in mind: prices are usually lower in the United States, and you must have a voltage converter in order to use the equipment at home (Japan uses 100 volts, whereas 110 volts is the U.S. standard).

There are some export models available, which are designed for use outside of Japan and will work fine at home. It is still fun to look at the most up-to-date electronic items, since some take time to reach the United States, and some models are not introduced abroad. Electronic and computer parts are sold individually at some stores, and these are very good bargains.

Finally, note that there is a 3 percent sales tax on all items.

GENERAL SHOPPING EXPRESSIONS

Where can I find _____?	_____はどこですか？	_____ wah DOH-koh dess KAH?
Can you help me? (lit., Excuse me, but …)	ちょっとすみませんが …	CHOHT-toh s'MIH-MAH-SEn gah…
I'm just browsing.	見てるだけです。	MIH-teh-lu dah-KEH dess.
Please show me…	_____を見せて下さい。	_____ OH MIH-seh-teh k'dah-sahy.
• this one.	• これ	• koh-LEH
• that one.	• それ	• soh-LEH
• the one in the window.	• ウィンドーの	• wiN-DOH NOH
• something less costly.	• もう少し安いの	• MOH-S'KOHsh yah-SU-ih noh
• something better.	• もう少しいいの	• MOH-S'KOHsh Ee noh
• something darker.	• もっと濃い色の	• MOHT-toh KOy ih-LOH noh
• something lighter.	• もっと薄い色の	• MOHT-toh u-SU-IH IH-LOH noh
• a different color.	• 他の色の	• hoh-KAH NOH IH-LOH noh
• a different style.	• 他のスタイルの	• hoh-KAH NOH S'TAHy-lu noh

I'm looking for a gift for…	_____へのプレゼントを捜してるんです。	_____ EH noh pu-LEH-zen-toh oh sah-GAH-SH'TEH LUn-dess.
• a woman.	• 女性	• joh-SEH
• a man.	• 男性	• DAHN-SEH
• a little [boy] / [girl].	• 小さい［男の子］／［女の子］	• CHEE-SAHy [oh-TOH-KOH noh koh] / [OHN-NAH noh koh]
• a [girl] / [boy] in the low teens.[1]	• 中学生位の[女の子]／［男の子］	• CHU-GAHK-SEH G'lahy noh [OHN-NAH noh koh] / [oh-TOH-KOH noh koh]
• a [boy] / [girl] in the high teens.	• 高校生位の[男の子]／［女の子］	• KOH-KOh-seh g'lahy noh [oh-TOH-KOH noh koh] / [OHN-NAH noh koh]
I prefer something …	_____物が欲しいんです。	_____ moh-NOH gah hoh-SHEEn-dess.
• locally made.	• この地方の	• koh-NOH chih-HOh noh
• handmade.	• 手作りの	• teh-ZU-k'lih noh
• more practical.	• もっと実用的な	• MOHT-toh jih-TS'YOH-TEH-KIH NAH
• less typical.	• もっと変った	• MOHT-toh kah-WAHT-TAH
• more typical.	• もっと典型的な	• MOHT-toh TEN-KEH-TEH-KIH NAH

[1]Note that in talking about children's age groups in general, the Japanese most often refer to them in terms of what kind of school the child attends (e. g., elementary school, junior high, high school). Therefore, a child in the low teens would be "a boy/girl in junior high."

Please show me your selection of ...	______を見せて下さい。	_____ oh MIH-seh-teh k'dah-sahy.
• ceramics.	• 陶器	• TOh-kih
• textiles.	• 布地	• nu-NOH-JIH
• folk art.	• 民芸品	• MIN-GEH-HIN
• lacquer ware.	• 塗物	• nu-LIH-MOH-NOH
• pearls.	• 真珠	• SHIN-JU
• portable radio-cassette players.	• ラジカセ	• lah-JIH-KAH-SEH
How much is this?	これはおいくらですか？	koh-LEH WAH oY-K'LAH DEss KAH?
Can you write down the price for me?	値段を紙に書いてもらえますか？	neh-DAHN OH kah-MIH NIH KAHy-teh moh-LAH-EH MAHss KAH?
I'll take it.	それを下さい。	soh-LEH OH K'DAH-SAHy.
I'll take two.	二つ下さい。	hu-TAHTS K'DAH-SAHy.
Will you take a ...	_____でよろしいですか？	_____ deh yoh-LOH-SHEe dess KAH?
• credit card?	• クレジットカード	• k'LEH-JIT-TOH KAh-doh
• traveler's check?	• トラベラーズチェック	• toh-LAH-BEH-LAH-ZU CHET-ku
Can you ...	_____もらえますか？	_____ moh-LAH-EH-MAHss KAH?
• order it?	• 注文して	• CHU-MOHN SH'TEH
• send it to me?	• 私宛に送って	• wah-TAHSH AH-TEH NIH oh-KUT-TEH
• deliver it to this address?	• この住所へ送って	• koh-NOH Ju-shoh eh oh-KUT-TEH

• gift-wrap it?[1]	• プレゼント用に包んでもらえますか？	• pu-LEH-ZEN-TOH YOH NIH TS'TSUn-deh moh-LAH-EH-MAHss KAH?
Is it out of stock?	品切れですか？	shih-NAH-GIH-LEH DEss KAH?
When do you close?	いつ閉まりますか？	IH-ts shih-MAH-LIH-MAHss KAH?
I bought this here yesterday.	これを昨日ここで買ったんです。	koh-LEH OH kih-NOh koh-KOH DEH kaht-TAHn-dess.
Can I exchange this?	交換出来ますか？	KOH-KAHN deh-KIH-MAHss KAH?
Can I return it?	返品出来ますか？	HEN-PIN deh-KIH-MAHss KAH?
I'd like my money back.	払い戻しして下さい。	hah-LAHY-MOH-DOHSH SH'TEH K'DAH-SAHy.
Here's my receipt.	レシートはこれです。	leh-SHEe-toh wah koh-LEH DEss.
Can I have a shopping bag?	ショッピングバッグをもらえますか？	shoht-PIN-GU BAHT-gu oh moh-LAH-EH MAHss KAH?
That will be all.	それだけです。	soh-LEH-DAH-KEH dess.

WESTERN-STYLE CLOTHING

Western clothes	洋服	yoh-hu-ku

[1] Almost everything you purchase will be wrapped neatly (almost to a point of excess), so you don't even need to ask for items to be gift-wrapped. However, if you tell the salesperson that it's a gift, he or she may wrap it in special paper, or put a ribbon around it for you.

I'd like to buy …	_____を買いたいんです。	_____ oh kahY-TAHy-n-dess.
• a bathrobe.	• バスローブ	• bah-SU LOh-bu
• a bathing cap.	• 水泳帽	• SU-IH-Eh-boh
• a bathing suit.	• 水着	• mih-ZU-GIH
• a belt.	• ベルト	• beh-LU-TOH
• a blouse.	• ブラウス	• bu-LAH-u-su
• a bra.	• ブラジャー	• bu-LAH-JAh
• a coat.	• コート	• KOh-toh
• a dress.	• ドレス	• DOH-leh-su
• a dressing gown.	• ガウン	• GAH-un
• an evening dress.	• イブニングドレス	• ih-BU-NING DOH-leh-su
• gloves.	• 手袋	• teh-BU-k'loh
• a handbag/ pocketbook.	• ハンドバッグ	• HAHN-DOH-BAHT-gu
• a hat/cap.	• 帽子	• boh-shih
• a jacket.	• ジャケット	• jah-KET-toh
• jeans.	• ジーンズ	• JEen-zu
• panties.	• パンティー	• PAHn-tee
• pants.	• ズボン	• ZU-bohn
• panty hose.	• パンティストッキング	• PAHN-TEE S'TOHT-kin-gu
• pajamas.	• パジャマ	• PAH-jah-mah
• a raincoat.	• レーンコート	• LEHN-KOh-toh
• a scarf.	• スカーフ	• s'KAh-hu
• a _____ shirt.	• _____のシャツ	• _____ NOH SHAH-tsu
long-sleeved	長袖	nah-GAH-SOH-DEH
short-sleeved	半袖	HAHN-SOH-DEH
sleeveless	ノースリーブ	NOH-S'LEe-bu
• shoes.	• 靴	• ku-TSU
• shorts.	• ショートパンツ	• SHOH-TOH-PAHn-tsu
• a skirt.	• スカート	• s'KAh-toh
• a pair of socks.	• 靴下	• k'TSU-sh'tah
• a sports jacket.	• ブレザーコート	• bu-LEH-ZAH-KOh-toh
• a suit (woman's).	• スーツ	• Su-tsu

• a suit (man's).	• 背広	• seh-BIH-LOH
• suspenders.	• サスペンダー	• sah-s'PEn-dah
• a sweater.	• セーター	• SEh-tah
• a tie.	• ネクタイ	• NEK-tahy
• tights.	• タイツ	• TAHy-tsu
• a turtleneck.	• タートルネック	• TAH-TOH-LU-NET-ku
• an umbrella.	• 傘	• KAH-sah
• an undershirt.	• アンダーシャツ	• AHN-DAH-SHAH-tsu
• underwear.	• パンツ	• PAHn-tsu
• a vest.	• ベスト	• BEH-s'toh

TRADITIONAL JAPANESE ATTIRE 和服 wah-HU-KU

You probably have already heard of kimonos, the traditional dress of Japan. The basic shape is a robe secured around the waist by a sash, but the formal versions are more complex. For women, both the *furisode* and the *homongi* (described below) require that you wear under-kimonos, Japanese socks, fancy Japanese sandals, and a complicated sash ensemble (including an above-sash tie, a sash brooch, etc.) that often necessitates professional help in putting it all together, even for Japanese women. The fabrics used are examples of the masterful techniques of Japanese textile production; there's a wide range, from the most exquisitely designed silks to cottons with more humble but attractive prints. Men's kimonos are more subdued in color, and for formal occasions, a jacket with the family crest is worn over a divided skirt. These days, it seems that kimonos have become special-occasion dress for the Japanese; Western clothes are the norm for most people, aside from some older people who still wear them regularly.

The most convenient way for you to try on a kimono for fun is to stay at a Japanese-style inn, which usually provides you with a *yukata* robe and sash for after your bath. It's truly an experience to come out of a refreshing bath and get into a crisp cotton yukata; it's acceptable to go out in public in your robe, so enjoy a nice stroll in the countryside if you like.

There are various types of kimonos. Most broadly, there are three kinds of kimonos for women:

Furisode (振袖 hu-LIH-SOH-DEH): An elaborate kimono in bright, vivid hues and with rich designs. It is characterized by the long "sleeves" that almost reach the ankle. Traditionally, only young women who are not yet married can wear furisodes.

Homongi (訪問着 hoh-mohn-gih): Less showy than the furisode, a homongi is more subtle in color and design, although it can still be quite striking. The "sleeves" are shorter; about hip-length. It is worn by married and older women.

Yukata (ゆかた yu-KAH-TAH): The yukata is a casual and simpler alternative kimono style. Yukatas often cost a lot less than formal kimonos, which can easily run double your airfare to and from Japan. Originally an after-bath robe and made of cotton, it is now a summer staple. It is a single-layer piece worn only with a simple sash. You can go barefoot with a simple Japanese sandal. If you are looking for just a flavor of kimonos, you should opt for a yukata.

There are two basic kimono variations for men:

Men's Kimono (男物の着物 oh-TOH-KOH-MOH-NOH NOH KIH-MOH-NOH): An informal attire in simple fabrics. The style of the garment is similar to a short-"sleeve" women's kimono, but the sash is thinner and tied at the lower waist, instead of the upper waist for women. Traditional Japanese clogs are worn on the feet.

Formal Wear (紋付羽織袴 mohn-ts'kih hah-oh-lih hah-kah-mah): For special occasions; this is the Japanese "black tie" attire. A divided skirt is worn over a kimono, then a light, crested jacket.

Japanese clothes	和服	wah-HU-KU
Please show me ...	______を見せて下さい。	_____ oh MIH-seh-teh k'dah-sahy.
• a hair ornament.	• 髪飾り	• kah-MIH-KAH-zah-lih
• a kimono.	• 着物	• kih-MOH-NOH
• a light overcoat/ men's formal "jacket."	• 羽織	• hah-OH-LIH
• a pair of Japanese sandals.	• 草履	• z<u>oh</u>-lih
• a sash.	• 帯	• OH-bih
• an above-sash tie.	• 帯揚げ	• oh-BIH-AH-geh
• an over-sash tie.	• 帯締め	• oh-BIH-SHIH-MEH
• a sash brooch.	• 帯留め	• oh-BIH-DOH-meh
• a sash shaper.	• 帯枕	• oh-BIH-MAH-k'lah
• a pair of Japanese socks.	• 足袋	• TAH-bih
• a yukata.	• ゆかた	• yu-KAH-TAH
• a long under-kimono.	• 長じゅばん	• nah-GAH JU-bahn
• a short under-kimono.	• じゅばん	• ju-BAHN
• a pair of Japanese clogs.	• 下駄	• geh-TAH
• a men's divided skirt.	• 袴	• hah-KAH-MAH

GENERAL CLOTHES-SHOPPING EXPRESSIONS

I'd like to try it on.	試着してみたいんですが。	shih-CHAHK SH'TEH MIH-TAHy-n-dess gah.
Do you have one that's…	もっと_____のはありますか？	MOHT-toh _____ noh wah ah-LIH-MAHss KAH?
• longer?	• 長い	• nah-GAHy
• shorter?	• 短い	• mih-JIH-KAHy
• bigger?	• 大きい	• OH-KEe
• smaller?	• 小さい	• CHEE-SAHy
I wear size _____.	サイズは_____です。	SAHy-zu wah _____ dess.
I don't know my size.[1]	サイズがわからないんですが。	SAHy-zu gah wah-KAH-LAH-nahy-n-dess gah.

COLORS AND PATTERNS

beige	ベージュ	beh-ju
black	黒	KU-loh
blue	青	AH-oh
brown	茶色	chah-IH-LOH
gray	グレー	gu-LEh
green	緑	MIH-doh-lih
orange	オレンジ	oh-LEn-jih
pink	ピンク	PIn-ku
purple	むらさき	mu-LAH-sah-kih

[1] The size charts on pages 164–65 should serve as a guide, but for a better fit, ask a salesperson at a department store or a boutique to take your measurements. He or she will then bring clothes in your size for you. It's always a good idea to try a garment on as well.

red	赤	AH-kah
silver	銀色	ghin-ih-loh
white	白	SHIH-loh
yellow	黄色	kee-loh
Do you have something …	_____のはありますか？	_____ NOH wah ah-LIH-MAH-Su KAH?
• in a solid color?	• 無地	• MU-jih
• with stripes?	• 縞	• shih-MAH
• with polka dots?	• 水玉	• miz-TAH-MAH
• checked?	• チェック	• CHET-ku
• plaid?	• 格子	• koh-shih

SHOES

I'm looking for a pair of …	_____を捜してるんです。	_____ oh sah-GAH-SH' TEH LUn-dess.
• boots.	• ブーツ	• Bu-tsu
• flats.	• フラット	• hu-LAHT-toh
• high heels.	• ハイヒール	• hahY-HEe-lu
• sandals.	• サンダル	• SAHn-dah-lu
• shoes.	• 靴	• ku-TSU
• slippers.	• スリッパ	• su-LIT-pah
• sneakers.	• スニーカー	• s'NEe-kah
They fit fine.	丁度いいです。	CHOH-DOH Ee dess.
They're too …	_____過ぎます。	_____ S'GIH-MAHss.
• small.	• 小さ	• CHEE-SAH-
• narrow.	• 幅が狭	• hah-BAH GAH seh-MAH-
• big.	• 大き	• OH-KIH-
• wide.	• 幅が広	• hah-BAH GAH hih-LOH-
I'd like the same in brown.	これの茶色いのを下さい。	koh-LEH NOH CHAHY-LOy noh oh k'dah-sahy.

WOMEN'S CLOTHING SIZES

Standard sizes; measurements in inches:

SIZE	3	5	7	9	11	13	15
BUST	29"	30"	31"	33"	35"	36"	38"
WAIST	22"	23"	24"	25"	26"	27"	30"
HIP	33"	34"	34.5"	35"	37"	39"	41"

I wear size 11.	11号です。	JU-IH-CHIH goh dess.

Sizes 3 through 7 are considered "small, " sizes 9 through 13 are considered "average/medium, " and sizes above 15 are considered "large" and are usually sold in a separate "plus" section. Imported items may be sized differently.

If you must buy lingerie, have yourself measured for the best fit because sizes run small.

MEN'S CLOTHING SIZES

Suits

Your "build/waist" and your chest measurement will determine your size.

Custom tailoring is available at many stores.

Height	Thin Build/Waist	Regular/Waist	Stocky Build/Waist
5'3"	YA-3/28"	A-3/30"	AB-3/32"
5'5"	YA-4/29"	A-4/31"	AB-4/33"
5'7"	YA-5/30"	A-5/31.5"	AB-5/34"
5'9"	YA-6/31"	A-6/32"	AB-6/35"
5'11"			AB-7/35.5"

Chest measurements							
U.S.	34	35	36	39	40	41	42
JAPAN	86	89	91	94	102	104	107

Shirts

NECK SIZE U.S.	14	14½	15	15½	15¾	16
NECK SIZE JAPAN	36 cm	37	38	39	40	41

Larger neck sizes (up to 45 cm) are available, though less common.

Sleeve lengths range from 76 cm (30") to 84 cm (33"). If you want to have a shirt made to order, sleeve length can be up to 90 cm (35").

Classifications: "YA"= thin build, "A"=regular, "AB"=stocky build.

Pants

Waist Size Conversion: Inches to Centimeters						
INCHES	28	30	32	34	36	38
CENTIMETERS	72	76	82	86	92	97

It might be difficult to find larger sizes.

SHOE/SOCK SIZES

JAPANESE SIZE	22	22.5	23	23.5	24	24.5	25	25.5	26
WOMEN'S U.S.	4½	5	5½	6	6½	7	7½	8	8½
JAPANESE SIZE	25	26	27	28	29				
MEN'S U.S.	7	8	9	10	11				

Note: It might be difficult to find sizes over 25 for women and 28 for men.

CERAMICS AND WARES 陶器／器 TOH-kih/u-TSU-WAH

I'd like to see a (n) …	_____をみせて下さい。	_____ oh MIH-seh-teh k' dah-sahy.
• chopstick rest. [1]	• 箸置き	• hah-SHIH-OH-KIH
• earthenware pot.	• 土鍋	• doh-NAH-BEH
• ironware pot.	• 鉄鍋	• teh-TS'NAH-BEH
• large bowl.	• どんぶり	• DOHN-BU-LIH
• lunch box.	• 弁当箱	• BEN-TOh-bah-koh
• pair of chopsticks.	• お箸	• oh-HAH-shih
• plate.	• お皿	• oh-SAH-LAH
• rice bowl.	• ご飯茶碗	• goh-HAHN JAH-wahn
• sake cup.	• 杯	• sah-KAHZ-KIH
• sake decanter.	• 徳利	• toht-KU-LIH

[1] A chopstick rest is used in setting the table. You place the narrow tips of the chopsticks upon one of these little pieces so that your chopsticks stay off the table. These are made from various materials, including ceramics and wood, and are quite whimsical and charming in design.

• small bowl.	• 小鉢	• KOH-bah-chih
• small plate.	• お小皿	• oh-KOH-zah-lah
• soup bowl.	• お椀	• oh-WAHN
• tea bowl.	• 茶碗	• chah-WAHN
• teacup.	• 湯のみ茶碗	• yu-NOH-MIH JAH-wahn
• teapot.	• 急須	• kyu-su
• toothpick holder.	• 楊子入れ	• YOH-JIH ih-leh

TEXTILES AND FABRICS 布地 nu-NOH-JIH

I'm looking for some …	_____を捜してるんです。	_____ oh sah-GAH-SH' TEH LUn-dess.
• cotton.	• 木綿	• moh-MEN
• crepe.	• クレープ	• k'LEH-PU
• denim.	• デニム	• DEH-nih-mu
• gabardine.	• ギャバジン	• GYAH-bah-jin
• lace.	• レース	• LEh-su
• leather.	• 革	• kah-WAH
• linen.	• 麻	• ah-SAH
• nylon.	• ナイロン	• NAHy-lohn
• poplin.	• ポプリン	• POH-pu-lin
• satin.	• サテン	• SAH-ten
• silk.	• 絹	• KIH-nu
• suede.	• スエード	• su-EH-DOH
• velvet.	• ビロード	• bih-LOH-DOH
• wool.	• ウール	• U-lu

CRAFTS AND FOLK ART 民芸品 min-geh-hin

What are the famous folk crafts of this region?	この辺の有名な民芸品は何ですか?	koh-NOH HEN NOH YU-MEH NAH MIN-GEH-HIN WAH NAHn-dess KAH?

Please show me your selection of …	＿＿を見せて下さい。	＿＿ OH MIH-seh-teh k'dah-sahy.
• bamboo crafts.	• 竹細工	• tah-KEH ZAHy-ku
• baskets.	• 籠	• kah-GOH
• brushes.	• 筆	• hu-DEH
• carvings.	• 彫刻	• choh-kohk
• cloisonnés.	• 七宝	• ship-POH
• cutlery.	• 刃物	• HAH-moh-noh
• dolls.	• 人形	• nin-gyoh
• fans.	• 扇子	• seN-SU
• ink stones.	• 硯	• s'ZU-LIH
• Japanese paper.	• 和紙	• WAH-shih
• paper lanterns.	• 提灯	• CHOH-CHIn
• paper umbrellas.	• 唐傘	• kah-LAH KAH-sah
• paperweights.	• 文鎮	• BUN-CHIn
• traditional toys.	• 玩具	• oh-MOH-chah
• wind chimes.	• 風鈴	• hu-lin

THE RECORD STORE　レコード屋　leh-KOH-DOH YAH

Do you have any …	＿＿はありますか？	＿＿ WAH ah-LIH-MAHssKAH?
• CDs by [Miles Davis]?	• [マイルズ　デービス]のＣＤ	• [MAHY-LU-ZU DEh-bih-su] noh SEE-Dee
• cassette tapes?	• カセットテープ	• kah-SET-TOH TEh-pu
• record albums?	• レコード	• leh-KOh-doh
Where is the section for …	＿＿はどこですか？	＿＿ wah DOH-koh dess KAH?
• classical music?	• クラシック	• ku-LAH-shik-ku
• Western folk music?	• フォークミュージック	• FOH-KU MYu-jit-ku
• Japanese pop music?	• 歌謡曲	• kah-YOh-kyohk
• jazz?	• ジャズ	• JAH-zu
• soundtracks?	• サウンドトラック	• sah-UN-DOH TOH-LAHT-ku

• traditional Japanese music?	• 邦楽	• HOH-GAHK
• Western rock?	• ロック	• LOHT-ku

THE PHOTO SHOP 写真屋 shah-SHIN-YAH

Do you sell …	_____はありますか？	_____ wah ah-LIH-MAHss KAH?
• cameras?	• カメラ	• KAH-meh-lah
• automatic cameras?	• オートカメラ	• OH-TOH KAH-meh-lah
• video camcorders?	• ビデオカメラ	• bih-DEH-OH KAH-meh-lah
• filters?	• フィルター	• fih-LU-TAH
• batteries?	• 電池	• DEn-chih
• light meters?	• 露出計	• loh-SHUTS-KEH
• lens caps?	• レンズキャップ	• LEN-ZU KYAHT-pu
• telephoto lenses?	• 望遠レンズ	• BOH-EN LEn-zu
• wide-angle lenses?	• 広角レンズ	• KOH-KAHK LEn-zu
• film?	• フィルム	• fih-LU-MU
• disposable cameras?	• 使い捨てのカメラ	• ts'KAHY-S'TEH NOH KAH-meh-lah
I'd like a roll of …	_____を下さい。	_____ oh k'DAH-SAHy.
• color film.	• カラーフィルム	• kah-LAH FIH-lu-mu
• black-and-white film.	• 黒白のフィルム	• k'LOH-SH'LOH NOH FIH-lu-mu
• 24 exposures.	• 24枚撮り	• NIH-ju-YOHN-MAHY-DOH-LIH
• 36 exposures.	• 36枚撮り	• SAHn-ju-loh-KU-MAHY-DOH-LIH
• slide film.	• スライド用フィルム	• s'LAHY-DOH YOH FIH-lu-mu

• film this ASA number.	• このＡＳＡのフィルム	• koh-NOH AY-ESS-Ay noh fih-LU-MU
• film for artificial light.	• 室内用フィルム	• shih-TS'NAHY-YOH FIH-lu-mu
• film for natural light.	• 自然光フィルム	• shih-ZEN-KOH FIH-lu-mu
How much is it to develop this roll of film?	このフィルムの現像料はいくらですか？	koh-NOH fih-LU-MU NOH GEN-ZOh-lyoh wah IH-k'lah-dess KAH?
I'd like …	_____お願いします。	_____ oh-NEH-GAHY SH'MAHss.
• to have this developed.	• 現像を	• GEN-ZOH OH
• 2 prints of each one.	• プリントを２枚ずつ	• pu-LIN-TOH OH nih-MAHY ZU-tsu
• an enlargement.	• 引き延ばし	• hih-KIH-NOH-BAHSH
• prints with a glossy finish.	• 光沢プリント	• KOH-TAHK P'LIn-toh
• prints with a matte finish.	• マットのプリント	• maht-TOH NOH P'LIn-toh
When will they be ready?	いつ出来ますか？	IH-ts deh-KIH-MAHss KAH?
I'm having a problem with the …	_____がおかしいんです。	_____ gah oh-KAH-SHEEn-dess.
• flash.	• フラッシュ	• hu-LAHSS-shu
• focus.	• フォーカス	• FOh-kahss
• shutter.	• シャッター	• SHAHT-tah
• winding mechanism.	• 巻き取り	• mah-KIH-TOH-LIH
Do you repair cameras?	カメラの修繕はやってますか？	KAH-meh-lah noh SHU-ZEN WAH yaht-TEH MAHss KAH?

ELECTRONICS/HOME APPLIANCES
エレクトロニクス／家庭用品
eh-LEK-TOH-LOH-NIK-su/kah-TEH YOH-hin

Both high-technology components and home appliances are available at department stores, but for a wider selection of the former, you can venture to a specialty store in an "electronic district" of a city, such as the Akihabara area in Tokyo. Also, keep in mind the difference in voltage (see page 153–54).

What is the voltage?	何ボルトですか？	NAHN-BOH-lu-toh dess KAH?
I need batteries for this.	これの電池がいるんです。	?koh-LEH NOH DEn-chih gah ih-LUn-dess.
It's broken; can you fix it?	壊れたんですが、直してもらえますか？	koh-WAH-leh-tahn-dess gah, nah-OHsh-teh moh-LAH-EH-MAHss KAH?
I'd like to see the newest models.	最新のモデルを見たいんです。	SAHY-SHIN NOH MOH-deh-lu oh mih-TAHy-n-dess.
Please show me your selection of ...	＿＿＿を見せて下さい。	＿＿＿ oh MIH-seh-teh k'dah-sahy.
• amplifiers.	• アンプ	• AHn-pu
• cassette decks.	• カセットデッキ	• kah-SET-TOH DET-kih
• CD players.	• ＣＤプレイヤー	• SEE-DEE P'LAy-yah
• blank computer discs.	• パソコンディスク	• pah-SOH-KOHN DIss-ku
• computer software.	• パソコンソフト	• pah-SOH-KOHN SOH-hu-toh
• personal computers.	• パソコン	• pah-SOH-KOHN

• receivers.	• レシーバー	• leh-SHEE-BAH
• speakers.	• スピーカー	• s'PEE-KAH
• turntables.	• ターンテーブル	• TAHN-TEh-bu-lu
• TVs.	• テレビ	• TEH-leh-bih
• VCRs.	• ビデオデッキ	• bih-DEH-OH DET-kih
I'd like to buy …	＿＿を買いたいんです。	＿＿ OH KAHY-TAHy-n-dess.
• a rice cooker.	• 電気釜	• DEN-KIH-GAH-mah
• a transformer.	• トランス	• toh-LAHN-SU
• a travel iron.	• 携帯用アイロン	• KEH-TAHY-YOH AHY-LOHN

BOOKS/MAGAZINES 本／雑誌 HOHn/zahss-SHIH

Small bookstores usually sell a selection of popular novels, comic books, magazines, maps and travel guides, children's books, and student study guides. Many larger stores will have a wider selection, including scholarly books, dictionaries, foreign-language books, coffee-table books, and books on specialized fields of interest.

You can buy newspapers and popular magazines at newsstand kiosks near and in train stations. You can also ask your hotel where you can get them.

Is there ＿＿ near here?	この近くに＿＿はありますか？	koh-NOH CHIH-KAHk nih ＿＿ wah ah-LIH- MAHss KAH?
• a bookstore	• 本屋	• HOHn-yah
• a newsstand	• キオスク	• kih-OHss-ku
Where are …	＿＿はどこですか？	＿＿ WAH DOH-koh-dess KAH?
• books in English?	• 英語の本	• AY-GOH NOH HOHn

• magazines in English?	• 英語の雑誌	• AY-GOH NOH ZAHSS-SHIH
• newspapers in English?	• 英語の新聞	• AY-GOH NOH SHIN-BUN
Do you have the book by [Abe Kobo] called [*Suna no Onna* (*Woman in the Dunes*)]?	[安部公房]の[砂の女]はありますか？	[ah-BEH KOh-boh] noh [*s'NAH NOH OHN-NAH*] wah ah-LIH-MAHss KAH?
Do you carry books by _____ ?	_____の本は売ってますか？	_____ noh HOHn wah ut-TEH MAHss KAH?
I'm looking for this title.	この題を捜してるんです。	koh-NOH DAHy oh sah-GAHSH-TEH LUn-dess.
Is there an English translation of this book?	この本の英訳はありますか？	koh-NOH HOHn noh AY-YAHK WAH ah-LIH-MAHss KAH?
Do you have it in paperback?	文庫本はありますか？	BUN-KOH-BOHN WAH ah-LIH-MAHss KAH?
I'd like …	_____を下さい。	_____ oh k'dah-sahy.
• a book on _____	• _____についての本	• _____ nih TS'ih-teh noh HOHn
• a calendar.	• カレンダー	• kah-LEn-dah
• an English-Japanese dictionary.	• 英和辞典	• AY-WAH JIH-ten
• a map of this area.	• この辺の地図	• koh-NOH-HEN NOH CHIH-zu
• a city map.	• 市街地図	• shih-GAHY CHIH-zu
• a detailed map.	• 詳しい地図	• k'WAH-SHEe chih-zu
• a road map.	• 道路地図	• DOH-LOH CHIH-zu

• a travel guide for Kyoto.	• 京都の旅行ガイド	• KYOh-toh noh lyoh-KOH GAHy-doh

STATIONERY STORE 文房具屋 bun-boh-g'yah

Smaller stationery stores may be limited in stock, but larger stores will have a wide selection of goods. Some products are quite nicely designed with traditional Japanese themes, making them appropriate as gifts. You can also find basic art supplies at some stores.

I'd like ...	_____を下さい。	_____ OH k'DAH-SAHy.
• an address book.	• 住所録	• JU-SHOH-lohk
• a ballpoint pen.	• ボールペン	• BOH-LU-PEN
• colored pencils.	• 色鉛筆	• ih-LOH En-pits
• crayons.	• クレヨン	• k'LEH-yohn
• envelopes.	• 封筒	• HU-TOH
• an eraser.	• 消ゴム	• keh-SHIH-GOHM
• glue.	• のり	• noh-LIH
• ink.	• インキ	• iN-KIH
• labels.	• ラベル	• LAH-beh-lu
• markers.	• サインペン	• sahY-N PEn
• a notebook.	• ノート	• NOh-toh
• origami[1] paper.	• 折り紙	• oh-LIH-GAH-mih
• paper.	• 紙	• kah-MIH
• paper clips.	• クリップ	• k'LIT-pu
• a pen.	• ペン	• PEn
• a pencil.	• 鉛筆	• EN-PITS
• a pencil sharpener.	• 鉛筆削り	• EN-PITS KEH-zu-lih
• a pocket appointment book.	• 手帳	• teh-CHOH
• a pocket calculator.	• 計算機	• KEH-SAHn-kih

[1] "Origami" (折り紙 oh-LIH-GAH-mih) stands both for the art of paper folding and the square pieces of paper used for this craft. They can be quite colorful, and are available in solid colors or prints.

• a ruler.	• ものさし	• moh-NOH-SAH-shih
• scissors.	• はさみ	• hah-SAH-mih
• Scotch tape.	• スコッチテープ	• s'KOHT-CHIH TEh-pu
• a sketchbook.	• スケッチブック	• s'KET-CHIH BUT-ku
• a stapler.	• ホッチキス	• HOHT-chih-kiss
• staples.	• ホッチキスの針	• HOHT-chih-kiss noh HAH-lih
• stationery.	• 便箋	• BIN-SEN
• thumbtacks.	• 画鋲	• gah-BY OH
• a typewriter.	• タイプライター	• tahY-PU-LAHy-tah
• a typewriter ribbon.	• タイプライターのリボン	• tahY-PU-LAHy-tah noh LIH-bohn
• a writing pad.	• メモ帳	• meh-MOH-CHOH

TOILETRIES AND COSMETICS

Imported products from Europe and the United States are astronomically priced. We don't recommend buying cosmetics or perfumes in Japan unless you find something special that's sold only in Japan. It is cheaper to buy cosmetics by a Japanese company (such as Shiseido) in the United States, although product lines may be different. If you run out of toiletries and need to buy some, less expensive items are available at local drugstores or supermarkets.

Do you have …	_____はありますか？	_____ wah ah-LIH-MAHss KAH?
• after-shave lotion?	• アフターシェーブローション	• ah-hu TAH-SHEH-BU LOh-shohn
• baby powder?	• ベビーパウダー	• beh-BEE PAH-u-dah
• blush?	• 頬紅	• HOH-BEH-nih
• bobby pins?	• ヘアピン	• heh-AH-PIn

• cleansing cream?	• クレンジングクリーム	• k'LEN-JIN-GU K'LEe-mu
• a comb?	• くし	• k'SHIH
• deodorant?	• デオドラント	• deh-OH-doh-lahn-toh
• curlers?	• カーラー	• KAh-lah
• an eyebrow pencil?	• まゆずみ	• mah-YU-ZU-mih
• eyeliner?	• アイライナー	• ahY-LAHy-nah
• eye shadow?	• アイシャドー	• ahY-SHAH-doh
• face powder?	• おしろい	• oh-SHIH-LOY
• facial soap?	• 洗顔用石鹸	• SEN-GAHN-YOH SET-ken
• foundation?	• ファンデーション	• FAHN-DEh-shohn
• a hairbrush?	• ヘアブラシ	• heh-AH-BU-lah-shih
• hair spray?	• ヘアスプレー	• heh-AH S'PU-LEh
• hand cream?	• ハンドクリーム	• HAHN-DOH K'LEe-mu
• lipstick?	• 口紅	• k'CHIH-BEH-NIH
• makeup?	• 化粧品	• keh-SHOH-HIN
• mascara?	• マスカラ	• mahss-KAH-LAH
• a mirror?	• 鏡	• kah-GAH-MIH
• moisturizing lotion?	• ローション	• LOh-shohn
• nail clippers?	• 爪切り	• ts'MEH-KIH-lih
• a nail file?	• 爪やすり	• ts'MEH YAH-su-lih
• nail polish?	• ネールエナメル	• NEH-LU EH-NAH-meh-lu
• nail polish remover?	• マニキュア落し	• mah-NIH-KYU-AH OH-toh-shih
• perfume?	• 香水	• KOH-SU-IH
• a razor?	• 剃刀	• kah-MIH-SOH-lih
• razor blades?	• 剃刀の刃	• kah-MIH-SOH-LIH noh HAH
• safety pins?	• 安全ピン	• AHN-ZEn-pin
• sanitary napkins?	• 生理用ナプキン	• SEH-LIH YOH NAHP-kin
• scissors?	• はさみ	• hah-SAH-mih
• shampoo?	• シャンプー	• SHAHN-Pu
• shaving cream?	• 髭剃りクリーム	• hih-GEH-SOH-LIH K'LEe-mu

• soap?	• 石鹸	• set-KEN
• suntan lotion?	• 日焼けクリーム	• hih-YAH-KEH K'LEe-mu
• suntan oil?	• 日焼けオイル	• hih-YAH-KEH Oy-lu
• tampons?	• タンポン	• TAHn-pohn
• tissues?	• ティッシュペーパー	• tiss-SHU PEh-pah
• toilet paper?	• トイレットペーパー	• toY-LET-TOH PEh-pah
• a toothbrush?	• 歯ブラシ	• hah-BU-lahsh
• toothpaste?	• 歯磨き粉	• hah-MIH-GAH-KIH KOH
• towels?	• タオル	• TAH-oh-lu
• tweezers?	• 毛抜き	• keh-NU- KIH

FOOD SHOPPING

Local supermarkets usually stock a good selection of fresh produce and other groceries. Twenty-four-hour convenience stores also keep a supply of foods, though they tend to be more ready-made (e.g., instant soups, bags of chips, etc.). Food prices are high in Japan, but a trip to one of these neighborhood stores might be an interesting experience. For a more complete list of food names, see chapter 6, "Dining Out."

Remember that the metric system is used in measuring weights. In counting quantities, you can get by with using the "quantity numbers" (see chapter 1, page 15) instead of using the precise system that differs according to the shape and type of object to be counted. In the phrases below you will see several examples of the actual counting system that you are likely to encounter, but keep in mind that you will be understood even if you use the simpler system. Also, Japanese nouns don't differentiate between singular and plural forms.

I'd like …	_____下さい。	_____ k'dah-sahy.
• 500 grams of apples.	• りんごを500グラム	• LIN-GOH OH goh-HYAHK-GU-lah-mu
• 200 grams of this.	• これを200グラム	• koh-LEH OH nih-HYAHK-GU-lah-mu
• a bottle of soda.	• ソーダを一ぽん	• SOh-dah oh IT-pohn
• a carton of milk.	• ミルクを一箱	• MIH-lu-ku oh hih-TOH-hah-koh
• a bunch of [spinach].	• [ほうれん草]を一把	• [HOH-LEN-SOH] OH IH-CHIH-wah
• a slice of [salmon].	• [鮭]を一切れ	• [SAH-keh] oh hih-TOH-kih-leh
Where can I find …	_____はどこですか？	_____ wah DOH-koh-dess KAH?
• bread?	• パン	• PAHn
• butter?	• バター	• BAH-tah
• canned food?	• 缶詰	• KAHN-ZU-meh
• coffee?	• コーヒー	• KOH-HEe
• fruit?	• 果物	• k'DAH-moh-noh
• fruit juices?	• ジュース	• Ju-su
• instant noodle packages?	• ラーメン	• LAh-men
• instant noodle soup in a disposable bowl?	• カップラーメン	• kaht-PU LAh-men
• potato chips?	• ポテトチップ	• poh-TEH-TOH CHIT-pu
• salt?	• 塩	• shih-OH
• soy sauce?	• お醤油	• oh-SHOH-YU
• sugar?	• 砂糖	• sah-TOh
• tea?	• 紅茶	• KOH-CHAH
• vegetables?	• 野菜	• yah-SAHY
• yogurt?	• ヨーグルト	• YOH-GU-lu-toh

METRIC CONVERSION CHARTS AND RULER

Metric Weight	U.S.
1 gram (g)	0.035 ounce
28.35 grams	1 ounce
100 grams	3.5 ounces
454 grams	1 pound
1 kilogram (kilo)	2.2 pounds
Liquids	**U.S.**
1 liter (l)	4.226 cups
1 liter	2.113 cups
1 liter	1.056 quarts
3.785 liters	1 gallon
Dry Measures	**U.S.**
1 liter	0.908 quart
1 decaliter	1.135 pecks
1 hectoliter	2.837 bushels

One inch = 2.54 centimeters
One centimeter = .39 inch

	inches	feet	yards
1 mm	0.039	0.003	0.001
1 cm	0.39	0.03	0.01
1 dm	3.94	0.32	0.10
1 m	39.40	3.28	1.09

.39 (# of centimeters) = (# of inches)
2.54 (# of inches) = (# of centimeters)

	mm	cm	m
1 in.	25.4	2.54	0.025
1 ft.	304.8	30.48	0.304
1 yd.	914.4	91.44	0.914

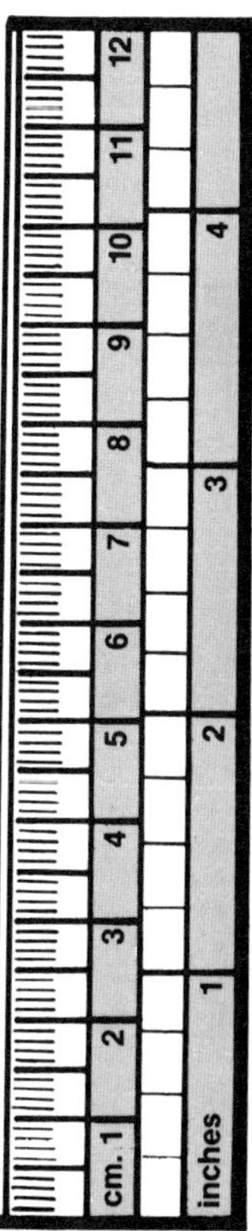

13 / ACTIVITIES AND ENTERTAINMENT

ACTIVITIES

DIALOGUE: AT THE TICKET OFFICE 入場券売場で NYU-JOH-KEN U-lih-bah deh

観光客：KAHN-KOh-kyahk	今日の切符はまだありますか？	KYOh noh kit-PU WAH MAH-dah ah-LIH-MAHss KAH?
係員：kah-KAH-LIH-in	はい、ございます。	HAHy, goh-ZAHY-MAHss.
観光客：KAHN-KOh-kyahk	二枚ほしいんですが。	NIH-mahy hoh-SHEen-dess gah.
係員：kah-KAH-LIH-in	どの辺の席がよろしいでしょうか？	doh-NOH-HEN NOH SEH-kih gah yoh-LOH-SHEe-deh-shoh KAH?
観光客：KAHN-KOh-kyahk	よく見える席をお願いします。	YOH-ku mih-EH-lu seh-kih oh oh-NEH-GAHY SH'MAHss.
係員：kah-KAH-LIH-in	かしこまりました。	kahsh-KOH-MAH-LIH-MAHsh-tah.

Tourist:	Are there still tickets left for today?
Employee:	Yes, there are.
Tourist:	I'd like to buy two.
Employee:	Where would you prefer to sit?
Tourist:	Where I can get a good view, please.
Employee:	Certainly.

SPORTS

You will find that a large majority of Japanese are enthusiastic about both spectator and participatory sports, especially the younger generation. If you plan to enjoy these activities yourself, one thing to expect is crowds (large crowds!)—unless you're lucky enough to hit an off-peak time, or are in a really out-of-the way place.

SPECTATOR SPORTS

Among the most popular spectator sports in Japan is baseball. Teams have a passionate and loyal following, and for fans, keeping track of their favorite team's records is a way of life. Tickets are available through Playguide (プレイガイド pu-LAY-GAHy-doh), a national advance-ticket sales agency, or at the stadium box office on the day of the game (if it's not sold out by then). A very popular attraction is the high school baseball tournament, held once in the spring and once in the summer, which is televised nationally and causes quite a stir (think of it as the equivalent of college basketball or football).

A traditional sport is sumo wrestling, which is said to have been practiced since ancient times. Enormous sumo players wrestle each other inside a circular ring. The atmosphere is quite unique (much different from a professional wrestling match in both the United States and Japan), and there are die-hard fans of the sport. Cheaper seats still give you a decent view, but it would be a memorable experience to sit in the better box seats, so that you can sit on a traditional cushion and enjoy refreshments. There are six tournaments throughout the year in different cities.

Aside from the two major spectator sports, there are other popular ones, such as soccer, volleyball, and judo, a traditional sport of self-defense.

I'd like to see ...	_____を観に行きたいんです。	_____OH MIH-nih ih-kih-TAHY-n-dess.
• a baseball game.	• 野球	• yah-KYU
• a judo match.	• 柔道	• Ju-doh
• a rugby game.	• ラグビー	• LAH-gu-bee
• a soccer game.	• サッカー	• SAHT-kah
• sumo wrestling.	• 相撲	• su-MOH
• a tennis match.	• テニス	• TEH-nih-su
How much do tickets cost?	入場料はいくらですか？	NYU-JOh-lyoh wah IH-k'lah dess KAH?
When does the game begin?	いつ始まりますか？	IH-ts hah-JIH-MAH-LIH-MAHss KAH?
Who's playing?	誰が出てますか？	DAH-leh gah deh-teh-mahss KAH?
Who's winning?	誰が勝ってますか？	DAH-leh gah KAHT-teh-mahss KAH?
What are the teams?	どこのチームですか？	DOH-koh noh CHEe-mu dess KAH?

PARTICIPATORY SPORTS

You can find most kinds of participatory sports in Japan, although access may be difficult and expensive. Golf, possibly the most popular sport, is played on courses that are usually for members only. The same is true for tennis courts and health-and-fitness clubs. If you stay at a resort hotel, these facilities might be available.

Beaches are characterized by the tremendous crowds they attract during peak season; you'll be lucky if you manage to get a spot of sand large enough for your beach towel! If you must go, opt for off-peak seasons in Okinawa, or weekdays in early July (before summer vacation) at any of the other beaches. In general, the beaches along the Japan Sea tend to be more rugged than those on the

Pacific side (see map of Japan on pages viii-ix). Watch out for jellyfish, especially after mid-August, when waves get higher due to the approaching typhoon season. As for swimming, your hotel's pool is the best bet, as public pools are also crowded.

You will notice that bicycles are a popular mode of transportation. (Caution: bicycles are ridden on the sidewalk!) You can rent a bicycle fairly cheaply; some hotels or inns have their own rental system, or the front desk can assist you in locating a store. City streets are probably too crowded for joggers, but rural areas offer quieter paths and interesting sights along the way.

There are some very good places to ski in Japan. Many mountains get terrific snowfall, but the long lift lines might be discouraging. The Japan "Alps," in the middle of Honshu island, offer excellent skiing and are fairly easy to get to from Tokyo. The northern parts of Japan, including Hokkaido, are also great for this sport.

Other fun sporting activities might include a swing at a local batting practice facility or driving range. A hike along a mountain path is also recommended; ask at your lodging about local trails.

SWIMMING

The Beach

Where are the best beaches?	いい浜辺はどこですか？	Ee hah-MAH-BEH WAH DOH-koh dess KAH?
How do we get there?	どう行けばいいですか？	DOh ih-keh bah Ee dess KAH?
Is there a lifeguard?	見張りの人はいますか？	mih-HAH-LIH NOH HIH-TOH wah ih-MAHss KAH?

Are the currents safe?	潮の流れは大丈夫ですか？	shih-OH NOH NAH-GAH-LEH wah DAHY-JOh-bu dess KAH?
Are the waves high?	波は高いですか？	nah-MIH wah tah-KAHy dess KAH?
No, they are low.	いいえ、低いですよ。	ee-EH, hih-KU-ih dess YOH.
Are there lots of jellyfish?	くらげは多いですか？	k'LAH-GEH WAH Oh-ih dess KAH?
I'd like to rent…	_____を借りたいんですが。	_____oh kah-LIH-TAHy-n-dess gah.
• a beach chair.	• ビーチチェアー	• BEE-CHIH CHEH-ah
• a beach towel.	• タオル	• TAH-oh-lu
• a beach umbrella.	• ビーチパラソル	• BEE-CHIH PAH-lah-soh-lu
• a rowboat.	• ボート	• BOh-toh
• a sailboat.	• ヨット	• YOHT-toh
• snorkeling equipment.	• シュノーケル	• shu-NOh-keh-lu
• a surfboard.	• サーフィンボード	• SAH-FIN-BOh-doh
• waterskis.	• 水上スキー	• SU-IH-JOH S'KEe
Where can I buy …	_____はどこで売ってますか？	_____wah DOH-koh deh ut-TEH MAHss KAH?
• sunglasses?	• サングラス	• SAHN-G'lahss
• suntan lotion?	• 日焼けクリーム	• hih-YAH-KEH K'LEe-mu

Poolside

Where is the pool?	プールはどこですか？	Pu-lu wah DOH-koh dess KAH?
Is the pool …	_____プールですか？	_____ Pu-lu dess KAH?

• outdoors? • indoors? • heated?	• 屋外 • 室内 • 温水	• oh-KU-GAHY • shih-TS'NAHY • OHN-SU-IH
When does the pool… • open? • close?	プールはいつ_____ますか？ • 開き • 終り	Pu-lu wah IH-ts ___ mahss KAH? • hih-LAH-KIH • oh-WAH-LIH
Do I need a bathing cap?	水泳帽はいりますか？	SU-IH-Eh-boh wah ih-LIH-MAHss KAH?

SKIING

Would you like to go skiing?	スキーに行きませんか？	s'KEe nih ih-KIH-MAH-SEn KAH?
What is the best ski area?	どのスキー場が一番いいですか？	DOH-noh s'KEE-JOH GAH ih-CHIH-BAHN Ee dess KAH?
Are there slopes for …	_____のスロープはありますか？	_____ NOH su-LOh-pu wah ah-LIH-MAHss KAH?
• beginners?	• 初心者用	• shoh-SHIN-SHAH YOH
• intermediates? • experts?	• 中級用 • 上級用	• CHU-KYU-YOH • JOH-KYU-YOH
I'd like to take a lesson.	レッスンを受けたいんですが。	LESS-sun oh u-KEH-TAHy-n-dess gah.
Does the instructor speak English?	先生は英語が出来ますか？	SEN-SEh wah AY-GOH GAH deh-KIH-MAHss KAH?
What are the conditions like now?	雪はどうですか？	yu-KIH wah DOh dess KAH?
There's lots of snow.	沢山積もっています。	tahk-SAHN TS'MOHT-teh ih-mahss.

Where are the lifts?	リフトはどこですか？	LIH-hu-toh wah DOH-koh dess KAH?
How much is the lift?	リフトはいくらですか？	LIH-hu-toh wah IH-k'lah dess KAH?
I'd like to rent ...	_____を借りたいんです。	_____ oh kah-LIH-TAHy-n-dess.
• ski equipment.	• スキー用具	• s'KEE YOh-gu
• skis.	• スキー	• s'KEe
• ski boots.	• スキー靴	• s'KEe gu-tsu
• poles.	• ストック	• s'TOHT-ku

OTHER ACTIVE SPORTS

I like ...	_____が好きです。	_____ GAH s'KIH dess.
• baseball.	• 野球	• yah-KYU
• basketball.	• バスケットボール	• bahss-KET-TOH-BOh-lu
• boxing.	• ボクシング	• BOHK-shin-gu
• cycling.	• サイクリング	• SAHy-ku-lin-gu
• fishing.	• 釣	• tsu-LIH
• football.	• フットボール	• hut-TOH-BOh-lu
• golf.	• ゴルフ	• GOH-lu-hu
• hiking.	• ハイキング	• HAHy-kin-gu
• jogging.	• ジョギング	• joh-GHIN-GU
• judo.	• 柔道	• Ju-doh
• karate[1].	• 空手	• kah-LAH-TEH
• kendo[2].	• 剣道	• KEn-doh
• rugby.	• ラグビー	• LAH-gu-bee
• scuba diving.	• スキューバダイビング	• s'KYU-BAH DAHy-bin-gu
• skiing.	• スキー	• s'KEe
• swimming.	• 水泳	• su-IH-AY

[1] Karate is a traditional martial art without the use of any weapons.
[2] Kendo is Japanese-style fencing that uses bamboo swords.

English	Japanese	Pronunciation
• tennis.	• テニス	• TEH-nih-su
• volleyball.	• バレーボール	• bah-LEH-BOh-lu
Where can I find …	_____はどこですか？	_____ wah DOH-koh dess KAH?
• a tennis court?	• テニスコート	• teh-NISS-KOh-toh
• a tennis racket?	• テニスラケット	• teh-NISS-LAH-KET-toh
• some tennis balls?	• テニスボール	• teh-NISS BOh-lu
• a golf course?	• ゴルフ場	• goh-LU-HU JOH
Would you like to play …	_____をしませんか？	_____ oh shih-MAH-SEn KAH?
• tennis?	• テニス	• TEH-nih-su
• golf?	• ゴルフ	• GOH-lu-hu
How much is it per hour?	一時間いくらですか？	ih-CHIH-JIH-kahn IH-k'lah dess KAH?
You play very well.	お上手ですね。	oh-JOH-ZU dess NEH.
What's the score?	スコアは何ですか？	s'KOH-ah wah NAHn-dess KAH?

CAMPING

There are designated campsites at some national parks and certain other parks. For a list of campsites with descriptions of facilities at each site, call JNTO (see page 2 for the phone number).

English	Japanese	Pronunciation
Is there a campsite in this area?	この辺にキャンプ場はありますか？	koh-NOH HEN NIH KYAHN-PU-JOH WAH ah-LIH-MAHss KAH?
Is the campsite equipped with …	キャンプ場には_____はありますか？	KYAHN-PU-JOH NIH-wah _____ WAH ah-LIH-MAHss KAH?

• running water?	• 水道	• SU-IH-DOH
• toilets?	• トイレ	• TOy-leh
• showers?	• シャワー	• SHAH-wah
• cooking gas?	• ガス	• GAH-su
What does it cost for one night?	一晩おいくらですか？	hih-TOH-bahn oY-K'LAH DEss KAH?

CULTURAL DIVERSIONS

Theater and Dance

You can enjoy a wide variety of theater in Japan. The more traditional kinds are No (能　noh), kyogen (狂言　KYOH-GEn), Bunraku (文楽　BUn-lahk), and Kabuki (歌舞伎　kah-BU-KIH). Their histories are complicated, but all represent the different aspects of traditional theater. To summarize briefly, No can be traced back to the medieval era. Haunting chants are accompanied by a small group of instruments, actors dance onstage in subdued motions, and masks are commonly used to represent characters. It is sometimes difficult for those with no prior exposure to or knowledge of this form of theater to fully appreciate its minimalist beauty. Kyogen is another old form of theater and is sometimes performed with No plays to provide some comic relief. The language is pre-modern, so it is sometimes hard for even native Japanese to understand the jokes. Bunraku is a puppet theater and can be visually exciting even though you may not understand the dialogue. The same can be said for Kabuki, which is the most action oriented and uses elaborate costumes and makeup. Though good seats aren't cheap, attending any of the above performances is sure to be a memorable experience. There's a full spectrum of modern theater forms from traditional Western styles to the very avant-garde. If you plan to attend a performance, it's a good idea to invest in a book that explains the theater genre and perhaps even the play itself.

As for dance, there's everything from traditional forms to ballet available, depending on the time of year.

Your hotel staff will be able to help you obtain theater or dance tickets.

What's playing at the theaters?	今どんな劇をやっていますか？	IH-mah DOHn-nah geh-kih oh yaht-TEH IH-MAHss KAH?
What kind of play is it?	どんな演しものですか？	DOHn-nah dah-SHIH-moh-noh dess KAH?
Who wrote it?	作者は誰ですか？	SAHK-SHAH wah DAH-leh DEss KAH?
What genre of dance is it?	どんな踊りですか？	DOHn-nah oh-DOH-LIH DEss KAH?
I'd like to see a ...	_____を観たいんですが。	_____oh mih-TAHy-n-DEss gah.
• ballet.	• バレー	• BAH-l<u>eh</u>
• Bunraku play.	• 文楽	• BUn-lahk
• Kabuki performance.	• 歌舞伎	• kah-BU-KIH
• kyogen play.	• 狂言	• KY<u>OH</u>-GEn
• musical.	• ミュージカル	• MY<u>u</u>-jih-kah-lu
• No play.	• 能	• n<u>oh</u>
• traditional Japanese dance performance.	• 日本舞踊	• nih-HOHN BU-y<u>oh</u>
• modern play (including Western-style).	• 新劇	• shin-geh-kih
Are there tickets for tonight?	今夜の切符はありますか？	KOHn-yah noh kit-PU WAH ah-LIH-MAHss KAH?

I'd like to buy a program[1].	プログラムを下さい。	pu-LOH-GU-lah-mu oh k'dah-sahy.

Concerts

The choice of concerts in Japan ranges from classical to traditional Japanese to rock. Several major cities have their own symphonies that hold concerts on a regular basis. Traditional music, such as *gagaku* (雅楽 GAH-gahk), is performed as part of a ceremonial ritual at shrines at certain festivals. Other concerts are koto (琴 KOH-toh) and shamisen (三味線 shah-MIH-SEN) (both traditional instruments), which offer a taste of traditional culture. For a more contemporary variety, try one of the Live Houses ライブハウス LAHY-BU-HAH-u-su (i.e., bars that have live music) in the entertainment districts. Musicians play anything from jazz to punk rock. Bigger pop concerts are played at concert halls, but these tend to be expensive, especially for a band from abroad, so if you can catch them back home, you should wait.

However, you might find that the difference in the crowds is something to see!

I want to go to …	_____に行きたいんです。	_____nih ih-KIH-TAHy- n-dess.
• a classical music concert.	• クラシックのコンサート	• k'LAH-SHIK-ku noh KOHN-SAh-toh
• a jazz concert.	• ジャズのコンサート	• JAH-zu noh KOHN-SAh-toh
• an opera.	• オペラ	• OH-peh-lah
• a rock concert.	• ロックコンサート	• loht-KU KOHn-sah-toh
• a gagaku performance.	• 雅楽を見	• GAH-gahk oh MIH-

[1] In Japan, you normally have to purchase a program for a performance.

• a traditional Japanese music concert.	• 邦楽のコンサート	• hoh-gahk noh KOHN-SAh-toh
What pieces are going to be played?	どんな曲をやりますか？	DOHn-nah kyohk oh yah-lih-mahss KAH?
Who is the performer?	誰がでますか？	DAH leh gah deh-mahss KAH?
What kind of music is it?	どんな音楽ですか？	DOHn-nah OHn-gahk dess KAH?
How much are the least expensive seats?	一番安い席はいくらですか？	ih-CHIH-BAHN YAH-SU-ih seh-kih wah IH-k'lah dess KAH?
Do I need a reservation?	予約がいりますか？	yoh-YAHK GAH ih-LIH-MAHss KAH?
I'd like …	_____を下さい。	_____ oh k'DAH-SAHy.
• an orchestra seat.	• A席を一枚	• Ay-seh-kih oh ih-CHIH-mahy
• a balcony seat.	• C席を一枚	• SHEe-seh-kih oh ih-CHIH-mahy
• two tickets.	• 切符を二枚	• kit-PU OH NIH-mahy

Movies

These days, movies from the West don't take too long to reach Japan. They are either dubbed in Japanese or subtitled (unless you're fluent in Japanese, look for films with English subtitles). Current features are expensive; expect to pay twice as much as you would at home. Japanese films, which are also shown for about the same price, are not usually subtitled or dubbed in English.

I'd like to see a movie.	映画を見たいんです。	AY-GAH OH mih-TAHy-n-dess.

What's playing?	何をやっていますか？	NAH-nih oh yaht-TEH IH-MAHss KAH?
What kind of film is it?	どんな映画ですか？	DOHn-nah ay-gah dess KAH?
Is it in Japanese or English?	日本語ですか英語ですか？	nih-HOHN-GOH DEss kah, AY-GOH DEss KAH?
Is it dubbed in Japanese?	日本語に吹替えてありますか？	nih-HOHN-GOH NIH HU-KIH-KAH-eh-teh ah-LIH-MAHss KAH?
Is it subtitled?	字幕付ですか？	jih-MAHK-TS'KIH DEss KAH?
I want to see …	＿＿＿を見たいんです。	＿＿＿ oh mih-TAHy-n-dess.
• an action film.	• アクション映画	• ahk-SHOHN-Ay-gah
• a comedy.	• 喜劇	• KIH-geh-kih
• a drama.	• 劇映画	• geh-KIH-AY-gah
• a love story.	• ロマンス映画	• loh-MAHN-SU Ay-gah
When does the show start?	何時からですか？	NAHn-jih kah-lah dess KAH?
How much are the tickets?	いくらですか？	IH-k'lah dess KAH?
What theater is showing the new film directed by _____with_____?	＿＿＿監督、＿＿＿主演の新しい映画はどこでやっていますか？	_____ kahn-tohk, _____shu-EN NOH ah-TAH-LAH-SHee ay-gah wah DOH-koh deh yaht-TEH IH-MAHss KAH?

CLUBS, DISCOS, AND CABARET

Nightlife in Tokyo is alive with excitement, and it won't be hard to find something entertaining. Some bars that have live acts are packed with young people (see the description of Live Houses above, under “Concerts”), while others attract a more nine-to-five crowd, such as “beer gardens” (ビアガーデン bih-AH GAh-den), which are often situated on a building rooftop (such as a department store), and are only open in the summer. You may have already heard of ***karaoke*** bars (カラオケバー kah-LAH-OH-KEH BAh), which are basically sing-along bars complete with state-of-the-art audio equipment. Some have booths or private rooms so you can sing with your own group, and others have a stage at the front of the bar so that you can sing to the entire bar. Discos are popular, but generally expensive (though some places may include a free buffet or drinks in the cover charge). Some might have restrictions (such as couples only) so call ahead to check.

Note that these descriptions apply mainly to larger cities, and that more rural cities and towns might not have a substantial nightlife (if any at all), and evening activities might end early.

I'd like to go to …	_____へ行きたいんですが。	_____eh ih-KIH-TAHy-n-dess gah.
• a disco.	• ディスコ	• DISS-koh
• a *karaoke* bar.	• カラオケバー	• kah-LAH-OH-KEH-BAh
How much is the cover charge?	カバーチャージはいくらですか？	kah-BAH-CHAh jih wah IH-k'lah dess KAH?
Are there any restrictions?	何か規則はありますか？	NAH-nih kah KIH-sohk wah ah-LIH-MAHss KAH?
Would you like to dance?	踊りませんか？	oh-DOH-LIH-MAH-SEn KAH?
Do you want to sing along?	一緒に歌いませんか？	iss-SHOH NIH u-TAHY-MAH-SEn KAH?

ACTIVITIES

HOT SPRINGS AND BATHS

Hot springs and baths have been briefly described in chapter 4, but they are worthy of mentioning again since a visit to one of these is a wonderful experience. Many small towns in the mountain regions thrive solely on the fame of the hot spring in that town. There are variations such as milk baths, herbal baths, and mineral baths, which are aimed at pampering you in general, as well as alleviating particular health problems, since baths are traditionally considered medicinal. Normally, you would bring your own soap, washcloth, pail, and towel, though some places do provide them for public use. Upon entering the bathing room, you will notice that there is a large tub full of hot water, and a sizable area on the side for scrubbing and rinsing yourself. Fill your pail with water from the tub and rinse yourself. Scrub down with soap, and rinse again with a pail of water, making sure that soap never gets into the tub. You can now enter the tub and enjoy a long soak. After a hot bath, you may want to enjoy a relaxing massage or a cold glass of Japanese beer.

I'd like to go to a …	_____に行きたいんですが。	_____ NIH IH-KIH-TAHy-n-dess gah.
• hot spring.	• 温泉	• OHN-SEN
• public bath.	• 銭湯	• SEn-toh
I'd like a massage.	マッサージをお願いします。	mahss-SAh-jih oh oh-NEH-GAHY-SH'mahss.

PACHINKO

One form of very popular entertainment is *pachinko* (パチンコ pah-CHIN-KOH), which is basically a vertical pinball machine. A *pachinko* parlor has rows and rows of these machines, and players sit in front of them (often for hours at a time) until they collect a big container full of balls that come out of the machines (if you play well, these balls come pouring out of a slot). They can be exchanged for various prizes at the cashier.

Is there a *pachinko* nearby?	この近くにパチンコ屋はありますか？	koh-NOH CHIH-KAHK nih pah-CHIN-KOH YAH WAH ah-LIH-MAHss KAH?

TRADITIONAL ARTS SCHOOLS

There are some organizations and individual experts throughout Japan that give demonstrations to tourists of various traditional arts of Japan, such as the tea ceremony and flower arrangement. For a list of them, contact a JNTO office (see page 2); some locations may require advance notice, so plan ahead.

ACTIVITIES FOR CHILDREN

A large percentage of activities in Japan are geared toward children. There are numerous museums, amusement parks, theme parks, and playgrounds throughout the country. Fun places to go in and around Tokyo include the Ueno Zoo and Tokyo Disneyland.

You will also find that children in Japan are taken almost everywhere their parents go, be it a classical music concert or an art museum. This means that the system of hiring baby-sitters is not very widespread, and in areas outside of Tokyo, you may encounter difficulties in finding a sitter. Some hotels in Tokyo offer baby-sitting arrangements (though reservations may have to be made far in advance), but many hotels do not have such services.

14 / GENERAL INFORMATION

DAYS, MONTHS, AND SEASONS

Days of the Week

Sunday	日曜日	nih-CHIH-YOh-bih
Monday	月曜日	geh-TSU-YOh-bih
Tuesday	火曜日	kah-YOh-bih
Wednesday	水曜日	su-IH-YOh-bih
Thursday	木曜日	moh-KU-YOh-bih
Friday	金曜日	KIN-YOh-bih
Saturday	土曜日	doh-YOh-bih

Days of the Month

the first	一日	tsu-ih-tahch
the second	二日	hu-TS'KAH
the third	三日	miht-KAH
the fourth	四日	yoht-KAH
the fifth	五日	ih-TS'KAH
the sixth	六日	mu-IH-KAH
the seventh	七日	nah-NOH-KAH
the eighth	八日	YOH-KAH
the ninth	九日	koh-KOH-NOH-KAH
the tenth	十日	TOH-KAH
the eleventh	十一日	JU-IH-CHIH-NICH
the twelfth	十二日	JU-NIH-NICH
the thirteenth	十三日	JU-SAHn-nich

the fourteenth	十四日	Ju-yoht-KAH
the fifteenth	十五日	JU-GOH-nich
the sixteenth	十六日	JU-LOHK-NICH
the seventeenth	十七日	JU-SHI-CHIH-NICH
the eighteenth	十八日	JU-HAH-CHIH-NICH
the nineteenth	十九日	JU-KU-nich
the twentieth	二十日	hah-ts'KAH
the twenty-first	二十一日	NIH-ju-ih-CHIH-NICH
the twenty-second	二十二日	NIH-ju-NIH-NICH
the twenty-third	二十三日	NIH-ju-SAHN-NICH
the twenty-fourth	二十四日	NIH-ju-yoht-KAH
the twenty-fifth	二十五日	NIH-ju-GOH-nich
the twenty-sixth	二十六日	NIH-ju-loh-KU-NICH
the twenty-seventh	二十七日	NIH-ju-shih-CHIH-NICH
the twenty-eighth	二十八日	NIH-ju-hah-CHIH-NICH
the twenty-ninth	二十九日	NIH-ju-KU-nich
the thirtieth	三十日	SAHN-Ju-nich
the thirty-first	三十一日	SAHn-ju-ih-CHIH-NICH

Months

January	一月	ih-CHIH-GAHTS
February	二月	NIH-GAHTS
March	三月	SAHn-gahts
April	四月	SHIH-GAHTS
May	五月	GOH-gahts

June	六月	loh-KU-GAHTS
July	七月	shih-CHIH-GAHTS
August	八月	hah-CHIH-GAHTS
September	九月	KU-gahts
October	十月	JU-GAHTS
November	十一月	JU-IH-CHIH-GAHTS
December	十二月	JU-NIH-GAHTS

Seasons

spring	春	HAH-lu
summer	夏	nah-TSU
fall	秋	AH-kih
winter	冬	hu-YU

THE DATE

What is today's date?	今日は何日ですか？	KYOh wah NAHn-nich dess KAH?
What day is it today?	今日は何曜日ですか？	KYOh wah NAHN-YOh-bih dess KAH?
Today is Friday, April 1.	今日は四月一日金曜日です。	KYOh wah SHIH-GAHTS TSU-IH-TACH KIN-YOh-bih dess.
Today is May 18, 1991.[1]	今日は平成三年五月十八日です。	KYOh wah HEH-SEH SAHN-NEN GOH-gahts JU-HAH-CHIH-NICH dess.

[1] Note: Although the Western year system is used in Japan, more often you'll hear people talk in terms of Japanese years, which are counted in reference to the emperor's reign. The year 1989 marked the beginning of the Heisei emperor's reign (i.e., the first year), thus 1991 is the third year of the Heisei. In this system, the Meiji period was from 1868 to 1912, the Taisho period was from 1912 to 1926, and the Showa period was from 1926 to 1988. Also, note that the year is said first, then the month and the date.

AGE

How old arc you?	おいくつですか？	oh-IH-K'TS DEss KAH?
I'm 36.	三十六才です。	SAHn-ju-loh-KU sahy dess.
How old is he/she?	おいくつの方ですか？	oh-IH-K'TS NOH KAH-TAH dess KAH?
She's 20.[1]	二十才です。	HAH-tahch dess.
I'm younger than he is.	私は彼より若いです。	wah-TAHSH WAH KAH-leh yoh-lih wah-KAHy dess.
A is [three] years older than B.	AはBより[三つ]年上です。	A wah B yoh-lih [mit-TSU] TOH-SHIH-U-EH DEss.
I was born in 1940.	一九四十年生まれです。	SEn-kyu-hyahk YOHN-JU-NEN U-mah-leh des.
Her birthday is December 2, 1956.	彼女の誕生日は一九五六年十二月二日です。	KAH-noh-joh noh TAHN-JOh-bih wah SEn-kyu-hyahk goh-JU-LOHK-nen JU-NIH-GAHTS hu-TS'KAH dess.

EXPRESSIONS OF TIME

now	今	IH-mah
earlier	前	MAH-eh
later/after	後	AH-toh
before	以前	IH-zen
from now on	今後／以後	KOHn-goh/IH-goh
soon	もうすぐ	MOH-S'gu

[1] Although age is expressed in the "counting number + sahy 才 (years old)" pattern, the age 20 is an exception. You can still say "nih-JUSS-sahy" (20 years old), but there is a set phrase called "HAH-tahch" which means the same, and is used often.

once	一度	ih-CHIH-DOH
in the morning	朝（に）[1]	AH-sah (nih)[1]
at noon	正午（に）	SHOh-goh (nih)
in the afternoon	午後（に）	GOH-goh (nih)
in the evening	夕方（に）	YU-GAH-TAH (NIH)
at night	夜（に）	YOH-lu (nih)
at midnight	真夜中（に）	mah-YOH-nah-kah (nih)
tomorrow	明日	ahsh-TAH/ah-SU
yesterday	昨日	kih-NOh
the day after tomorrow	明後日	ah-SAHT-teh
the day before yesterday	一昨日	oh-TOH-TOy
this week	今週	kohn-shu
next week	来週	lahy-shu
last week	先週	sen-shu
every day	毎日	MAHy-nich
in three days	三日後	miht-KAH GOH
two days ago	二日前	hu-TS'KAH MAH-eh
every Saturday	毎週土曜日	mahy-shu doh-YOh-bih
weekend	週末	shu-mahts
weekday(s)	平日[2]	heh-jits[2]

[1] The word *nih* follows these words depending on the context. You might hear *nih* being used in conjunction with them, or you might not. For further explanation of this word (called a particle), see page 216 in the Grammar section.

[2] This term sometimes includes Saturdays (traditionally a workday in Japan).

a working day	勤めのある日	ts'TOH-MEH noh AH-lu hih
a day off	休み（の日）	yah-SU-MIH (NOH-HIH)
in January	一月（に）	ih-CHIH-gahts nih
last January	去年の一月	KYOH-nen noh ih-CHIH-gahts
next January	来年の一月	lahY-NEN NOH IH-CHIH-gahts
every month	毎月	mahY-TS'KIH
since August	八月から	hah-CHIH-GAHTS kah-lah
this month	今月	kohn-gets
next month	来月	LAHy-gets
last month	先月	SEn-gets
this year	今年	koh-TOHSH
next year	来年	lahy-nen
last year	去年	KYOH-nen
every year	毎年	mahy-tohsh
In what year…	何年に	NAHn-nen nih
In 1980…	1980年に	SEn-KYu-hyahk hah-CHIH-Ju-nen nih
In the nineteenth century…	19世紀に	JU-KYU-SEh-kih nih
In the forties…	1940年代に[1]	SEn-KYu-hyahk YOHN-JU-NEn-dahy nih[1]

[1] Note that one doesn't normally say "forties" in Japan; rather, it is clearer to say "the nineteen forties."

HOLIDAYS

Below is a list of national holidays in Japan. Be aware that many establishments are closed during the big holiday season around New Year's Day. See page 143–144 for a brief description of a few festivals; Japan has numerous other regional festivals, so consult your guidebook or JNTO for more information.

January 1	元日 gahn-jits	New Year's Day
January 15	成人の日 SEh-jin noh hih	Coming-of-Age Day
February 11	建国記念日 KEN-KOHK KIH-NEn-bih	National Foundation Day
March 21	春分の日 shun-bun noh hih	Vernal Equinox
April 29	みどりの日 MIH-doh-lih noh hih	"Green Day"
May 3	憲法記念日 KEN-POH KIH-NEn-bih	Constitution Day
May 5	こどもの日 koh-DOH-MOH NOH HIH	Children's Day
September 15	敬老の日 keh-loh noh hih	Senior Citizens' Day
September 23	秋分の日 shu-bun noh hih	Autumnal Equinox
October 10	体育の日 TAHy-ku noh hih	Athletics Day
November 3	文化の日 BUn-kah noh hih	Culture Day

November 23	勤労感謝の日 KIN-LOH KAHn-shah noh hih	Labor Day
December 23	天皇誕生日 TEN-NOH TAHN-JOh-bih	Emperor's Birthday

WEATHER

What's the weather today?	今日の天気はどうですか？	KYOh noh TEn-kih wah DOh dess KAH?
It is… • raining. • snowing.	_____います。 • 雨が降って • 雪が降って	_____ ih-mahss. • AH-meh gah hut-teh • yu-KIH gah hut-teh
It's… • cold. • cool. • cloudy. • foggy. • warm.	_____です。 • 寒い • 涼しい • 曇り • 霧 • 暖かい	_____ dess. • sah-MU-ih • su-ZU-SHEe • ku-MOH-LIH • kih-LIH • ah-TAH-TAH-KAHy
• hot. • nice. • sunny. • windy.	• 暑い • いい天気 • 晴 • 風が強い	• ah-TSU-ih • Ee ten-kih • hah-LEH • kah-ZEH GAH TS'YOy
What's the forecast for tomorrow?	明日の予報はどうですか？	ah-SU NOH YOH-HOH WAH DOh dess KAH?
It will probably rain.	雨でしょう。	AH-meh deh-shoh.
What is the average temperature at this time of year?	毎年今ごろの気温は何度ぐらいですか？	MAHY-TOHSH ih-MAH-GOH-LOH NOH kih-OHN WAH NAHn-doh-g'lahy dess KAH?

TEMPERATURE CONVERSIONS

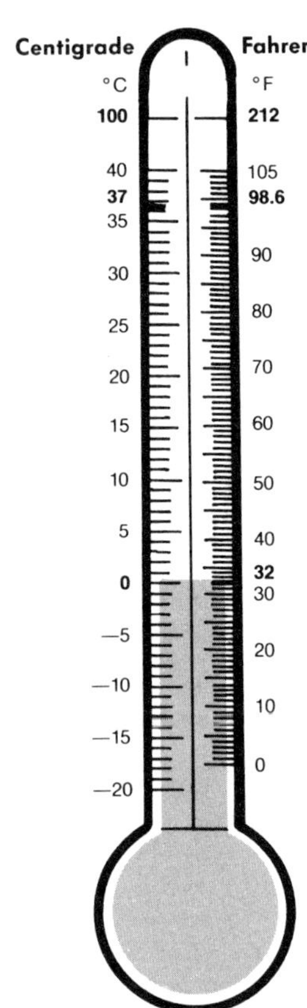

Temperature Conversions

In Japan, temperature is measured in degrees Celsius, or centigrade. To convert degrees Celsius into degrees Fahrenheit, use this formula:

To Convert Centigrade to Fahrenheit

$(\frac{9}{5})C^\circ + 32 = F^\circ$

1. Divide by 5.
2. Multiply by 9.
3. Add 32.

To Convert Fahrenheit to Centigrade

$(F^\circ - 32)\frac{5}{9} = C^\circ$

1. Subtract 32.
2. Divide by 9.
3. Multiply by 5.

ORIGINS AND DESTINATIONS

Where are you from?	どちらからいらっしゃいましたか？	DOH-ch'lah kah-lah ih-LAHSS-SHAHY-MAHsh-tah KAH?
I'm from…	＿＿＿から来ました。	＿＿＿ kah-lah kih-MAHsh-tah.
• the United States. • New York. • Los Angeles.	• アメリカ • ニューヨーク • ロスアンジェルス	• ah-MEH-LIH-KAH • NYU-YOh-ku • loh-SU-AHN-JEH-lu-su
To where are you going?	どこへ行かれるんですか？	DOH-koh eh ih-KAH-LEH-LUn-dess KAH?
I'm going to…	＿＿＿へ行きます。	＿＿＿ eh ih-kih-mahss.
• Kyoto. • Hong Kong.	• 京都 • 香港	• KYOh-toh • HOHN-KOHn

CONTINENTS AND REGIONS

continent	大陸	tahy-lik
region	地方	chih-HOh
Africa	アフリカ	ah-HU-LIH-KAH
Antarctica	南極	nahn-kyohk
Asia	アジア	AH-jih-ah
Australia	オーストラリア	OH-S'TOH-LAH-lih-ah
Europe	ヨーロッパ	YOH-LOHP-pah
Middle East	中東	chu-toh
North America	北アメリカ	kih-TAH AH-MEH-lih-kah

North Pole	北極	hoht-KYOHK
South America	南アメリカ	mih-NAH-MIH AH-MEH-lih-kah

COUNTRIES AND NATIONALITIES

To make a country into a nationality, simply add *jin* at the end of the name of the country. *Jin* 人 means "person/people," so the literal meaning is "people/person (of) that country." Example:
ah-MEH-LIH-KAH アメリカ (America/the United States) → ah-MEH-LIH-KAH-jin アメリカ人 (American).

One term that is used often to describe foreigners is *gaijin* (外人 gahY-JIN, or more formally, 外国人 GAHY-KOHK-jin), which literally means "person/people from the outside." This term is not particularly flattering but used very commonly and generally without any harmful intentions.

Afghanistan	アフガニスタン	ah-HU-GAH-NIss-tahn
Algeria	アルジェリア	ah-LU-JEH-LIH-AH
Angola	アンゴラ	ahn-goh-lah
Argentina	アルゼンチン	ah-LU-ZEN-CHIn
Australia	オーストラリア	OH-S'TOH-LAH-lih-ah
Austria	オーストリア	OH-S'TOH-lih-ah
Bangladesh	バングラデッシュ	bahN-GU-LAH-DESS-shu
Belgium	ベルギー	beh-LU-GHEe
Bhutan	ブータン	Bu-tahn
Brazil	ブラジル	bu-LAH-JIH-LU
Cameroon	カメルーン	kah-MEH-LUn

Canada	カナダ	KAH-nah-dah
Chile	チリ	CHIH-lih
China	中国	CH<u>u</u>-gohk
Colombia	コロンビア	koh-LOHN-BIH-AH
Costa Rica	コスタリカ	kohss-TAH-LIH-kah
Cuba	キューバ	KY<u>u</u>-bah
Czechoslovakia	チェコスロバキア	CHEH-KOH-S'LOH-BAH-kih-ah
Denmark	デンマーク	DEN-M<u>Ah</u>-ku
Dominican Republic	ドミニカ共和国	doh-MIH-NIH-KAH KY<u>OH</u>-WAH-kohk
Ecuador	エクアドール	eh-KU-AH D<u>Oh</u>-lu
Egypt	エジプト	eh-JIH-PU-TOH
El Salvador	エルサルバドール	eh-LU-SAH-LU-BAH-D<u>Oh</u>-lu
England/Great Britain	イギリス	ih-GIH-LIH-SU
Ethiopia	エチオピア	eh-CHIH-OH-pih-ah
Finland	フィンランド	FIN-LAHn-doh
France	フランス	hu-LAHN-SU
Germany	ドイツ	DOy-tsu
Ghana	ガーナ	G<u>Ah</u>-nah
Greece	ギリシャ	GIH-lih-shah
Guatemala	ガテマラ	gah-TEH-MAH-LAH
Guinea	ギニア	GIH-nih-ah
Haiti	ハイチ	HAHy-chih
Honduras	ホンジュラス	HOHN-JU-lahss
Hungary	ハンガリー	HAHN-GAH-LEe

India	インド	In-doh
Indonesia	インドネシア	IN-DOH-NEH-shih-ah
Iran	イラン	IH-lahn
Iraq	イラク	IH-lahk
Ireland	アイルランド	ahY-LU-LAHn-doh
Israel	イスラエル	ih-SU-LAH-eh-lu
Italy	イタリア	ih-TAH-LIH-AH
Ivory Coast	コートジボアール	KOH-TOH JIH-BOH-Ah-lu
Japan	日本	nih-HOHn/nit-POHn
Jordan	ヨルダン	YOH-lu-dahn
Kampuchea	カンプチア	KAHN-PU-chih-ah
Kenya	ケニア	KEH-nih-ah
Korea, Soc. Rep. of	北朝鮮	kih-TAH CHOH-SEn
Korea, Republic of	韓国	KAHn-kohk
Laos	ラオス	LAH-oh-su
Lebanon	レバノン	leh-BAH-nohn
Madagascar	マダガスカル	mah-DAH-GAHss-kah-lu
Malawi	マラウイ	mah-LAH-U-IH
Malaysia	マレイシア	mah-LAy-shih-ah
Mali	マリ	mah-LIH
Mexico	メキシコ	meh-KIH-SHIH-KOH
Mongolia	蒙古	MOh-koh
Morocco	モロッコ	moh-LOHT-koh
Mozambique	モザンビーク	moh-ZAHN-BEe-ku

Myanmar (Burma)	ミャンマー	mih-YAHN-MAh
Nepal	ネパール	neh-PAh-lu
Netherlands	オランダ	oh-LAHN-DAH
New Zealand	ニュージーランド	NYU-JEE-LAHn-doh
Nigeria	ナイジェリア	nahY-JEH-LIH-AH
Norway	ノルウェー	noh-LU-WEh
Pakistan	パキスタン	pah KIss-tahn
Papua New Guinea	パプアニューギニア	pah-PU-AH NYU-GIH-nih-ah
Peru	ペルー	PEH-lu
Philippines	フィリピン	fih-LIH-PIn
Poland	ポーランド	POH-LAHn-doh
Portugal	ポルトガル	poh-LU-TOH-GAH-LU
Puerto Rico	プエルトリコ	pu-EH-LU-TOH-LIH-koh
Romania	ルーマニア	lu-mah-nih-ah
Russia	ロシア	LOH-shi-ah
Saudi Arabia	サウジアラビア	SAH-U-JIH AH-LAH-bih-ah
Scotland	スコットランド	s'KOHT-TOH-LAHn-doh
Senegal	セネガル	SEH-neh-gah-lu
Singapore	シンガポール	SHIN-GAH-POh-lu
South Africa	南アフリカ	mih-NAH-MIH AH-hu-lih-kah
Spain	スペイン	s'PEH-in
Sri Lanka	スリランカ	s'LIH-LAHn-kah
Sudan	スーダン	Su-dahn

Sweden	スエーデン	s'Eh-den
Switzerland	スイス	SU-ih-su
Syria	シリア	SHIH-lih-ah
Taiwan	台湾	TAHY-WAHn
Tanzania	タンザニア	tahn-zah-nih-ah
Thailand	タイ	TAHy
Turkey	トルコ	TOH-lu-koh
Uganda	ウガンダ	u-GAHn-dah
United States/America	アメリカ	ah-MEH-LIH-KAH
Venezuela	ベネズエラ	beh-NEH-ZU-eh-lah
Vietnam	ベトナム	beh-TOH-NAH-MU
Zaire	ザイール	zah-EE-lu
Zimbabwe	ジンバブエ	JIN-BAH-bu-eh

LANGUAGES

As a rule, add *goh* 語 (the language of) at the end of a country name to describe its language. Therefore, Japanese is "Japan" (nih-HOHn 日本) + "language of" (goh 語) = "Japanese" (nih-HOHN-GOH 日本語). There are exceptions, however, and below are some examples that you might encounter:

Arabic	アラビア語	ah-LAH-BIH-AH-GOH
Chinese	中国語	chu-gohk-goh
English	英語	ay-goh
French	フランス語	hu-LAHN-SU-GOH
German	ドイツ語	doY-TSU-GOH

Japanese	日本語	nih-HOHN-GOH
Korean	韓国語	kahn-kohk-goh
Russian	ロシア語	loh-SHIH-AH-GOH
Spanish	スペイン語	s'PEH-IN-GOH
I can speak Japanese.	日本語を話せます。	nih-HON-GOH OH HAH-NAH-SEH-MAHss.
I like Japanese.	日本語は好きです。	nih-HOHN-GOH WAH s'KIH dess.

OCCUPATIONS

accountant	計理士	KEH-LIH-shih
architect	建築家	ken-chik-kah
artist	画家	gah-KAH
bank employee	銀行員	GHIN-KOh-in
butcher	肉屋	nih-KU-yah
carpenter	大工	DAHy-ku
chef	シェフ	SHEH-hu
clerk	書記	shoh-KIH
dentist	歯医者	HAHy-shah
doctor	医者	ih-SHAH
electrician	電機屋	den-kih-yah
engineer	技師	GIH-shih
lawyer	弁護士	BEN-GOH-shih
maid	お手伝いさん	oh-TEH-tsu-dahy sahn
nurse	看護婦	KAHN-GOH-hu
plumber	水道屋	su-ih-doh-yah

professor	教授	kyoh-ju
researcher	研究員	KEN-KYu-in
salesperson	セールス担当	SEh-lu-su TAHN-TOH
schoolteacher	先生	SEN-SEh
shopkeeper	店主	TEn-shu
waiter	ウェイター	waY-TAH
waitress	ウェイトレス	WAy-toh-less
writer	作家	saht-KAH

EMERGENCY EXPRESSIONS

Help!	助けて！	tahss-KEH-TEH!
Fire!	火事だ！	KAH-JIH DAH!
Hurry!	早く！	HAH-yah-ku!
Police!	警察！	kay-sahts!
Stop!	止まれ！	toh-MAH-LEH!
Call the police!	警察を呼んで！	kay-sahts oh yohn-deh!
Call the fire department!	消防署に連絡を！	SHOH-BOH-SHOH nih LEN-LAHK OH!
I feel sick.	気分が悪いんです。	KIH-bun gah wah-LU-in-dess.
Call a doctor!	医者を呼んで！	ih-SHAH OH YOHN-DEH!
I'm lost.	道に迷ったんです。	mih-CHIH NIH mah-YOHT-tahn-dess.
Please help me.	助けてください。	tahss-KEH-teh k'dah-sahy.
Thief!	泥棒！	doh-LOH-BOH!

My______was stolen!	______を盗まれたんです！	______OH nu-SU-MAH-leh-tahn-dess!
• camera	• カメラ	• KAH-meh-lah
• car	• 車	• ku-LU-MAH
• handbag	• ハンドバッグ	• HAHN-DOH BAHT-gu
• money	• お金	• oh-KAH-NEH
• passport	• パスポート	• pahss-POh-toh
• suitcase	• スーツケース	• SU-TSU KEh-su
• wallet	• 財布	• SAHY-HU
• watch	• 時計	• toh-KAY
That's the thief!	あれが泥棒です！	ah-LEH GAH DOH-LOH-BOH DEss!
Catch him/her!	捕まえて！	ts'KAH-MAH-eh-teh!
I'm going to call the police.	警察を呼びますよ。	KAY-SAHTS OH yoh-BIH-MAHss YOH.
Where's the police (station)?	警察はどこですか？	KAY-SAHTS WAH DOH-koh dess KAH?
Please get me…	______を頼みます。	______ oh tah-NOH-MIH-MAHss.
• a lawyer.	• 弁護士	• BEN-GOH-shih
• an interpreter.	• 通訳	• TSu-yahk
Is there someone here who speaks English?	英語のわかる人はいますか？	AY-GOH NOH WAH-KAH-lu hih-toh wah ih-MAHss KAH?
I want to go to the American consulate.	アメリカ領事館へ行きたいんです。	ah-MEH-LIH-KAH LYOH-JIH-kahn eh ih-KIH-TAHy-n-dess.

15 / GRAMMAR IN BRIEF

Traveltalk™: Japanese is designed to help you to find and use Japanese phrases without formal grammar study. However, this chapter will provide you with some basic grammatical building blocks of the language so that you can increase your range of expression. Of course, it's impossible to condense all the essential points of Japanese grammar into one short chapter; it is a complicated language that is entirely different from English, and there are numerous exceptions to any broad rule. The explanations below are intended as guides for you to be able to construct some simple sentences on your own.

WORD ORDER

The order of words in a Japanese sentence differs from that of English sentences. The basic things to keep in mind are the following:

1) In general, a predicate word (such as a verb) is placed at the end of the clause or a sentence.

    English order: I am John.
    Japanese order: I John am.

2) A modifier always precedes the word or clause it modifies.

    English order: The apple she bought at that store yesterday was tasty.

    All of the words in the box modify *apple*.

    Japanese order: She yesterday that store at bought the apple tasty was.

    Note how the modifier comes before the modified word *apple*, no matter how long it may be.

NOUNS AND PARTICLES

1) There is no distinction between a singular and plural noun, and nouns are not preceded by articles, such as *the* and *a/an* in English.

   apple, apples, an apple, the apple ＝りんご liN-GOH

2) Nouns in a sentence are usually accompanied by *particles*. A particle is very often not translatable. It indicates the relationship of the word it accompanies to another word or part of the sentence. All particles follow the words to which they refer. Some frequently-used particles that follow nouns are (particles are in bold type):

a) は **wah** shows that the noun it follows is the topic of the sentence. It can be compared to the occasional practice in English of beginning a sentence with "As for… " or " Speaking of …"

(As for) apples, (I) like it. (i. e., I like apples.)	りんごは好きです。	liN-GOH **WAH** S'KIH-dess.

b) が **gah** emphasizes the noun it follows.

I want the apple (emphasis on *apple*).	りんごがほしいんです。	liN-GOh **GAH** hoh-SHEEn-dess.

c) を **oh** shows that the noun it follows is the object of the verb.

I buy an apple.	りんごを買う	liN-GOH **OH** kah-U

d) か **kah** forms a question at the end of a positively stated sentence.

This is an apple.	これはりんごです。	koh-LEH WAH LIN-GOH DEss.

Is this an apple?	これはりんごですか。	koh-LEH WAH LIN-GOH DEss **KAH**?

e) の **noh** is most frequently used for the possessive and shows that the noun it follows modifies another noun that comes after it.

the apple's core	りんごの芯	liN-GOH **NOH** SHIn

Other particles include **nih** に, **deh** で, and **eh** へ. Like the particles above, these and other particles function similarly to English word order and prepositions to show the relation of parts of phrases to the whole phrase.

PRONOUNS

Japanese pronouns function like regular nouns, taking the same particles and modified by the same type of words, phrases, and clauses. Note that:

1) A pronoun that is the subject of a sentence, and the topic marker *wah,* is often omitted. It is assumed from the context.

(I) am going to Tokyo today.	(私は) 今日東京に行きます。	(wah-TAHSH WAH) KYOh TOH-KYOH NIH ih-KIH-MAHss.

2) There are many different ways to say *I* or *you* in Japanese. This is a complicated issue that relates to the various degrees of politeness that exist in the language and the relative social status of the speaker and the listener. Below are some standard ways of saying *I* and *you* in most everyday situations. Keep in mind that you may encounter other variations.

I (standard level of politeness for both men and women; also used more casually by women)	私	wah-TAHSH/wah-TAH-SHIH
I (used casually by men only)	僕	BOH-ku/BOHK
we (standard/ casual women)	私達	wah-TAHSH-tahch
we (casual men)	僕達	BOHK-tahch
you (singular)[1]	あなた	ah-NAH-tah
you (plural)[1]	あなた方	ah-NAH-TAH-GAH-tah
he[2]	彼	KAH-leh
she[2]	彼女	KAH-noh-joh
that person	あの人	ah-NOH hih-toh
that person (polite)	あの方	ah-NOH KAH-TAH
they	あの人達	ah-NOH-HIH-TOH-tahch
they (polite)	あの方達	ah-NOH-KAH-TAH-tahch

3) Demonstrative pronouns also function like nouns. A few popular demonstrative pronouns are:

this one	これ	koh-LEH

[1] You will notice that *you* is used a lot less often than it is in English. More often, in referring to someone, the last name + *sahn* (Mr./Ms) pattern is used (or the first name, if on a very casual basis).
[2] *He* and *she* are not as common as they are in English as well, especially when talking about someone you don't know.

GRAMMAR

that one	それ	soh-LEH
that one (farther away)	あれ	ah-LEH

ADJECTIVES

Adjectives come before the nouns that they modify, as do all modifiers.

Regular Adjectives

Adjectives are conjugated according to their usage in the following way:

Example: The adjective *inexpensive.*

the stem		安 yah-SU-
present tense	is inexpensive	安い yah-SU-ih
past tense	was inexpensive	安かった yah-SU-kaht-tah
"-te" form	is/was inexpensive and…	安くて yah-SU-ku-teh
conditional	if it is inexpensive	安かったら yah-SU-kaht-tah-lah
tentative	is probably inexpensive	安いでしょう yah-SU-ih-deh-sh<u>oh</u>

Nominal Adjectives

Many words that are considered adjectives in English are, in Japanese, composed of "stems" that function like nouns, followed by the particle *nah*.

beautiful	きれいな	KIH-l<u>eh</u> nah
wonderful	素敵な	s'TEH-KIH NAH

GRAMMAR

Possessive Adjectives

There is no separate set of possessive adjectives as in English. To form the possessive, simply attach the particle *noh* after the subject pronoun:

my, mine	私の	wah-TAHSH NOH
your, yours (singular)	あなたの	ah-NAH-tah noh
your, yours (plural)	あなた方の	ah-NAH-TAH-GAH-tah noh
his	彼の	KAH-leh noh
hers	彼女の	KAH-noh-joh noh
that person's	あの人の	ah-NOH-HIH-toh noh
their, theirs	あの人達の	ah-NOH-HIH-TOH-tahch noh
my book	私の本	wah-TAHSH NOH HOHn
his camera	彼のカメラ	KAH-leh noh KAH-meh-lah

Demonstrative Adjectives

These words do not need particles to separate them from the nouns they modify. Remember that they must be followed by nouns; for words such as *this one* and *that one*, see the section on pronouns on page 216. A few demonstrative adjectives are:

this	この	koh-NOH
that	その	soh-NOH
that (farther away)	あの	ah-NOH
which	どの	DOH-noh

ADVERBS

Adverbs precede the verbs they modify.

1) One way to form an adverb is to take the stem of an adjective and add a *-ku* after it instead of *-ih,* which would form an adjective.

the adjective *inexpensive*	安い	yah-SU-ih
the adverb *inexpensively*	安く	yah-SU-**ku**

2) As in the case of adjectives, there are some adverbs that are formed by taking noun stems and adding the particle *nih* after them (instead of *nah*, which would form an adjective).

beautiful (adj.)	きれいな	KIH-l<u>eh</u> nah
beautifully (adv.)	きれいに	KIH-l<u>eh</u> **nih**

VERBS

There are basically two categories of regular verbs, plus two common irregular verbs and what is called a "copula." Practically speaking, learning which verbs belong to which group is a matter of memorization. All conjugations below are at the standard level of politeness, exccpt where noted.

The "Copula"

The equivalent of the English verb *to be* is *deh-su* (です dess). It is called a copula, and changes according to its usage in the following manner:

is/am/are	です	DEss
isn't/am not/aren't	じゃありません／ではありません	JAH ah-LIH-MAH-SEn/DEH-wah ah-LIH-MAH-SEn

was/were	でした	DEsh-tah
wasn't/weren't	じゃありませんでした／ではありませんでした	JAH ah-LIH-MAH-SEn-desh-tah/DEH-wah ah-LIH-MAH-SEn-desh-tah[1]
I am John.	私はジョンです。	wah-TAHSH WAH JOHn dess.
They aren't Americans.	あの人達はアメリカ人じゃありません。	ah-NOH-hih-toh-tahch wah ah-MEH-LIH-KAH-JIn jah ah-LIH-MAH-SEn.
(It) was beautiful.	きれいでした。	KIH-leh desh-tah.
The room wasn't quiet.	部屋は静かではありませんでした。	heh-YAH wah SHIH-zu-kah deh-wah ah-LIH-MAH-SEn-desh-tah.

Regular Verbs

***-Lu* verbs:** Certain verbs ending in *-lu* (in *romaji*, *-ru* verbs[2]) belong in this group. The stem of these verbs is the informal present/future from minus the *lu* at the end; conjugations are achieved through the addition of various endings to these stems. Only the present/future, past, gerund, and conditional forms, and the negatives, are listed below.

Example: the verb *to eat*.

The Stem		tah-BEH-
informal[3] present/future	eat/will eat	食べる tah-BEH-lu

[1]The latter of these is more formal.
[2] Note that most dictionaries use the *romaji* system to phoneticize Japanese.
Therefore you should look for *-lu* verbs under *-ru* verbs in these dictionaries.
[3] The "informal" form can be considered a kind of "basic form"; verbs are listed in this form in dictionaries.

formal present/ future[1]	eat/will eat	食べます tah-BEH-MAHss
past	ate	食べました tah-BEH-MAHsh-tah
gerund[2]	(followed by certain verb particles)	食べて TAH-beh-teh
negative (present/ future)	don't/won't eat	食べません tah-BEH-MAH-SEn
negative (past)	did not eat/have not eaten	食べませんでした tah-BEH-MAH-SEn-desh-tah
conditional	if (I) eat	食べたら TAH-beh-tah-lah

***-U* verbs**. This group consists of verbs that end in *-u*, including some that end in *-lu*. The stem for these verbs is the informal present/future form minus the *u* at the end. Again, only the present/future, past, gerund, and conditional forms, and the negatives, are listed.

Example : the verb *to speak/talk.*

The Stem		hah-NAH-s-
informal present/future	speak/will speak	話す hah-NAH-su
formal present / future	speak/will speak	話します hah-NAH-SHIH-MAHss
past	spoke	話しました hah-NAH-SHIH-MAHsh-tah

[1] The more formal present/future form represents the standard level of politeness used in this book; while it is more polite than the informal form, it is not extremely formal.
[2] The gerund form is followed by certain verb particles or *k'dah-sahy*; see page 225.

gerund	(followed by certain verb particles)	話して hah-NAHsh-teh
negative (present/ future)	don't/won't speak	話しません hah-NAH-SHIH-MAH-SEn
negative (past)	didn't speak	話しませんでした hah-NAH-SHIH-MAH-SEn-de-shi-tah
conditional	if (I) speak	話したら hah-NAHsh-tah-lah

Irregular Verbs

There are two common irregular verbs, *to come* and *to do*.

to come

informal present future	come/will come	来る KU-lu
formal present/ future	come/will come	来ます kih-MAHss
past	came	来ました kih-MAHsh-tah
gerund	(followed by certain verb particles)	来て KIH-teh
negative (present/ future)	don't/won't come	来ません kih-MAH-SEn
negative (past)	didn't come	来ませんでした kih-MAH-SEn-desh-tah
conditional	if (I) come	来たら KIH-tah-lah

to do

informal present/ future	do/will do	する su-LU
formal present/ future	do/will do	します shih-MAHss

past	did	しました shih-MAHsh-tah
gerund	(followed by certain verb particles)	して shih-TEH
negative (present future)	don't/won't do	しません shih-MAH-SEn
negative (past)	didn't do	しませんでした shih-MAH-SEn-desh-tah
conditional	if (I) do	したら shih-TAH-lah

Verbs may be followed by particles too, which can be used with adjectives as well. Three examples are:

1) だけ **dah-keh** *only* or *just*

I (will) only look.	見るだけです。	MIH-lu **dah-KEH** dess.

2) が **gah** *but* or *in spite of doing* (verb)

I'm listening, but I don't understand.	聞いていますが、わかりません。	KEE-TEH IH-MAHss **gah**, wah-KAH-LIH-MAH-SEn-desh-tah.

3) から **kah-lah**

- Following a gerund form, meaning *after / since doing* (something)

After (I) do it, (I) will go.	してから行きます。	shih-TEH **KAH-lah** ih-KIH-MAHss.

- After a verb / adjective ending of a sentence, meaning *and so,* or *therefore*

I wrote a letter so I'll mail it.	手紙を書きましたから送ります。	teh-GAH-MIH OH KAH-KIH-MAHsh-tah **kah-lah** oh-KU-LIH-MAHss.

COMPARISONS

1) Use **noh HOh gah** after the subject to show what is being compared.

Tokyo is better.	東京のほうがいいです。	TOH-KYOH **NOH HOh gah** Ee dess.

2) Use **yoh-lih** after the subject to mark the standard against which a comparison is made.

It is better than Tokyo.	東京よりいいです。	TOH-KYOH **YOH-lih** Ee dess.

3) Combine the use of **noh-HOh gah** and **yoh-lih** to make a complete comparison.

Tokyo is colder than Kyoto.	東京のほうが京都より寒いです。	TOH-KYOH **NOH HOh gah** KYOh-toh **yoh-lih** sah-MU-ih dess.

4) To express the superlative ("the most"), use **ih-CHIH-BAHN** (lit., number one) before the adjective.

the tallest building	一番高いビル	**ih-CHIH-BAHN** TAH-KAHy bih-lu

MAKING REQUESTS

There are several ways of expressing a request in Japanese. The most practical are the following:
1) Gerund form of verb + **k'dah-sahy** = *Please do* (verb).

Please come here.	ここへ来て下さい。	koh-KOH EH KIH-teh k'dah-sahy.

2) Noun + **oh** + **k'dah-sahy** = *Please give me* (noun).

Please give me a ticket.	切符を下さい。	kit-PU OH K'DAH-SAHy.

3) Noun + **oh** + **oh-NEH-GAHY-SH'MAHss** = *I'd like to get* (noun). This pattern is sometimes interchangeable with pattern 2 above; both express your request for something.

I'd like to get a haircut.	ヘアカットをお願いします。	heh-AH-KAHT-toh oh oh-NEH-GAHY-SH' MAHss.

LEVELS OF LANGUAGE

This is one of the most difficult concepts in learning Japanese since there is no equivalent in English. In Japanese, there are three basic levels of language: casual, standard, and polite. Within each of these levels, there are subtleties and nuances; in addition, there are differences between the language used by men and that used by women. Furthermore, regional dialects, still alive in many places (e.g. Osaka), contribute different vocabulary and intonations to the language. In order to choose the correct language for any given situation, you must consider not only the situation but your social position as well as your audience's. While complete explanation is beyond the scope of this book, below are just five examples to give you an idea.

English sentence: "I gave that (male) person a book."

standard	私はあの人に本をあげました。	wah-TAHSH WAH ah-NOH-hih-toh nih HOHn oh ah-GEH-MAHsh-tah.

GRAMMAR

polite	私はあの方に本を差し上げました。	wah-TAHK-SHIH WAH ah-NOH-KAH-TAH nih HOHn oh sah-SHIH-AH-GEH-MAHsh-tah.
less formal	私はあの人に本をあげた。	wah-TAHSH WAH ah-NOH-hih-toh nih HOHn oh ah-geh-tah.
casual situation, male speaker	僕は彼に本をあげた。	BOH-ku wah KAH-leh nih HOHn oh ah-geh-tah.
casual situation, female speaker	私はあの人に本をあげたわ。	wah-TAHSH WAH ah-NOH-hih-toh nih HOHn oh ah-GEH-TAH wah.

ENGLISH-JAPANESE DICTIONARY

List of Abbreviations

Verbs:

-u v. conjugate as a *-u* verb

-lu v. conjugate as a *-lu* verb *(-ru* in standard *romaji)*

irreg. irregular verb; the ending indicates whether it is a *ku-lu* verb form or a *su-lu* verb form

cop. conjugate as a copula

nom. a nominal form that can be changed into:
an adjective, by adding a *nah* to the end
an adverb, by adding a *nih* to the end

part. particle
For details, see Grammar, chapter 15.

Note: The transcription system of this book uses *l* to represent sounds that are traditionally written with *r* in the *romaji* system. You may also find that the letter *f* is found in some dictionaries instead of the *h* used in this book.

A

able, to be 出来る deh-KIH-lu *(-lu v.)*
above ____の上 ____noh u-EH
accident 事故 JIH-koh
address 住所 Ju-shoh
adult 大人 oh-TOH-NAH
after 後 AH-toh
again また mah-TAH
AIDS エイズ Ay-zu
air conditioner エアコン eh-AH-KOHN／クーラー Ku-lah
airmail 航空便 koh-ku-bin
airplane 飛行機 hih-KOh-kih
airport 空港 ku-koh
aisle 通路 TSu-loh
alarm clock 目覚し時計 meh-ZAH-MAHSH-DOH-keh
all 全部 ZEn-bu

allergies アレルギー ah-LEH-LU-ghee
almost 殆ど hoh-TOHn-doh
although けれど KEH-leh-doh *(part.)*／のに noh-nih *(part.)*
always いつも IH-ts'moh
A.M. 午前 GOH-zen
American person アメリカ人 ah-MEH-LIH-KAH-JIn
and と toh *(part.)*
ankle くるぶし ku-LU-bu-shih
another 他の hoh-KAH NOH
to answer 答える koh-TAH-eh-lu *(-lu v.)*
anybody 誰でも DAH-leh-deh-moh
anything 何でも nahn-deh-moh
apartment アパート ah-PAh-toh
apple りんご lin-goh
April 四月 shih-gahts
to arrive 着く TSU-ku *(-u v.)*
art 美術 BIH-juts
to ask 聞く kih-KU *(-u v.)*
aspirin アスピリン ahss-PIH-LIN
at に nih *(part.)*／で deh *(part.)*
August 八月 hah-CHIH-GAHTS
autumn 秋 AH-kih

B

baby 赤ちゃん AH-kah-chahn
back (body part) 背中 seh-NAH-KAH
back (rear) 後ろ u-SHIH-LOH
bad 悪い wah-LU-ih
bag バッグ BAHT-gu
baggage 手荷物 teh-NIH-mohts
ball ボール boh-lu
banana バナナ BAH-nah-nah
bank 銀行 ghin-koh
bank notes お札 oh-SAH-TSU
bar バー BAh
barber 床屋 toh-KOH-YAH
bath (お)風呂 (oh)-HU-LOH
bathing suit 水着 mih-ZU-GIH
bathroom お手洗 oh-TEH-AH-lahy
battery (automobile) バッテリー baht-TEH-LEE
batteries 電池 DEn-chih
be です DEss *(cop.)*
to be in a place (for inanimate objects) ある AH-lu *(-u v.)*
to be in a place (for living things) いる ih-LU *(-lu v.)*
beautiful 美しい u-TSUK-SHee／きれい KIH-leh *(nom.)*
beauty parlor 美容室 bih-YOh-shih-tsu
because から kah-lah *(part.)*／ので NOH-deh *(part.)*

bed ベッド BET-doh
beef 牛肉 gyu-nik
beer ビール BEe-lu
before 前 MAH-eh
to believe 信じる SHIN-JIH-lu *(-lu v.)*
below 下 shih-TAH
belt ベルト beh-LU-TOH
best 一番いい ih-CHIH-BAHN Ee
better もっといい MOHT-toh Ee
between _____の間_____NOH ahY-DAH
beverage 飲物 noh-MIH-moh-noh
bicycle 自転車 jih-TEN-SHAH
big 大きい OH-KEe
bill (check) お勘定 oh-KAHN-JOH
bird 鳥 toh-LIH
bitter 苦い nih-GAHy
black 黒 KU-loh
blanket 毛布 MOh-hu
blood 血 chih
blouse ブラウス bu-LAH-u-su
blue 青 AH-oh
body 体 kah-LAH-DAH
bone 骨 hoh-NEH
book 本 HOHn
bookstore 本屋 HOHn-yah
booth, telephone 電話ボックス DEN-WAH-BOHT-ku-su
to be born 生まれる u-MAH-LEH-LU *(-lu v.)*
bottle ビン BIn
box 箱 hah-KOH
boy 男の子 oh-TOH-KOH-noh-koh
bread パン PAHn
breakfast 朝食 choh-shohk
bridge 橋 hah-SHIH
to be broken 壊れる koh-WAH-LEH-lu *(-lu v.)*
brother (older) 兄 AH-nih
brother (younger) 弟 oh-TOH-TOH
brown 茶色 chahy-loh
bruise うちみ u-CHIH-MIH
building ビル BIH-lu／建物 tah-TEH-moh-noh
burn (injury) 火傷 yah-KEH-DOH
to burn 燃える moh-EH-LU *(-lu v.)*
bus バス BAHss
bus stop バス停 bahss-TEH
business card 名刺 meh-shih
business hours 営業時間 EH-GYOH-JIH-kahn
busy 忙しい ih-SOH-GAH-SHEe
but が gah *(part.)*／しかし shih-KAHsh
to buy 買う kah-U *(-u v.)*
by (means of) で deh *(part.)*

C

to call out 呼ぶ yoh-BU *(-u v.)*

camera カメラ KAH-meh-lah
can 缶詰 KAHN ZU meh
to cancel キャンセルする KYAHn-seh-lu su-lu *(irreg.)*
candle ろうそく loh-sohk
candy キャンデー KYAHn-deh
car (automobile) 車 k'LU-MAH
car (railroad) 車両 shah-LYOH
card (playing) トランプ toh-LAHn-pu
card (greeting) カード kah-doh
to be careful 気を付ける kih-OH-TS'KEH-lu *(-lu v.)*
carpet 絨毯 Ju-tahn
cart カート KAH-toh
to carry 運ぶ hah-KOH-BU *(-u v.)*
carry-on luggage 持ち込み手荷物 moh-CHIH-KOH-MIH TEH-NIH-mohts
cash 現金 GHEN-KIn
cashier お勘定(場) oh-KAHN-JOH-(BAH)／レジ LEH-jih
castle (お)城 (oh)-SHIH-LOH
cat 猫 NEH-koh
caution 注意 CHu-ih
ceiling 天井 ten-joh
center 中央 CHU-Oh
certainly もちろん moh-CHIH-lohn
chain 鎖 k'SAH-LIH
chair 椅子 ih-SU
to change 変える kah-EH-LU
chest 胸 mu-NEH
chicken 鶏肉 keh-nik／チキン CHIH-kin
child 子供 koh-DOH-MOH
China 中国 CHu-gohk
chopsticks (お)箸 (oh)-HAH-shih
to choose 選ぶ eh-LAH-bu *(-u v.)*
church 教会 kyoh-kahy
cigarette タバコ tah-BAH-KOH
city 市 shih
class クラス KU-lahss
clean きれい KIH-leh *(nom.)*
to climb 登る noh-BOH-LU *(-u v.)*
to close 閉める shih-MEH-lu *(-lu v.)*
clothing 服 hu-KU
coat コート KOh-toh
coffee コーヒー KOH-HEe
coin locker コインロッカー koYN-LOHT-k ah
coins 小銭 koh-ZEH-NIH
cold (temperature) 寒い sah-MU-ih
cold (illness) 風邪 kah-ZEH
collar 衿 eh-LIH
to collect 集める ah-TS'MEH-lu *(lu v.)*
color 色 ih-LOH
color film カラーフィルム kah-LAH FIH-lu-mu
to come 来る KU-lu *(irreg.)*

to come out 出て来る DEH-teh ku-lu *(irreg.)*
comfortable 楽 lah-KU *(nom.)*
company (firm) 会社 kahy-shah
complaint 苦情 ku-JOH
concert コンサート kohN-SAh-toh
conductor (train) 車掌 shah-SHOH
conference 会議 KAHy-gih
to confirm 確認する kah-KU-NIN SU-LU *(irreg.)*
consulate 領事館 LYOH-JIH-kahn
to continue 続ける ts'ZU-KEH-LU *(-lu v.)*
conversation 会話 kahy-wah
cool (weather) 涼しい su-ZU-SHEe
corner 角 KAH-doh
to correct 直す nah-OH-su *(-u v.)*
cosmetics 化粧品 keh-SHOH-HIN
cough 咳 seh-KIH
to count 数える kah-ZOH-EH-lu *(-lu v.)*
country 国 ku-NIH
countryside 田舎 ih-NAH-KAH
credit card クレジットカード ku-LEH-JIT-TOH KAh-doh
cucumber きゅうり KYu-lih
cup コップ koht-PU
curtain カーテン KAh-ten
curve カーブ KAh-bu
customer (お)客 (oh)-KYAHK
custom (habit) 習慣 shu-kahn
customs (at airports) 税関 zeh-kahn
to cut 切る KIH-lu *(-u v.)*

D

daily 毎日 MAHy-nich
dance 踊り oh-DOH-LIH／ダンス DAHn-su
to dance 踊る oh-DOH-LU *(-u v.)*
danger 危険 kih-KEN *(nom.)*
dark 暗い ku-LAHy
date (calendar) 日付 hih-Z'KEH
daughter 娘 mu-SU-MEH
day 日 hih
December 十二月 JU-NIH-gahts
to decide 決める kih-MEH-LU *(-lu v.)*
to declare 申告する shin-kohk su-lu *(irreg.)*
deep 深い hu-KAHy
to deliver 届ける toh-DOH-KEH-lu *(-lu v.)*
dentist 歯医者 HAHy-shah
denture 入れ歯 ih-LEH-BAH
to depart 発つ TAH-tsu *(-u v.)*
department store デパート deh-PAh-toh
desk 机 ts'KU-EH
dessert デザート deh-ZAh-toh

to develop (film) 現像する gen-z<u>oh</u> su-lu *(irreg.)*
diapers おしめ oh-SHIH-meh
dictionary 辞書 JIH-shoh
to die 死ぬ shih-NU *(-u v.)*
different 違う chih-GAH-U
difficult 難しい mu-ZU-KAH-SHEe
dining room ダイニング DAHY-nin-gu
dinner 夕食 y<u>u</u>-shohk
direction 方角 h<u>oh</u>-gahk
dirty 汚い kih-TAH-NAHy
discount 割り引き wah-LIH-BIH-KIH
to feel dizzy めまいがする meh-MAHy gah su-lu *(irreg.)*
to do する su-LU *(irreg.)*
do not enter 立入禁止 tah-CHIH-IH-LIH KIN-SHIH
dock ドック DOHT-ku
doctor 医者 ih-SHAH
document 書類 shoh-LU-IH
dog 犬 ih-NU
dollar ドル DOH-lu
door ドア DOH-ah／戸 toh
down 下 shih-TAH
dozen ダース D<u>Ah</u>-su
to draw 画く KAH-ku *(-u v.)*
drawer 引きだし hih-KIH-DAHSH
dress ドレス DOH-leh-su
to drink 飲む NOH-mu *(-u v.)*
drinkable 飲める noh-MEH-lu
to drive 運転する un-ten su-lu *(irreg.)*
driver 運転手 UN-TEn-shu
to be drunk 酔う YOH-u *(-u v.)*
dry 乾いた kah-WAHy-tah
dry cleaning ドライクリーニング doh-LAHY K'LEe-nin gu

E

each one 一つ hih-TOHts
ear 耳 mih-MIH
early 早い hah-YAHy
east 東 hih-GAH-SHIH
easy やさしい yah-SAH-SHEE
to eat 食べる tah-BEH-lu *(-lu v.)*
egg 卵 tah-MAH-goh
elbow 肘 hih-JIH
electricity 電気 DEn-kih
elevator エレベーター eh-LEH-B<u>Eh</u>-t<u>ah</u>
embassy 大使館 TAHY-SHIH-kahn
emergency 緊急 kin-ky<u>u</u>
emergency exit 非常口 hih-J<u>Oh</u>-g'chih
empty 空 kah-LAH
end 終り oh-WAH-LIH
endorse 裏書する u-LAH-GAH-KIH SU-LU *(irreg.)*
engine エンジン En-jin
English language 英語 ay-goh
enjoyable 楽しい tah-NOH-SHEe
enlargement 引き延ばし hih-KIH-NOH-BAH-SHIH

ENGLISH–JAPANESE

enough 充分 JU-BUn
to enter 入る HAHy-lu *(-u v.)*
entrance 入口 ih-LIH-G'CHIH
escalator エスカレーター ess-KAH-LEh-tah
evening 夕方 yu-gah-tah
everybody 皆 miN-NAH
to examine 調べる shih-LAH-BEH-lu *(-lu v.)*
to exchange 替える kah-EH-LU *(-lu v.)*
excuse me 失礼します shih-TS'lay-sh'mahss／すみません s'MIH-MAH-SEn
exhaust (automobile) 排気 hahy-kih
exit 出口 DEH-g'chih
to expect 期待する kih-TAHY SU-LU *(irreg.)*
expensive 高い tah-KAHy
express train 急行 kyu-koh
express train (super express) 特急 toht-KYU
extra 余分 yoh-BUN
eye 目 meh
eyebrow 眉毛 MAH-yu-geh
eyeglasses めがね MEH-gah-neh
eyelash 睫毛 MAH-tsu-geh
eyelid まぶた MAH-bu-tah

F

face (body part) 顔 kah-OH
facial (massage) フェーシャル FEh-shah-lu／美顔 bih-GAHN
to fall 落ちる oh-CHIH-lu *(-lu v.)*
false 偽の nih-SEH NOH
family 家族 KAH-zohk
family name 名字 MYOh-jih
famous 有名 yu-meh *(nom.)*
fan (electric) 扇風機 SEN-Pu-kih
far 遠い toh-ih
fare (fee) 料金 LYOh-kin
fast 速い hah-YAHy
father 父 chih-CHIH
faucet 蛇口 jah-G'CHIH
to fear 恐れる oh-SOH-LEH-lu *(-lu v.)*
February 二月 nih-gahts
to feel (sensation) 感じる kahn-jih-lu *(-lu v.)*
feeling 気持ち kih-MOH-CHIH
fender フェンダー feN-DAH
festival (お)祭り (oh)-MAH-TS'LIH
fever 熱 neh-TSU
few 少し s'KOHsh
to fill 満たす mih-TAH-su *(-u v.)*
film (photographic) フィルム fih-LU-MU
to find 見つける mih-TS'KEH-lu *(-lu v.)*
fine (penalty) 罰金 baht-KIN
fine (quality) よい YOy
finger 指 yu-BIH
to finish 終える oh-EH-LU *(-lu v.)*

fire 火 hih
fire (destructive) 火事 KAH-jih
first 一番 ih-CHIH-bahn／最初 sahy-shoh
first aid 応急手当 OH-KYU TEH-ah-teh
first time 初めて hah-JIH-meh-teh
fish 魚 sah-KAH-NAH
to fit 合う AH-u *(-u v.)*
fix 直す nah-OH-su *(-u v.)*
flashlight 懐中電灯 KAHY-CHU-DEn-toh
flat 平ら tahy-lah *(nom.)*
to get a flat tire パンクする pahN-KU SU-LU *(irreg.)*
flight (plane) 便 BIn
floor 床 yu-KAH
flower 花 hah-NAH
fog 霧 kih-LIH
to follow ついて行く TSU-ih-teh ih-ku *(-u v.)*
foot 足 ah-SHIH
for (exchange) _____ の代りに _____noh kah-WAH-LIH NIH
for (purpose) に nih *(part.)*／の為に_____noh tah-MEH nih
forehead 額 hih-TAHY
foreign country 外国 gahy-kohk
to forget 忘れる wah-SU-LEH-LU *(-lu v.)*
fork フォーク FOh-ku
forty 四十 YOHn-ju
forward 前方 zen-poh
fountain 噴水 hun-su-ih
fountain pen 万年筆 MAHN-NEn-hits
free (independent) 自由 jih-Yu *(nom.)*
free of charge ただ TAH-dah
Friday 金曜日 KIN-YOh-bih
friend 友達 toh-MOH-DAHCH
from から kah-lah *(part.)*
front 前 MAH-eh
fruit 果物 k'DAH-moh-noh
full いっぱい it-PAHY
funny おかしい oh-KAH-SHEe
furniture 家具 KAH-gu

G

game ゲーム GEh-mu
garden 庭 nih-WAH
gasoline ガソリン gah-SOH-LIN
gas station ガソリンスタンド gah-SOH-LIN S'TAHn-doh
gauze ガーゼ GAh-zeh
gear (automobile) ギアー GHIH-ah
to get (obtain) 手に入れる TEH nih ih-leh-lu *(-lu v.)*
gift プレゼント pu-LEH-zen-toh／贈物 oh-KU-LIH-MOH-NOH
girl 女の子 OHN-NAH-noh-koh
to give あげる ah-GEH-LU *(-lu v.)*
glad うれしい u-LEH-SHEe
glass (material) ガラス gah-LAHSS

ENGLISH–JAPANESE

glove 手袋 teh-BU-k'loh

to go 行く ih-KU *(-u v.)*

to go back 帰る KAH-eh-lu *(-u v.)*

to go down 降りる oh-LIH-lu *(-lu v.)*

to go into 入る HAHy-lu *(-u v.)*

to go out 出る DEH-lu *(-lu v.)*

to go up 上がる ah-GAH-LU (-u v.)

gold 金 KIn

good いい Ee

good-bye さようなら sah-YOH-NAH-lah

gram グラム GU-lah-mu

grapes ぶどう bu-DOH

grass 草 ku-SAH

grateful 有難い ah-LIH-GAH-TAHy

gray グレー g'LEh

green グリーン g'LEEn

greeting 挨拶 AHy-sahts

to act as a guide 案内する AHN-NAHy su-lu *(irreg.)*

guide (person) ガイド GAHy-doh

guidebook ガイドブック gahY-DOH BUt-ku

gum (chewing) チューインガム CHU-IN-GAH-mu

H

hair 髪 kah-MIH

hairbrush ヘアブラシ heh-AH-BU-lah-shih

haircut (ヘア)カット (heh-AH)-KAHT-toh

hairpin ヘアピン heh-AH-PIN

half 半分 HAHN-BUn

ham ハム HAH-mu

hammer かなづち kah-NAH-Z'chih

hand 手 teh

handbag ハンドバッグ HAHN-DOH BAHT-gu

handkerchief ハンカチ hahn-kah-chih

handmade 手作り teh-ZU-k'lih

hanger ハンガー HAHn-gah

to happen (occur) 起こる oh-KOH-lu *(-u v.)*

happiness 幸せ shih-AH-WAH-SEH *(nom.)*

harbor 港 mih-NAH-TOH

hat 帽子 boh-shih

to have (possess) 持つ MOH-tsu *(-u v.)*

he 彼 KAH-leh

head 頭 ah-TAH-mah

headache 頭痛 zu-TSU

headlight ヘッドライト het-DOH-LAHy-toh

health 健康 ken-koh *(nom.)*

to be able to hear 聞こえる kih-KOH-EH-LU *(-lu v.)*

heart (organ) 心臓 shin-zoh

heart (as seat of emotions) 心 koh-KOH-LOH

heat 熱 neh-TSU

heater ヒーター HEE-tah

heavy 重い oh-MOY

heel かかと kah-KAH-TOH

hello こんにちは kohN-NIH-CH'-WAH
hello (phone conversations only) もしもし MOHsh-mosh
to help (aid) 助ける tahss-KEH-lu *(-lu v.)*
to help (lend a hand, act as an assistant) 手伝う teh-TSU-DAH-u *(-u v.)*
here ここ koh-KOH
high 高い tah-KAHy
highway 高速道路 KOH-SOHK-DOh-loh
hip 腰 koh-SHIH
to hire 雇う yah-TOH-u *(-u v.)*
history 歴史 leh-KIH-SHIH
hook フック HUT-ku
to hope 願う neh-GAH-u *(-u v.)*
horn (automobile) クラクション k'LAHK-shohn
horse 馬 u-MAH
hospital 病院 byoh-in
hostel (youth) ユースホステル YU-SU HOHss-teh-lu
hot (temperature) 熱い ah-TSU-ih
hot (weather) 暑い ah-TSU-ih
hot springs 温泉 ohn-sen
hot water お湯 oh-YU
hotel ホテル HOH-teh-lu
hour 時間 jih-KAHN
house, home 家 ih-EH
how どうやって DOh-yaht-teh
How do you do? 始めまして hah-JIH-MEH-MAHsh-teh
How far? どこまで DOH-koh mah-deh
How long? いつまで IH-ts mah-deh
How many (things)? いくつ IH-k'ts; (people) 何人 NAHn-nin
How much? いくら IH-k'lah
to be hungry お腹が空く oh-NAH-KAH GAH SU-KU *(-u v.)*
to hurry 急ぐ ih-SOH-gu *(-u v.)*
to hurt oneself 怪我をする keh-GAH oh su-lu *(irreg.)*
husband (generic term) 夫 oht-TOH
husband (your husband) 主人 SHU-jin

I

I 私 wah-TAHSH
ice 氷 koh-lih
identification 身分証明書 mih-BUN SHOH-MEH-SHOH
if もし MOHsh
ignition (automobile) イグニション ih-GU-NIH-shohn
illness 病気 byoh-kih
imported product 輸入品 yu-NYU-HIN
in に nih *(part.)*／で deh *(part.)*
to be included 入っている HAHyt-teh ih-lu *(-lu v.)*
to get indigestion お腹をこわす oh-NAH-KAH OH KOH-WAH-su *(-u v.)*
inexpensive 安い yah-SU-ih

information 情報 joh-hoh
information booth 案内所 ahN-NAHY-JOH
injection (shot) 注射 chu-shah
ink インキ iN-KIH
to inquire 尋ねる tah-ZU-NEH-lu *(-lu v.)*
insect 虫 mu-SHIH
inside 中 NAH-kah
instead of ______の代りに ______ noh kah-WAH-LIH NIH
insurance 保険 hoh-KEN
to be interested in 興味がある KYOh-mih gah AH-lu *(-u v.)*
interpreter 通訳 TSu-yahk
intersection 交差点 koh-sah-ten
into ______の中へ ______ noh NAH-kah eh
to introduce 紹介する shoh-kahy su-lu *(irreg.)*
to invite 招く mah-NEH-ku *(-u v.)*
iron (appliance) アイロン ahY-LOHN
iron (metal) 鉄 teh-TSU
is です DEss *(cop.)*

J

jack (automobile) ジャッキ JAHT-kih
January 一月 ih-CHIH-GAHTS
Japan 日本 nih-HOHn／nit-POHn
Japanese language 日本語 nih-HOHN-GOH
Japanese person 日本人 nih-HOHN-JIn
Japanese-style inn 旅館 lyoh-KAHN
jaw 顎 ah-GOH
jewel 宝石 hoh-seh-kih
journey 旅 tah-BIH
juice ジュース Ju-su
July 七月 shih-CHIH-GAHTS
June 六月 loh-KU-GAHTS

K

to keep (hold on to) 取っておく TOHT-teh oh-ku *(-u v.)*
key 鍵 kah-GIH
kilogram キログラム kih-LOH-G'lah-mu
kilometer キロメーター kih-LOH-MEh-tah
kimono 着物 kih-MOH-NOH
kindness 親切 SHIn-sets *(nom.)*
kitchen キッチン KIT-chin
knee 膝 hih-ZAH
knife ナイフ NAHy-hu
to know 知る shih-LU *(u v.)*
Korea, Republic of 韓国 KAHn-kohk

L

label ラベル LAH-beh-lu
lamp, lighting 電灯 den-toh
land (ground) 地面 JIH-men
land (property) 土地 toh-CHIH

to land (by plane) 着陸する chah-KU-LIK SU-LU *(irreg.)*
language 言葉 koh-TOH-BAII
last 最後 SAHy-goh
late 遅い oh-SOy
to laugh 笑う wah-LAH-U *(-u v.)*
laundry ランドリー LAHn-doh-lee
lawyer 弁護士 BEN-GOH-shih
laxative 下剤 geh-ZAHY
to leak 洩る MOH-lu *(-u v.)*
to lean on よりかかる yoh-LIH-KAH-KAH-lu *(-u v.)*
to learn 習う nah-LAH-u *(-u v.)*
to leave 発つ TAH-tsu *(-u v.)*
left 左 hih-DAH-LIH
leg 脚 ah-SHIH
length 長さ NAH-gah-sah
lens レンズ LEn-zu
letter 手紙 teh-GAH-MIH
library 図書館 toh-SHOH-kahn
lid 蓋 hu-TAH
to lie down 横になる yoh-KOH NIH NAH lu *(-u v.)*
life, one's 人生 JIn-seh
life preserver 救命道具 KYU-MEH-DOh-gu
to lift 持ち上げる moh-CHIH-AH-GEH-lu *(-lu v.)*
light (brightness) 明るい ah-KAH-LU-ih
light (color) 薄い u-SU-ih
lighter (cigarette) ライター LAHy-tah
lightweight 軽い kah-LU-ih
like (as) _____のような _____ noh YOh nah
like (favor) 好き su-KIH *(nom.)*
limit, speed 最高速度 SAHY-KOH-SOHk-doh
line 線 SEn
line (of people) 列 LEH-tsu
lip 唇 k'CHIH-BIH-LU
lipstick 口紅 k'CHIH-BEH-NIH
liquor (Japanese) 酒 sah-KEH
liquor (Western) 洋酒 yoh-shu
list リスト LISS-toh
to listen 聞く kih-KU *(-u v.)*
liter リッター lit-TAH
little 小さい CHEE-SAHy
to live in a place 住む SU-mu *(-u v.)*
living room 居間 ih-MAH
lobby ロビー LOH-bee
lock ロック LOHT-ku
long 長い nah-GAHy
long-distance 長距離 CHOH-KYOH-lih
to look 見る MIH-lu *(-lu v.)*
to lose なくす nah-KU-su *(-u v.)*
loud うるさい u-LU-SAHy
low 低い hih-KU-ih
luck 運 Un
lunch 昼食 chu-shohk／ランチ LAHn-chih
lung 肺 hahY

M

machine 機械 kih-KAHy
magazine 雑誌 zahss-SHIH

maid メードさん meh-doh sahn
mailbox ポスト POHss-toh
to make 作る ts'KU-lu *(-u v.)*
man 男 oh-toh-koh／男性 dahn-seh
manager マネージャー mah-NEh-jah
many たくさん tahk-SAHn
map 地図 CHIH-zu
March 三月 SAHn-gahts
market 市場 IH-chih-bah
marriage 結婚 ket-KOHN
massage マッサージ mahss-SAh-jih
It doesn't matter. かまいません kah-MAHY-MAH-SEn.
What's the matter? どうしたんですか？ DOh sh'tahn-dess KAH?
meal 食事 shoh-KU-JIH
meaning 意味 IH-mih
measurement 寸法 sun-poh
meat 肉 nih-KU
to meet 会う AH-u *(-u v.)*
medicine 薬 k'SU-LIH
menu メニュー MEH-nyu
message 伝言 den-gohn／言付け koh-TOH-Z'KEH
meter メートル meh-toh-lu
middle 真中 mahn-nah-kah
midnight 真夜中 mah-YOH-nah-kah
milk ミルク MIH-lu-ku／牛乳 gyu-nyu
mine 私の wah-TAHSH NOH
minute 分 HUn
mirror 鏡 kah-GAH-MIH
to miss (a vehicle) 乗り遅れる noh-LIH OH-KU-LEH-lu *(-lu v.)*
missing 無い NAHy
mistake 間違い mah-CHIH-GAHy
Monday 月曜日 geh-TSU-YOh-bih
money (お)金 oh-KAH-NEH
month 月 tsu-KIH
monument 記念碑 kih-NEn-hih
moon 月 tsu-KIH
more もっと MOHT-toh
morning 朝 AH-sah
mosquito 蚊 kah
mother 母 HAH-hah
mouth 口 k'CHIH
to move 動く u-GOH-ku *(-u v.)*
movie 映画 ay-gah
Mr. _____さん _____sahn
Ms _____さん _____sahn
museum 博物館 hah-KU-BUTS-kahn; (**art**) 美術館 bih-JUTS-kahn
mushroom きのこ KIH-noh-koh
music 音楽 OHn-gahk
must ____なければならない ____ NAH-keh-leh bah nah-LAH-nahy
my 私の wah-TAHSH NOH

N

nail (body part) 爪 ts'MEH
name 名前 nah-MAH-EH
narrow 狭い seh-MAHy
nationality 国籍 kohk-SEH-KIH

nearby 近く chih-KAHk
nearest 一番近い ih-CHIH-BAHN CH'KAHy
necessary 必要 hih-TS'YOH *(nom.)*
neck 首 ku-BIH
necktie ネクタイ NEK-tahy
needle 針 HAH-lih
nerve 神経 SHIn-kay
never 決して kess-SHIH-TEH
new 新しい ah-TAH-LAH-SHEe
new year 新年 SHIn-nen
newspaper 新聞 shin-bun
newsstand キオスク kih-OHss-ku
next 次 ts'GIH
nice いい Ee
night 夜 YOH-lu
nightclub (disco) ディスコ DISS- koh
night rate 夜間料金 yah-KAHN LYOh-kin
no いいえ ee-EH
no smoking 禁煙 kin-en
noise 音 oh-TOH
noon 正午 SHOh-goh／昼 hih-LU
north 北 kih-TAH
nose 鼻 hah-NAH
notice (announcement) お知らせ oh-SHIH-LAH-SEH
novel (book) 小説 shoh-sets
November 十一月 JU-IH-CHIH-gahts
now 今 IH-mah
number 数 KAH-zu
nurse 看護婦 KAHN-GOH-hu

O

occupied 使用中 shih-YOH-CHU
October 十月 ju-gahts
of の noh *(part.)*
of course もちろん moh-CHIH-lohn
office オフィス OH-fih-su
often たびたび tah-BIH TAH-BIH
oil 油 ah-BU-LAH
It's okay いいです Ee dess
old 古い hu-LU-ih
How old are you? おいくつですか？ oY-K'T S DEss KAH?
on top ____の上 ____NOH u-EH
once 一度 ih-CHIH-DOH ／一回 it-KAHY
once more もう一度 moh-ih-chih-doh
one 一 ih-CHIH
oneself 自分 jih-BUN
onion 玉葱 tah-MAH-NEH-gih
only ____だけ ____dah-KEH *(part.)*
to open 開ける ah-KEH-LU *(-lu v.)*
operator (phone) オペレーター oh-PEH-LEh-tah
orange オレンジ oh-LEn-jih
order (turn) 順番 jun-bahn

to order 注文する chu-mohn su-lu *(irreg.)*
other 他 hoh-KAH
ouch! 痛い！ ih-TAHy!
outlet (electrical) コンセント KONH-SEN-toh
outside 外 SOH-toh
over (above) 上 u-EH
over (finished) 終り oh-WAH-LIH
overheat (automobile) オーバーヒート OH-BAH-HEe-toh
overnight 泊り掛け toh-MAH-LIH-GAH-KEH
to owe 借りがある kah-LIHGAH AH-lu *(-u v.)*
to own 持つ MOH-tsu *(-u v.)*

P

to pack 詰める ts'MEH-lu *(-lu v.)*
package (mail) 小包 koh-ZU-ts'mih
page (book) ページ peh-jih
to page 呼び出す yoh-BIH-DAH-su *(-u v.)*
pain 痛み ih-TAH-MIH
wet paint ペンキ塗たて peN-KIH nu-LIH-TAH-TEH
pajamas パジャマ PAH-jah-mah
pants ズボン ZU-bohn
paper 紙 kah-MIH
park 公園 koh-en
parking lot 駐車場 chu-shah-joh
no parking 駐車禁止 chu-shah kin-shih
part (section) 部分 BU-bun
to part 分ける wah-KEH-lu *(-lu v.)*
parts 部品 bu-HIN
pass (permit) パス PAHss
passenger 乗客 joh-kyahk
passport パスポート pahss-POh-toh
past 過去 KAH-koh
patient 患者 kahn-jah
to pay 払う hah-LAH-u *(-u v.)*
pea 豆 mah-MEH
pedestrian 歩行者 hoh-KOh-shah
pen ペン PEn
pencil 鉛筆 en-pits
peppers ピーマン PEe-mahn
perhaps 多分 TAH-bun
permit (license) 免許 MEn-kyoh
person, people 人 hih-TOH
personal check 小切手 koh-GHIT-teh
pet ペット PET-toh
photograph 写真 shah-SHIN
pickle 漬物 ts'KEH-MOH-NOH
picture (art) 絵 eh
pier 埠頭 hu-TOH
pillow 枕 MAH-k'lah
pilot パイロット PAHY-LOHT-toh

pin ピン PIn
safety pin 安全ピン AHN-ZEn-pin
pink ピンク PIn-ku
place 場所 bah-SHOH
to place 置く oh-KU *(-u v.)*
plate (お)皿 (oh)-SAH-LAH
platform ホーム HOh-mu
play (drama) 劇 GEH-kih
to play 遊ぶ ah-SOH-BU *(-u v.)*
to play (an instrument) 弾く hih-KU *(-u v.)*
please (in offering something) どうぞ DOh-zoh
pleasure よろこび yoh-LOH-KOH-BIH
pliers ペンチ PEn-chih
P.M. 午後 GOH-goh
pocket ポケット poh-KET-toh
point 点 ten
poison 毒 doh-KU
police 警察 kay-sahts
police person 警察官 KAY-SAHTS-kahn
polite 丁寧 TEh-neh *(nom.)*
pork ポーク POh-ku
porter ポーター POh-tah
to be possible 出来る deh-KIH-lu *(-lu v.)*
possibility 可能性 kah-NOH-SEH
postage stamp 切手 kit-TEH
postcard 絵はがき eh-HAH-gah-kih
potato じゃがいも jah-GAHY-MOH
powder パウダー PAH-u-dah
prefer ____の方がいい ____noh HOh gah Ee
to prepare 用意する YOh-ih su-lu *(irreg.)*
prescription 処方箋 shoh-HOH-SEN
pretty きれい KIH-leh *(nom.)*
price 値段 neh-DAHN
print (photography) プリント pu-LIN-TOH
program プログラム pu-LOH-GU-lah-mu
to promise 約束する yahk-SOHK SU-LU *(irreg.)*
to pull 引く hih-KU *(-u v.)*
to purchase 買う kah-U *(-u v.)*
to push 押す oh-SU *(-u v.)*
to put 置く oh-KU *(-u v.)*
to put in 入れる ih-LEH-LU *(-lu v.)*
to put (clothes) on 着る kih-LU (-lu v.)

Q

quarter (fraction) 四分の一 yohn-bun noh ih-chih
quick 速い hah-YAHy
quickly 速く HAH-yahk
quiet 静か SHIH-zu-kah *(nom.)*

quite かなり KAH-nah-lih ／大変 tahy-hen *(nom.)*

R

radio ラジオ LAH-jih-oh
radish (Japanese) 大根 DAHY-KOHn
railroad 鉄道 teh-TSU-DOH
rain 雨 AH-meh
rate (of exchange) レート LEh-toh
raw 生 NAH-mah
razor 剃刀 kah-MIH-SOH-lih
to reach 届く toh-DOH-ku *(-u v.)*
to read 読む YOH-mu *(-u v.)*
real 本当 hohn-toh
receipt レシート leh-SHEe-toh
to recover (get back) 取り戻す toh-LIH-MOH-DOH-su *(-u v.)*
to recover (health) 回復する kahy-hu-ku su-lu *(irreg.)*
red 赤 AH-kah
refund 払い戻し hah-LAHY-MOH-DOH-SHIH
to refuse 断る koh-TOH-WAH-lu *(-u v.)*
regular 普通 hu-TSU
to remember 覚える oh-BOH-EH-lu *(-lu v.)*
to rent 借りる kah-LIH-LU *(-lu v.)*
rent-a-car レンタカー leN-TAH-KAh
to repair 直す nah-OH-su *(-u v.)*
to repeat 繰り返す k'LIH-KAH-eh-su *(-u v.)*
to replace 取り替える toh-LIH-KAH-EH-LU *(-lu v.)*
to reply 返事をする HEN-JIH oh su-lu *(irreg.)*
reservation 予約 yoh-YAHK
to rest 休む yah-SU-mu *(-u v.)*
restaurant レストラン LEH-s'toh-lahn
rest room お手洗い oh-TEH-AH-lahy
to return (give back) 返す KAH-eh-su *(-u v.)*
rice (cooked) ご飯 GOH-hahn
rice (uncooked) 米 koh-MEH
rich 金持ち kah-NEH-MOH-chih
to ride 乗る noh-LU *(-u v.)*
right (correct) 正しい tah-DAH-SHEe
right (direction) 右 mih-GIH
to rip 破る yah-BU-lu *(-u v.)*
river 川 kah-WAH
road 道 mih-CHIH
room 部屋 heh-YAH
rope 縄 nah-WAH
round 丸い mah-LU-ih
round trip 往復 oh-hu-ku
to rush 急ぐ ih-SOH-gu *(-u v.)*

rubber ゴム GOH-mu
rubber band 輪ゴム wah-GOH-MU
to run 走る hah-SHIH-lu *(-u v.)*

S

safety 安全 ahn-zen *(nom.)*
safe (cashbox) 金庫 KIn-koh
sale セール SEh-lu／大売出し OH-U-lih-dahsh
salt 塩 shih-OH
same 同じ oh-NAH-JIH
sand 砂 s'NAH
Saturday 土曜日 doh-YOh-bih
to say 言う ih-U *(-u v.)*
school 学校 gaht-KOH
scissors はさみ hah-SAH-mih
sea 海 U-mih
season 季節 KIH-sets
seasonings 調味料 CHOH-MIH-lyoh
seat 席 SEH-kih
second 二番 NIH-bahn
secretary 秘書 HIH-shoh
to see 見る MIH-lu *(-lu v.)*
to select 選ぶ eh-LAH-bu *(-u v.)*
to sell 売る u-LU *(-u v.)*
to send 送る oh-KU-LU *(-u v.)*
September 九月 KU-gahts
service charge サービス料 SAH-BISS-lyoh
in the shade 日蔭 hih-KAH GEH
shampoo シャンプー SHAhn-pu
she 彼女 KAH-noh-joh
sheet (bedding) シーツ SHEE-tsu
to shine (shoes) 磨く mih-GAH-KU *(-u v.)*
ship 船 HU-neh
shirt シャツ SHAH-tsu
shoe 靴 ku-TSU
shoelace 靴紐 ku-TSU HIH-MOH
shop, store (お)店 (oh)-MIH-SEH
to shop 買物をする kahY-MOH-NOH OH SU-LU *(irreg.)*
short 短い mih-JIH-KAHy
shoulder 肩 KAH-tah
show (art) 展覧会 TEN-LAHn-kahy
show (performance) ショー SHOh
to show 見せる mih-SEH-lu *(-lu v.)*
shower シャワー SHAH-wah
shrimp 海老 eh-BIH
shrine 神社 JIn-jah
sickness 病気 byoh-kih
side 横 yoh-KOH
sidewalk 歩道 hoh-DOH
sign 看板 kahn-bahn／サイン SAHy-n
to sign one's name サインする SAHy-n su-lu *(irreg.)*
silver 銀 GHIn

since から kah-lah *(part.)*
to sing 歌う u-TAH-U *(-u v.)*
single room シングル SHIn-gu-lu
single (not married) 独身 dohk-SHIN
sink (basin) ながし nah-GAHSH
sister (older) 姉 ah-NEH
sister (younger) 妹 ih-MOH-TOH
to sit 座る su-WAH-LU *(-u v.)*
size サイズ SAHy-zu
skin 肌 HAH-dah／皮膚 HIH-hu
skirt スカート s'KAh-toh
sky 空 SOH-lah
to sleep 眠る neh-MU-LU *(-u v.)*
sleeping car 寝台車 SHIN-DAHy-shah
sleepy 眠い neh-MU-ih
slope 坂 sah-KAH
slow ゆっくり yut-KU-lih
small 小さい CHEE-SAHy
smoke 煙り keh-MU-LIH
to smoke タバコを吸う tah-BAH-KOH OH SU *(-u v.)*
snow 雪 yu-KIH
so (thus) ですから DESS-kah-lah
soap 石鹸 set-KEN
socks 靴下 k'TSU-sh'tah
soda ソーダ SOh-dah
sofa ソファー SOH-fah
soft 柔らかい yah-WAH-LAH-KAHy
some (a little) 少し s'KOHsh
someone 誰か DAH-leh-kah
something 何か NAH-nih-kah
sometimes 時々 toh-KIH-DOH-KIH
son 息子 muss-KOH
song 歌 u-TAH
soon もうすぐ MOH-S'gu
I am sorry ごめんなさい goh-MEN-NAH-SAHy
sour 酸っぱい sut-PAHy
south 南 mih-NAH-MIH
souvenir (お)みやげ (oh)-MIH-YAH-GEH
soy sauce 醤油 shoh-yu
to speak 話す hah-NAH-su *(-u v.)*
special 特別 toh-KU-BETS *(nom.)*
to spend (money) 使う ts'KAH-U *(-u v.)*
to spend (time) 過ごす s'GOH-su *(-u v.)*
spoon スプーン s'PU-n
sports スポーツ s'POh-tsu
sprain 捻挫 nen-zah
spring (mechanical) バネ BAH-neh
spring (season) 春 HAH-lu
square 四角 shih-KAHK
stairs 階段 kahy-dahn
stamp (postage) 切手 kit-TEH
to stand 立つ TAH-tsu *(-u v.)*
star 星 hoh-SHIH
to start 始まる hah-JIH-MAH-LU *(-u v.)*

station (bus) バスターミナル bahss-TAh-mih-nah-lu
station (train) 駅 EH-kih
stationery supplies 文房具 BUN-BOh-gu
to stay (overnight) 泊まる toh-MAH-LU *(-u v.)*
to stay (at a place) 滞在する tahy-zahy su-lu *(irreg.)*
to steal 盗む nu-SU-mu *(-u v.)*
steering wheel ハンドル hahN-DOH-LU
still (not yet) まだ MAH-dah
stomach (body part) お腹 oh-NAH-KAH; **(organ)** 胃 ih
to stop 止まる toh-MAH-LU *(-u v.)*
Stop it! やめて！ yah-MEH-TEH!
straight 真っ直ぐ mahss-SU-gu
strange 変 HEn *(nom.)*
street 道 mih-CHIH
string 紐 hih-MOH
strong 強い ts'YOy
student 学生 gahk-SEH
style スタイル s'TAHy-lu
sudden 突然 toh-TS'ZEN *(nom.)*
sugar 砂糖 sah-TOh
suit (men's) 背広 seh-BIH-LOH; **(women's)** スーツ Su-tsu
suitcase スーツケース SU-TSU-KEh-su
summer 夏 nah-TSU
sun 太陽 TAHy-yoh
sunglasses サングラス SAHN-G'lahss
Sunday 日曜日 nih-CHIH-YOh-bih
sunny 晴れ HAH-leh
sweater セーター SEh-tah
sweet 甘い ah-MAHy
sweets (お)菓子 (oh)-KAH-shih
to swell 腫れる hah-LEH-LU *(-lu v.)*
to swim 泳ぐ oh-YOH-gu *(-u v.)*
swimming pool プール Pu-lu
switch (electric) スイッチ su-IT-chih

T

table テーブル teh-bu-lu
tablet 錠剤 joh-zahy
taillight (automobile) テールランプ TEH-LU-LAHn-pu
to take (carry) 持って行く MOHT-teh ih-ku *(-u v.)*
to take (a person) 連れて行く ts'LEH-TEH IH-KU *(-u v.)*
takes time 時間がかかる jih-KAHN GAH KAH-KAH-lu *(-u v.)*
tall 高い tah-KAHy
tank タンク TAHn-ku
tape テープ TEh-pu
tasty おいしい OY-SHEe
tax 税金 zeh-kin

taxi タクシー TAHK-shee
tea (green) お茶 oh-CHAH
tea (Western) 紅茶 koh-chah
to teach 教える oh-SHIH-EH-LU *(-lu v.)*
teacher 先生 SEN-SEh
telegram 電報 den-poh
telephone 電話 den-wah
to telephone 電話する den-wah su-lu *(irreg.)*
telephone number 電話番号 DEN-WAH BAHn-goh
television テレビ TEH-leh-bih
temperature (weather) 気温 kih-OHN
temple (お)寺 (oh)-TEH-LAH
temporary 一時的 ih-CHIH-JIH TEH-KIH *(nom.)*
terminal ターミナル TAh-mih-nah-lu
thank you 有難う(ございます) ah-LIH-gah-toh (goh-ZAHY-MAHss)
that, those それ soh-LEH
that, those (farther away than soh-LEH) あれ ah-LEH
theater (building) 劇場 geh-KIH-JOH
there そこ soh-KOH
there (farther away than soh-KOH) あそこ ah-SOH-KOH
therefore だから DAH-kah-lah／ので NOH-deh *(part.)*／から kah-lah *(part.)*
they あの人達 ah-NOH HIH-TOH tahch
thick 厚い ah-TSU-ih
thief 泥棒 doh-LOH-BOH
thing 物 moh-NOH
to think 考える KAHN-GAH-eh-lu *(-lu v.)*／思う oh-MOH-u *(-u v.)*
to be thirsty 咽が乾く NOH-doh gah kah-wah-ku *(-u v.)*
this, these これ koh-LEH
thousand 千 SEn
thread 糸 IH-toh
throat のど NOH-doh
through (by the medium of) で deh *(part.)*／_____を通して _____oh TOh-shih-teh
thunder 雷 kah-MIH-NAH-LIH
Thursday 木曜日 moh-KU-YOh-bih
ticket 切符 kit-PU
ticket booth 切符売場 kit-PU U-lih-bah
tight きつい kih-TSU-IH
till まで MAH-deh *(part.)*
time 時間 jih-KAHN
timetable 時刻表 jih-KOHK-HYOH
tip チップ CHIT-pu
tire タイヤ tahY-YAH
to be tired 疲れる ts'KAH-LEH-lu *(-lu v.)*
tissues ティッシュペーパー tiss-SHU-PEh-pah
to へ eh *(part.)*
today 今日 KYOh
together 一緒 iss-SHOH
toilet トイレ TOy-leh

toilet paper トイレットペーパー toY-LET-TOH PEh-pah
tomato トマト TOH-mah-toh
tomorrow 明日 ahsh-TAH/ah-SU
tongue 舌 shih-TAH
tonight 今夜 KOHn-yah／今晩 KOHn-bahn
too も moh *(part.)*
tool 道具 doh-gu
tooth 歯 hah
toothbrush 歯ブラシ hah-BU-lah-shih
to touch 触る sah-WAH-LU *(-u v.)*
tour ツアー TSU-ah
tourist 観光客 KAHN-KOh-kyahk
tourist information office 観光案内所 kahn-koh-ahn-nahy-joh
to tow (automobile) 牽引する ken-in su-lu *(irreg.)*
towel タオル TAH-oh-lu
town 町 mah-CHIH
track no.______(train)_____ 番線 ______bahn-sen
traffic light 信号 shin-goh
train 電車 DEn-shah
transfer (transportation) 乗り換え noh-LIH-KAH-EH
to translate 訳す yah-KU-su *(-u v.)*
to travel 旅行する lyoh-KOH SU-LU *(irreg.)*
traveler's checks トラベラーズチェック toh-LAH-BEH-LAH-ZU CHET-ku
tree 木 kih
trip 旅行 lyoh-KOH
to be in trouble 困る koh MAH-lu *(-u v.)*
truck トラック toh-LAHT-ku
true 本当 hohn-toh
trunk (automobile) トランク toh-LAHn-ku
to try 試す tah-MEH-su *(-u v.)*
to try on 試着する shih-CHAHK SU-LU *(irreg.)*
Tuesday 火曜日 kah-YOh-bih
turn 番 BAHn
to turn 回る mah-WAH-LU *(-u v.)*

U

ugly 醜い mih-NIH-KU-ih
umbrella 傘 KAH-sah
under 下 shih-TAH
to understand わかる wah-KAH-lu *(-u v.)*
undergarments 下着 shih-TAH-GIH
United States of America アメリカ ah-MEH-LIH-KAH
university 大学 dahy-gahk
until まで MAH-deh *(part.)*
up 上 u-EH
to use 使う ts'KAH-U *(-u v.)*

V

vacant 空き ah-KIH

various 色々 ih-LOH IH-LOH *(nom.)*
vegetables 野菜 yah-SAHY
vending machine 自動販売機 jih-DOH-HAHN-BAHy-kih
very とても toh-TEH-MOH／大変 tahy-hen *(nom.)*
veterinarian 獣医 Ju-ih
view 眺め nah-GAH-MEH
voltage ボルト boh-LU-TOH
to visit 訪問する hoh-mohn su-lu *(irreg.)*
to go visit (casual) 遊びに行く ah-SOH-BIH NIH IH-KU *(-u v.)*

W

waist ウエスト u-EH-s'toh
to wait 待つ MAH-tsu *(-u v.)*
waiter ウェイター waY-TAH
waiting room 待合室 mah-CHIH-AHy-shih-tsu
waitress ウェイトレス WAy-toh-less
to wake 起こす oh-KOH-su *(-u v.)*
to wake up 起きる oh-KIH-lu *(-lu v.)*
to take a walk 散歩する sahN-POH SU-LU *(irreg.)*
to walk 歩く ah-LU-ku *(-u v.)*
wallet 財布 sahy-hu
to want 欲しいです hoh-SHEe dess *(cop.)*
warm 暖かい ah-TAH-TAH-KAHy
was でした DEH-sh'tah *(cop.)*
to wash 洗う ah-LAH-U *(-u v.)*
watch (timepiece) 時計 toh-KAY
to watch 見る MIH-lu *(-lu v.)*
watch out! 危ない！ ah-BU-NAHy!
water 水 mih-ZU
way (method) 方法 hoh-hoh
way (path) 道 mih-CHIH
one-way 一方通行 it-POH-TSu-koh
Which way? どちら DOH-ch'lah
we 私達 wah-TAHSH-tahch
weak 弱い yoh-WAHy
to wear 着る kih-LU *(-lu v.)*
weather 天気 TEn-kih
Wednesday 水曜日 su-IH-YOh-bih
week ____週間 ____SHu-kahn
weight 重さ oh-MOH-SAH
welcome ようこそ YOh-koh-soh
You're welcome. どういたしまして DOh-ih-TAHSH-MAHSH-teh
well いい Ee
west 西 nih-SHIH
what 何 NAH-nih
wheel 車輪 shah-LIN
when いつ IH-ts

where どこ DOH-koh
which どれ DOH-leh
while (during) ながら NAH-gah-lah
whiskey ウィスキー WISS-kee
white 白 SHIH-loh
who 誰 DAH-leh
why なぜ NAH-zeh
wide 広い hih-LOY
wife (generic term) 妻 TSU-mah
wife (your wife) ワイフ WAHy-hu／家内 KAH-nahy
wind 風 kah-ZEH
window 窓 MAH-doh
winter 冬 hu-YU
to wish 願う neh-GAH-u *(-u v.)*
with と toh *(part.)*／で deh *(part.)*
without ___なしで ___ NAH-shih deh
woman 女 ohn-nah／女性 joh-SEH
wonderful 素晴らしい s'BAH-LAH-SIIEe
wood 木 kih
word 言葉 koh-TOH-BAH
work (job) 仕事 shih-GOH-TOH
to work 働く hah-TAH-LAH-KU *(-u v.)*
to worry 心配する shin-pahy su-lu *(irreg.)*
worse もっと悪い MOHT-toh wah-LU-ih
worst 一番悪い ih-CHIH-BAHN WAH-LU-ih
wound (injury) 傷 kih-ZU
to wrap 包む ts'TSU-mu *(-u v.)*
wrapping paper 包み紙 ts'TSU-MIH-GAH-mih
wrist 手首 TEH-k'bih
to write 書く KAH-ku *(-u v.)*
to be wrong 違う chih-GAH-U *(-u v.)*

X

X ray レントゲン len-toh-ghen

Y

year 年 toh-SHIH
yellow 黄色 kee-loh
yen 円 En
yes はい HAHy／ええ Eh
yesterday 昨日 kih-NOh
yet まだ MAH-dah
you あなた ah-NAH-tah
young 若い wah-KAHy
your, yours あなたの ah-NAH-tah noh

Z

zipper ファスナー FAHss-nah
zoo 動物園 DOH-BUTS-en

JAPANESE - ENGLISH DICTIONARY

List of Abbreviations

Verbs:

-u v. conjugate as a *-u* verb

-lu v. conjugate as a *-lu verb (-ru* in standard *romaji)*

irreg. irregular verb; the ending indicates whether it is a *ku-lu* verb form or a *su-lu* verb form

cop. conjugate as a copula

nom. a nominal form that can be changed into:
an adjective, by adding a *nah* to the end
an adverb, by adding a *nih* to the end

part. particle
For details, see Grammar, chapter 15.

Note: The transcription system of this book uses *l* to represent sounds that are traditionally written with *r* in the *romaji* system. You may also find that the letter *f* is found in some dictionaries instead of the *h* used in this book.

A

ah-BU-LAH 油 oil
ah-BU-NAHy! 危ない！ Watch out!
ah-GAH-LU *(-u v.)* 上がる to go up
ah-GEH-LU *(-lu v.)* あげる to give
ah-GOH 顎 jaw
AH-kah 赤 red
AH-kah-chahn 赤ちゃん baby
ah-KAH-LU-ih 明るい light (brightness)
ah-KEH-LU *(-lu v.)* 開ける to open
AH-kih 秋 autumn
ah-KIH 空き vacant
ah-LAH-U *(-u v.)* 洗う to wash
ah-LEH あれ that; those (farther away than soh-LEH)
ah-LEH-LU-ghee アレルギ

— allergies
ah-LIH-GAH-TAHy 有難い grateful
ah-LIH-gah-toh (goh-ZAHY-MAHss) 有難う（ございます） thank you
AH-lu *(-u v.)* ある to be in a place (for inanimate objects)
ah-LU-ku *(-u v.)* 歩く to walk
ah-MAHy 甘い sweet
AH-meh 雨 rain
ah-MEH-LIH-KAH アメリカ United States of America
ah-MEH-LIH-KAH-JIn アメリカ人 American person
ah-NAH-tah あなた you
ah-NAH-tah-noh あなたの your; yours
ah-NEH 姉 older sister
AH-nih 兄 older brother
ahN-NAHY-JOH 案内所 information booth
AHN-NAHy su-lu *(irreg.)* 案内する to act as a guide
ah-NOH HIH-TOH tahch あの人達 they
ahn-zen *(nom.)* 安全 safety
AHN-ZEn-pin 安全ピン safety pin
AH-oh 青 blue
ah-PAh-toh アパート apartment
AH-sah 朝 morning
ah-SHIH 足 foot
ah-SHIH 脚 leg
ahsh-TAH 明日 tomorrow
ah-SOH-BIH NIH IH-KU *(-u v.)* 遊びに行く to go visit (casual)
ah-SOH-BU *(-u v.)* 遊ぶ to play
ah-SOH-KOH あそこ there (farther away than soh-KOH)
ahss-PIH-LIN アスピリン aspirin
ah-SU 明日 tomorrow
ah-TAH-LAH-SHEe 新しい new
ah-TAH-mah 頭 head
ah-TAH-TAH-KAHy 暖かい warm
AH-toh 後 after
ah-TS'MEH-lu *(-lu v.)* 集める to collect
ah-TSU-ih 暑い hot (weather); 熱い hot (temperature)
ah-TSU-ih 厚い thick
AH-u *(-u v.)* 合う to fit
AH-u 会う to meet
ahY-LOHN アイロン iron (appliance)
AHy-sahts 挨拶 greeting
ay-gah 映画 movie
ay-goh 英語 English language
Ay-zu エイズ AIDS

B

BAh バー bar
BAHT-gu バッグ bag
baht-KIN 罰金 fine (penalty)
BAHn 番 turn

BAH-nah-nah バナナ banana
BAH-neh バネ spring (mechanical)
_____bahn-sen _____番線 track no._____(train)
bah-SHOH 場所 place
BAHss バス bus
bahss-TAh-mih-nah-lu バスターミナル bus station
bahss-TEH バス停 bus stop
baht-TEH-LEE バッテリー battery (automobile)
BET-doh ベッド bed
BEe-lu ビール beer
beh-LU-TOH ベルト belt
BEN-GOH-shih 弁護士 lawyer
bih-GAHN 美顔 facial (massage)
BIH-juts 美術 art
bih-JUTS-kahn 美術館 art museum
BIH-lu ビル building
bih-YOh-shih-tsu 美容室 beauty parlor
BIn ビン bottle
BIn 便 flight (plane)
BIn-boh *(nom.)* 貧乏 poor
boh-lu ボール ball
boh-LU-TOH ボルト voltage
boh-shih 帽子 hat
BU-bun 部分 part; section
bu-DOH ぶどう grapes
bu-HIN 部品 parts
bu-LAH-u-su ブラウス blouse
BUN-BOh-gu 文房具 stationery supplies
byoh-in 病院 hospital
byoh-kih 病気 illness; sickness

C

chah-KU-LIK SU-LU *(irreg.)* 着陸する to land (by plane)
chahy-loh 茶色 brown
CHEE-SAHy 小さい little; small
chih 血 blood
chih-CHIH 父 father
chih-GAH-U *(-u v.)* 違う different; to be wrong
chih-KAHk 近く nearby
CHIH-kin チキン chicken
CHIH-zu 地図 map
CHIT-pu チップ tip
CHOH-KYOH-lih 長距離 long-distance
CHOH-MIH-lyoh 調味料 seasonings
choh-shohk 朝食 breakfast
CHu-gohk 中国 China
CHu-ih 注意 caution
CHU-IN-GAH-mu チューインガム chewing gum
chu-mohn su-lu *(irreg.)* 注文する to order
CHU-Oh 中央 center
chu-shah 注射 injection (shot)
chu-shah-joh 駐車場 parking lot
chu-shah kin-shih 駐車禁止 no parking

chu-shohk 昼食 lunch

D

DAH-kah-lah だから therefore
_____ **dah-KEH** *(part.)*_____ だけ only
DAH-leh 誰 who
DAH-leh deh-moh 誰でも anybody
DAH-leh-kah 誰か someone
dahn-seh 男性 man
DAHn-su ダンス dance
DAh-su ダース dozen
dahy-gahk 大学 university
DAHY-KOHn 大根 Japanese radish
DAHY-nin-gu ダイニング dining room
deh *(part.)* で at; by (means of); with; in; through (by the medium of)
DEH-g'chih 出口 exit
deh-KIH-lu *(-lu v.)* 出来る to be able; to be possible
DEH-lu *(-lu v.)* 出る to go out
deh-PAh-toh デパート department store
DEH-sh'tah *(cop.)* でした was, were
DEH-teh ku-lu *(irreg.)* 出て来る to come out
deh-ZAh-toh デザート dessert
DEn-chih 電池 batteries
den-gohn 伝言 message
DEn-kih 電気 electricity
den-poh 電報 telegram
DEn-shah 電車 train
den-toh 電灯 lamp; lighting
den-wah 電話 telephone
DEN-WAH BAHn-goh 電話番号 telephone number
DEN-WAH-BOHT-ku-su 電話ボックス telephone booth
den-wah su-lu *(irreg.)* 電話する to telephone
DEss *(cop.)* です be; is; are
DESS kah-lah ですから so; thus
DISS-koh ディスコ nightclub (disco)
DOH-ah ドア door
DOH-BUTS-en 動物園 zoo
DOH-ch'lah どちら which way?
doh-gu 道具 tool
DOh-ih-TAHSH-MAHSH-teh どういたしまして you're welcome
DOHT-ku ドック dock
DOH-koh どこ where
DOH-koh mah-deh どこまで how far?
dohk-SHIN 独身 single (not married)
doh-KU 毒 poison
doh-LAHY K'LEe-nin-gu ドライクリーニング dry cleaning
DOH-leh どれ which
DOH-leh-su ドレス dress
doh-LOH-BOH 泥棒 thief

DOH-lu ドル dollar
DOh sh'tahn-dess KAH? どうしたんですか？ what's the matter?
DOh-yaht-teh どうやって how
doh-YOh-bih 土曜日 Saturday
DOh-zoh どうぞ please (in offering something)

E

Ee いい good; well; nice
Ee dess いいです it's okay
ee-EH いいえ no
eh 絵 picture (art)
eh *(part.)* へ to
Eh ええ yes
eh-AH-KOHN エアコン air conditioner
eh-BIH 海老 shrimp
EH-GYOH-JIH-kahn 営業時間 business hours
eh-HAH-gah-kih 絵はがき picture postcard
EH-kih 駅 train station
eh-LAH-bu *(-u v.)* 選ぶ to choose; to select
eh-LEH-BEh-tah エレベーター elevator
eh-LIH 衿 collar
En 円 yen
En-jin エンジン engine
en-pits 鉛筆 pencil
ess-KAH-LEh-tah エスカレーター escalator

F

FAHss-nah ファスナー zipper
FEh-shah-lu フェーシャル facial (massage)
feN-DAH フェンダー fender
fih-LU-MU フィルム film (photographic)
FOh-ku フォーク fork

G

gah *(part.)* が but
gaht-KOH 学校 school
gahk-SEH 学生 student
gah-LAHSS ガラス glass (material)
gah-SOH-LIN ガソリン gasoline
gah-SOH-LIN S'TAHn-doh ガソリンスタンド gas station
GAHy-doh ガイド a guide
gahY-DOH BUT-ku ガイドブック guidebook
gahy-kohk 外国 foreign country
GAh-zeh ガーゼ gauze
GEH-kih 劇 play (drama)
geh-KIH-JOH 劇場 theater (building)
GEh-mu ゲーム game
geh-ZAHY 下剤 laxative
GEN-KIn 現金 cash
geh-TSU-YOh-bih 月曜日 Monday
gen-zoh su-lu *(irreg.)* 現像する to develop (film)
GHIn 銀 silver
ghin-koh 銀行 bank

GIH-ah ギアー gear (automobile)
g'LEEn グリーン green
g'LEh グレー gray
GOH-goh 午後 P.M.
GOH-hahn ご飯 cooked rice
goh-MEN-NAH-SAHy ごめんなさい I am sorry
GOH-mu ゴム rubber
GOH-zen 午前 A.M.
GU-lah-mu グラム gram
gyu-nik 牛肉 beef
gyu-nyu 牛乳 milk

H

hah 歯 tooth
hah-BU-lah-shih 歯ブラシ toothbrush
hah-CHIH-GAHTS 八月 August
HAH-dah 肌 skin
HAH-hah 母 mother
hah-JIH-MAH-LU *(-u v.)* 始まる to start
hah-JIH-MEH-MAHsh-teh 始めまして how do you do
hah-JIH-meh-teh 初めて first time
hah-KOH 箱 box
hah-KOH-BU *(-u v.)* 運ぶ to carry
hah-KU-BUTS-kahn 博物館 museum
hah-LAHY-MOH-DOH-SHIH 払い戻し refund
hah-LAH-u *(-u v.)* 払う to pay
HAH-leh 晴れ sunny
hah-LEH-LU *(-lu v.)* 腫れる to swell
HAH-lih 針 needle
HAH-lu 春 spring (season)
HAH-mu ハム ham
hah-NAH 花 flower
hah-NAH 鼻 nose
hah-NAH-su *(-u v.)* 話す to speak
HAHN-BUn 半分 half
HAHN-DOH BAHT-gu ハンドバッグ handbag
hahN-DOH-LU ハンドル steering wheel
HAHn-gah ハンガー hanger
hahn-kah-chih ハンカチ handkerchief
hah-SAH-mih はさみ scissors
hah-SHIH 橋 bridge
hah-SHIH-lu *(-u v.)* 走る to run
hah-TAH-LAH-KU *(-u v.)* 働く to work
hahY 肺 lung
HAHy はい yes
HAH-yahk 速く quickly
hah-YAHy 早い early
hah-YAHy 速い fast; quick
hahy-kih 排気 exhaust (automobile)
HAHy-lu *(-u v.)* 入る to enter; to go into
HAHy-shah 歯医者 dentist
HAHyt-teh ih-lu *(-lu v.)* 入っている to be included

heh-AH-BU-lah-shih ヘアブラシ hairbrush
(heh-AH)-KAHT-toh （ヘア）カット haircut
heh-AH-PIN ヘアピン hairpin
het-DOH-LAHy-toh ヘッドライト headlight
heh-YAH 部屋 room
HEE-tah ヒーター heater
HEn *(nom.)* 変 strange
HEN-JIH oh su-lu *(irreg.)* 返事をする to reply
hih 日 day
hih 火 fire
hih-DAH-LIH 左 left
hih-GAH-SHIH 東 east
HIH-hu 皮膚 skin
hih-JIH 肘 elbow
hih-JOh-g'chih 非常口 emergency exit
hih-KAH-GEH 日蔭 in the shade
hih-KIH-DAHSH 引きだし drawer
hih-KIH-NOH-BAH-SHIH 引き延ばし enlargement
hih-KOh-kih 飛行機 airplane
hih-KU *(-u v.)* 弾く to play an instrument
hih-KU 引く to pull
hih-KU-ih 低い low
hih-LOY 広い wide
hih-LU 昼 noon
hih-MOH 紐 string
HIH-shoh 秘書 secretary
hih-TAHY 額 forehead
hih-TOH 人 person; people
hih-TOHts 一つ each one
hih-TS'YOH *(nom.)* 必要 necessary
hih-ZAH 膝 knee
hih-Z'KEH 日付 date (calendar)
hoh-DOH 歩道 sidewalk
hoh-gahk 方角 direction
hoh-hoh 方法 way; method
hoh-KAH 他 other
hoh-KAH NOH 他の another
hoh-KEN 保険 insurance
hoh-KOh-shah 歩行者 pedestrian
hoh-mohn su-lu *(irreg.)* 訪問する to visit
HOh-mu ホーム platform
hoh-NEH 骨 bone
HOHn 本 book
hohn-toh 本当 real; true
HOHn-yah 本屋 bookstore
hoh-seh-kih 宝石 jewel
hoh-SHEe dess *(cop.)* 欲しいです to want
hoh-SHIH 星 star
HOH-teh-lu ホテル hotel
hoh-TOHn-doh 殆ど almost
hu-KAHy 深い deep
HUT-ku フック hook
hu-KU 服 clothing
hu-LU-ih 古い old
HUn 分 minute
HU-neh 船 ship
hun-su-ih 噴水 fountain
hu-TAH 蓋 lid
hu-TOH 埠頭 pier

hu-TSU 普通 regular
hu-YU 冬 winter
hyah-KU 百 hundred
hyah-KU-MAHn 百万 million

I

ih 胃 stomach (organ)
ih-CHIH 一 one
IH-chih-bah 市場 market
ih-CHIH-bahn 一番 first
ih-CHIH-BAHN CH'KAHy 一番近い nearest
ih-CHIH-BAHN Ee 一番いい best
ih-CHIH-BAHN WAH-LU-ih 一番悪い worst
ih-CHIH-DOH 一度 once
ih-CHIH-GAHTS 一月 January
ih-CHIH-JIH TEH-KIH *(nom.)* 一時的 temporary
ih-EH 家 house; home
ih-GU-NIH-shohn イグニション ignition (automobile)
it-KAHY 一回 once
IH-k'lah いくら how much?
IH-k'ts いくつ how many?
ih-KU *(-u v.)* 行く to go
ih-LEH-BAH 入れ歯 denture
ih-LEH-LU *(-lu v.)* 入れる to put in
ih-LIH-G'CHIH 入口 entrance
ih-LOH 色 color
ih-LOH IH-LOH *(nom.)* 色々 various
ih-LU *(-lu v.)* いる to be in a place (for living things)
ih-MAH 居間 living room
IH-mah 今 now
IH-mih 意味 meaning
ih-MOH-TOH 妹 younger sister
ih-NAH-KAH 田舎 countryside
ih-NU 犬 dog
ih-SHAH 医者 doctor
ih-SOH-GAH-SHEe 忙しい busy
ih-SOH-gu *(-u v.)* 急ぐ to hurry; to rush
ih-SU 椅子 chair
ih-TAH-MIH 痛み pain
ih-TAHy! 痛い！ ouch!
IH-toh 糸 thread
IH-ts いつ when
IH-ts mah-deh? いつまで how long?
IH-ts'moh いつも always
ih-U *(-u v.)* 言う to say
iN-KIH インキ ink
iss-SHOH 一緒 together
it-PAHY いっぱい full
it-POH-TSu-koh 一方通行 one-way

J

jah-GAHY-MOH じゃがいも potato
jah-G'CHIH 蛇口 faucet
JAHT-kih ジャッキ jack (automobile)
jih-BUN 自分 oneself
jih-DOH-HAHN-BAHy-kih 自動販売機 vending machine

jih-KAHN 時間 hour; time
jih-KAHN GAH KAH-KAH-lu *(-u v.)* 時間がかかる to take time
JIH-koh 事故 accident
jih-KOHK-HYOH 時刻表 timetable
JIH-men 地面 land (ground)
JIH-shoh 辞書 dictionary
jih-TEN-SHAH 自転車 bicycle
jih-Yu *(nom.)* 自由 free (independent)
JIn-jah 神社 shrine
JIn-seh 人生 one's life
joh-hoh 情報 information
joh-kyahk 乗客 passenger
joh-SEH 女性 woman
joh-zahy 錠剤 tablet
JU-BUn 充分 enough
ju-gahts 十月 October
Ju-ih 獣医 veterinarian
JU-IH-CHIH-gahts 十一月 November
jun-bahn 順番 order (turn)
JU-NIH-gahts 十二月 December
Ju-shoh 住所 address
Ju-su ジュース juice
Ju-tahn 絨毯 carpet

K

kah 蚊 mosquito
KAh-bu カーブ curve
KAH-doh 角 corner
kah-doh カード greeting card
kah-EH-LU *(-lu v.)* 変える to change
kah-EH-LU *(-lu v.)* 替える to exchange
KAH-eh-lu *(-u v.)* 帰る to go back
KAH-eh-su *(-u v)* 返す to return; to give back
kah-GAH-MIH 鏡 mirror
kah-GIH 鍵 key
KAH-gu 家具 furniture
KAH-jih 火事 fire (destructive)
kah-KAH-TOH かかと heel
KAH-koh 過去 past
KAH-ku *(-u v.)* 画く to draw
KAH-ku *(-u v.)* 書く to write
kah-KU-NIN SU-LU *(irreg)* 確認する to confirm
kah-lah *(part)* から because; from; since; therefore
kah-LAH 空 empty
kah-LAH-DAH 体 body
kah-LAH FIH-lu-mu カラーフィルム color film
KAH-leh 彼 he
kah-LIH-GAH AH-lu *(-u v.)* 借りがある to owe
kah-LIH-LU *(-lu v.)* 借りる to rent
kah-LU-ih 軽い lightweight
kah-MAHY-MAH-SEn かまいません it doesn't matter
KAH-meh-lah カメラ camera

kah-MIH 髪 hair
kah-MIH 紙 paper
kah-MIH-NAH-LIH 雷 thunder
kah-MIH-SOH-lih 剃刀 razor
KAH-nah-lih かなり quite
KAH-nahy 家内 wife (yours)
kah-NAH-Z'chih かなづち hammer
kahn-bahn 看板 sign
kah-NEH-MOH-chih 金持ち rich
KAHN-GAH-eh-lu *(-lu v.)* 考える to think
KAHN-GOH-hu 看護婦 nurse
kahn-jah 患者 patient
kahn-jih-lu *(-lu v.)* 感じる to feel (sensation)
KAHN-KIH-lih 缶切 can opener
kahn-koh-ahn-nahy-joh 観光案内所 tourist information office
KAHn-kohk 韓国 Republic of Korea
KAHN-KOh-kyahk 観光客 tourist
KAH-noh-joh 彼女 she
kah-NOH-SEH 可能性 possibility
KAHN-ZU-meh 缶詰 can
kah-OH 顔 face (body part)
KAH-sah 傘 umbrella
kahsh-KOH-MAH-LIH-MAHsh-tah かしこまりました certainly (set phrase)
KAH-tah 肩 shoulder
KAh-ten カーテン curtain
KAH-toh カート cart
kah-U *(-u v.)* 買う to buy; to purchase
kah-WAH 川 river
kah-WAHy-tah 乾いた dry
KAHY-CHU-DEn-toh 懐中電灯 flashlight
kahy-dahn 階段 stairs
KAHy-gih 会議 conference
kahy-hu-ku su-lu *(irreg.)* 回復する to recover (health)
kahY-MOH-NOH OH SU-LU *(irreg.)* 買物をする to shop
kah-YOh-bih 火曜日 Tuesday
kahy-shah 会社 company (firm)
kahy-wah 会話 conversation
kah-ZEH 風邪 cold (illness)
kah-ZEH 風 wind
kah-ZOH-EH-lu *(-lu v.)* 数える to count
KAH-zohk 家族 family
KAH-zu 数 number
kay-sahts 警察 police
KAY-SAHTS-kahn 警察官 police person
k'CHIH 口 mouth
k'CHIH-BEH-NIH 口紅 lipstick
k'CHIH-BIH-LU 唇 lip
k'DAH-moh-noh 果物 fruit

kee-loh 黄色 yellow
keh-GAH oh su-lu *(irreg.)* 怪我をする to hurt oneself
KEH-leh-doh *(part.)* けれど although
keh-MU-LIH 煙り smoke
keh-nik 鶏肉 chicken
keh-SHOH-HIN 化粧品 cosmetics
ket-KOHN 結婚 marriage
ken-in su-lu *(irreg.)* 牽引する to tow
ken-koh *(nom.)* 健康 health
kess-SHIH-TEH 決して never
KIT-chin キッチン kitchen
kih 木 tree; wood
kih-KAHy 機械 machine
kih-KEN *(nom.)* 危険 danger
kih-KOH-EH-LU *(-lu v.)* 聞こえる to be able to hear
kih-KU *(-u v.)* 聞く to ask; to listen
KIH-leh *(nom.)* きれい beautiful; pretty; clean
kih-LIH 霧 fog
kih-LOH-G'lah-mu キログラム kilogram
kih-LOH-MEh-tah キロメーター kilometer
KIH-lu *(-u v.)* 切る to cut
kih-LU *(-lu v.)* 着る to put clothes on; to wear
kih-MEH-LU *(-lu v.)* 決める to decide
kih-MOH-CHIH 気持ち feeling
kih-MOH-NOH 着物 kimono
kih-NEn-hih 記念碑 monument
kih-NOh 昨日 yesterday
KIH-noh-koh きのこ mushroom
kih-OHN 気温 temperature (weather)
kih-OHss-ku キオスク newsstand
kih-OH-TS'KEH-lu *(-lu v.)* 気を付ける to be careful
KIH-sets 季節 season
kih-TAH 北 north
kih-TAH-NAHy 汚い dirty
kih-TAHY SU-LU *(irreg.)* 期待する to expect
kih-TSU-IH きつい tight
kih-ZU 傷 wound (injury)
KIn 金 gold
kin-en 禁煙 no smoking
KIn-koh 金庫 safe, cashbox
kin-kyu 緊急 emergency
KIN-YOh-bih 金曜日 Friday
kit-PU 切符 ticket
kit-PU U-lih-bah 切符売場 ticket booth
kit-TEH 切手 postage stamp
k'LAHK-shohn クラクション horn (automobile)
k'LIH-KAH-eh-su *(-u v.)* 繰り返す to repeat
k'LU-MAH 車 car (automobile)
koh-chah 紅茶 tea (Western)

koh-DOH-MOH 子供 child
koh-en 公園 park
koh-GHIT-teh 小切手 personal check
KOH-HEe コーヒー coffee
koh-KOH ここ here
koh-KOH-LOH 心 heart (as seat of emotions)
koh-ku-bin 航空便 airmail
kohk-SEH-KIH 国籍 nationality
koh-LEH これ this; these
koh-lih 氷 ice
koh-MAH-lu *(-u v.)* 困る to be in trouble
koh-MEH 米 uncooked rice
KOHn-bahn 今晩 tonight
kohN-NIH-CH'WAH こんにちは hello
kohN-SAh-toh コンサート concert
KOHN-SEN-toh コンセント outlet (electrical)
KOHn-yah 今夜 tonight
koht-PU コップ cup
koh-sah-ten 交差点 intersection
koh-SHIH 腰 hip
KOH-SOHK-DOh-loh 高速道路 highway
koh-TAH-eh-lu *(-lu v.)* 答える to answer
KOh-toh コート coat
koh-TOH-BAH 言葉 language; word
koh-TOH-WAH-lu *(-u v.)* 断る to refuse
koh-TOH-Z'KEH 言付け message
koh-WAH-LEH-lu *(-lu v.)* 壊れる to be broken
koh-ZEH-NIH 小銭 coins
koh-ZU-ts'mih 小包 package (mail)
koYN-LOHT-kah コインロッカー coin locker
k'SAH-LIH 鎖 chain
k'TSu-sh'tah 靴下 socks
ku-BIH 首 neck
KU-gahts 九月 September
ku-JOH 苦情 complaint
ku-koh 空港 airport
Ku-lah クーラー air conditioner
KU-lahss クラス class
ku-LAHy 暗い dark
ku-LEH-JIT-TOH KAh-doh クレジットカード credit card
KU-loh 黒 black
KU-lu *(irreg.)* 来る to come
ku-LU-bu-shih くるぶし ankle
ku-NIH 国 country
k'SU-LIH 薬 medicine
ku-SAH 草 grass
ku-TSU 靴 shoe
ku-TSU HIH-MOH 靴紐 shoelace
kyah-BU-LEH-tah キャブレター carburetor
KYAHn-deh キャンデー candy
KYAHn-seh-lu su-lu *(irreg.)* キャンセルする to cancel
KYOh 今日 today

kyoh-kahy 教会 church
KYOh-mih gah AH-lu *(-u v.)* 興味がある to be interested in
kyu-koh 急行 express train
KYu-lih きゅうり cucumber
KYU-MEH-DOh-gu 救命道具 life preserver

L

LAH-beh-lu ラベル label
LAH-jih-oh ラジオ radio
lah-KU *(nom.)* 楽 comfortable
LAHn-chih ランチ lunch
LAHn-doh-lee ランドリー laundry
LAHy-tah ライター lighter (cigarette)
LEh 零 zero
LEH-jih レジ cashier
leh-KIH-SHIH 歴史 history
leh-SHEe-toh レシート reccipt
LEH-s'toh-lahn レストラン restaurant
LEh-toh レート rate (of exchange)
LEH-tsu 列 line (of people)
leN-TAH-KAh レンタカー rent-a-car
len-toh-gen レントゲン X ray
LEn-zu レンズ lens
lin-goh りんご apple
LISS-toh リスト list
lit-TAH リッター liter
LOH-bee ロビー lobby
LOHT-ku ロック lock
loh-KU-GAHTS 六月 June
loh-sohk ろうそく candle
LYOH-JIH-kahn 領事館 consulate
lyoh-KAHN 旅館 Japanese-style inn
LYOh-kin 料金 fare (fee)
lyoh-KOH 旅行 trip
lyoh-KOH SU-LU *(irreg.)* 旅行する to travel

M

MAH-bu-tah まぶた eyelid
mah-CHIH 町 town
mah-CHIH-AHy-shih-tsu 待合室 waiting room
mah-CHIH-GAHy 間違い mistake
MAH-dah まだ still; yet; not yet
MAH-deh *(part.)* まで till; until
MAH-doh 窓 window
MAH-eh 前 before; front
MAH-k'lah 枕 pillow
mah-LU-ih 丸い round
mah-MEH 豆 pea
mah-NEh-jah マネージャー manager
mah-NEH-ku *(-u v.)* 招く to invite
mahn-nah-kah 真中 middle
MAHN-NEn-hits 万年筆 fountain pen

mahss-SAh-jih マッサージ massage
mahss-SU-gu 真っ直ぐ straight
mah-TAH また again
MAH-tsu *(-u v.)* 待つ to wait
MAH-tsu-geh 睫毛 eyelash
mah-WAH-LU *(-u v.)* 回る to turn
MAHy-nich 毎日 daily
mah-YOH-nah-kah 真夜中 midnight
MAH-yu-geh 眉毛 eyebrow
meh 目 eye
meh-doh sahn メードさん maid
MEH-gah-neh めがね eyeglasses
meh-MAHy gah su-lu *(irreg.)* めまいがする to feel dizzy
MEH-nyu メニュー menu
meh-shih 名刺 business card
meh toh-lu メートル meter
meh-ZAH-MAHSH-DOH-keh 目覚し時計 alarm clock
MEn-kyoh 免許 permit (license)
mih-BUN SHOH-MEH-SHOH 身分証明書 identification
mih-CHIH 道 road, street, path
mih-GAH-KU *(-u v.)* 磨く to shine an object
mih-GIH 右 right (direction)
mih-JIH-KAHy 短い short
MIH-lu *(-lu v.)* 見る to look; to see; to watch
MIH-lu-ku ミルク milk
mih-MIH 耳 ear
mih-NAH-MIH 南 south
mih-NAH-TOH 港 harbor
mih-NIH-KU-ih 醜い ugly
mih-SEH-lu *(-lu v.)* 見せる to show
mih-TAH-su *(-u v.)* 満たす to fill
mih-TS'KEH-lu *(-lu v.)* 見つける to find
mih-ZU 水 water
mih-ZU-GIH 水着 bathing suit
miN-NAH 皆 everybody
moh *(part.)* も too
moh-CHIH-AH-GEH-lu *(-lu v.)* 持ち上げる to lift
moh-CHIH-KOH-MIH TEH-NIH-mohts 持ち込み手荷物 carry-on luggage
moh-CHIH-lohn もちろん certainly; of course
moh-EH-LU *(-lu v.)* 燃える to burn
MOh-hu 毛布 blanket
moh-ih-chih-doh もう一度 once more
moh-KU-YOh-bih 木曜日 Thursday
MOH-lu *(-u v.)* 洩る to leak
moh-NOH 物 thing

JAPANESE–ENGLISH

MOH-S'gu もうすぐ soon
MOHsh もし if
MOHsh-mohsh もしもし hello (phone conversations only)
MOHT-teh ih-ku *(-u v.)* 持って行く to take; to carry
MOHT-toh もっと more
MOHT-toh Ee もっといい better
MOHT-toh wah-LU-ih もっと悪い worse
MOH-tsu *(-u v.)* 持つ to have; to possess; to own
mu-NEH 胸 chest
mu-SHIH 虫 insect
muss-KOH 息子 son
mu-SU-MEH 娘 daughter
mu-ZU-KAH-SHEe 難しい difficult
MYOh-jih 名字 family name

N

NAH-gah-lah ながら while (during)
nah-GAH-MEH 眺め view
NAH-gah-sah 長さ length
nah-GAHSH ながし sink (basin)
nah-GAHy 長い long
NAH-kah 中 inside
_____NAH-keh-leh bah nah-LAH-nahy_____ なければならない must
nah-KU-su *(-u v.)* なくす to lose
nah-LAH-u *(-u v.)* 習う to learn
NAH-mah 生 raw
nah-MAH-EH 名前 name
NAH-nih 何 what
NAH-nih-kah 何か something
nah-OH-su *(-u v.)* 直す to correct; to fix; to repair
_____ NAH-shih deh_____ なしで without
nah-TSU 夏 summer
nah-WAH 縄 rope
NAHy 無い missing
NAHy-hu ナイフ knife
NAH-zeh なぜ why
nan-deh-moh 何でも anything
neh-DAHN 値段 price
neh-GAH-u *(-u v.)* 願う to hope; to wish
NEH-koh 猫 cat
neh-MU-ih 眠い sleepy
neh-MU-LU *(-u v.)* 眠る to sleep
neh-TSU 熱 fever; heat
NEK-tahy ネクタイ necktie
nen-zah 捻挫 sprain
nih *(part.)* に at; for (purpose); in
NIH-bahn 二番 second
nih-CHIH-YOh-bih 日曜日 Sunday
nih-gahts 二月 February
nih-GAHy 苦い bitter
nih-HOHn 日本 Japan
nih-HOHN-GOH 日本語 Japanese language
nih-HOHN-JIn 日本人 Japanese person

nih-KU 肉 meat
nih-SEH NOH 偽の false
nih-SHIH 西 west
nih-WAH 庭 garden
nit-POHn 日本 Japan
noh *(part.)* の of
_____NOH ahY-DAH _____の間 between
noh-BOH-LU *(-u v.)* 登る to climb
NOH-deh *(part.)* ので because; therefore
NOH-doh のど throat
NOH-doh gah kah-wah-ku *(-u v.)* 咽が乾く to be thirsty
______ noh HOh gah Ee ______の方がいい prefer
______ noh kah-WAH-LIH NIH ______の代わりに for (exchange); instead of
noh-LIH-KAH-EH 乗り換え transfer (transportation)
noh-LU *(-u v.)* 乗る to ride
noh-MEH-lu 飲める drinkable
noh-MIH-moh-noh 飲物 beverage
NOH-mu *(-u v.)* 飲む to drink
______noh NAH-kah eh ______の中へ into
noh-nih *(part.)* のに although
noh-LIH OH-KU-LEH-lu *(-lu v.)* 乗り遅れる to miss (a vehicle)
______noh tah-MEH nih ______の為に for (purpose)
_____ noh u-EH ______の上 above; on top
_____ noh YOh nah ______のような like (as)
nu-SU-mu *(-u v.)* 盗む to steal

O

OH-BAH-HEe-toh オーバーヒート overheat (automobile)
oh-BOH-EH-lu *(-lu v.)* 覚える to remember
oh-CHAH お茶 tea (green)
oh-CHIH-lu *(-lu v.)* 落ちる to fall
oh-DOH-LIH 踊り dance
oh-DOH-LU *(-u v.)* 踊る to dance
oh-EH-LU *(-lu v.)* 終える to finish
OH-fih-su オフィス office
(oh)-HAH-shih （お）箸 chopsticks
oh-hu-ku 往復 round trip
(oh)-HU-LOH （お）風呂 bath
oh-KAH-NEH （お）金 money
oh-KAHN-JOH お勘定 bill (check)
oh-KAHN-JOH-(BAH) お勘定（場） cashier
oh-KAH-SHEe おかしい funny
(oh)-KAH-shih （お）菓子 sweets
OH-KEe 大きい big

oh-KIH-lu *(-lu v.)* 起きる to wake up
oh-KOH-lu *(-u v.)* 起こる to happen; to occur
oh-KOH-su *(-u v.)* 起こす to wake
OH-ku 億 one-hundred million
oh-KU *(-u v.)* 置く to place; to put
oh-KU-LIH-MOH-NOH 贈物 gift
oh-KU-LU *(-u v.)* 送る to send
(oh)-KYAHK (お)客 customer
OH-KYU TEH-ah-teh 応急手当 first aid
oh-LEn-jih オレンジ orange
oh-LIH-lu *(-lu v.)* 降りる to go down
(oh)-MAH-TS'LIH (お)祭り festival
(oh)-MIH-SEH (お)店 shop; store
(oh)-MIH-YAH-GEH (お)みやげ souvenir
oh-MOH-SAH 重さ weight
oh-MOH-u *(-u v.)* 思う to think
oh-MOY 重い heavy
oh-NAH-JIH 同じ same
oh-NAH-KAH お腹 stomach (body part)
oh-NAH-KAH GAH SU-KU *(-u v.)* お腹が空く to be hungry
oh-NAH-KAH OH KOH-WAH-su *(-u v.)* お腹をこわす to get indigestion
OHn-gahk 音楽 music
ohn-nah 女 woman
OHN-NAH-noh-koh 女の子 girl
ohn-sen 温泉 hot springs
oh-PEH-LEh-tah オペレーター telephone operator
(oh)-SAH-LAH (お)皿 plate
oh-SAH-TSU お札 bank notes
oh-SHIH-EH-LU *(-lu v.)* 教える to teach
oh-SHIH-LAH-SEH お知らせ notice (announcement)
(oh)-SHIH-LOH (お)城 castle
oh-SHIH-meh おしめ diapers
oh-SOH-LEH-lu *(-lu v.)* 恐れる to fear
oh-SOy 遅い late
oh-SU *(-u v.)* 押す to push
oh-TEH-AH-lahy お手洗 bathroom; restroom
(oh)-TEH-LAH (お)寺 temple
oh-TOH 音 noise; sound
oh-toh-koh 男 man
oh-TOH-KOH-noh-koh 男の子 boy
oh-TOH-NAH 大人 adult
_____ oh TOh-shih-teh _____を通して through (by the medium of)
oh-TOH-TOH 弟 younger brother
oht-TOH 夫 husband (generic term)

<u>OH</u>-U-lih-dahsh 大売出し sale
oh-WAH-LIH 終り end; over (finished)
oh-YOH-gu *(-u v.)* 泳ぐ to swim
oh-YU お湯 hot water
OY-K'TS DEss KAH? おいくつですか？ how old are you?
OY-SHEe おいしい tasty

P

PAH-jah-mah パジャマ pajamas
PAHn パン bread
pahN-KU SU-LU *(irreg.)* パンクする to get a flat tire
PAHss パス pass (permit)
pahss-P<u>Oh</u>-toh パスポート passport
PAH-u-d<u>ah</u> パウダー powder
PAHY-LOHT-toh パイロット pilot
PEe-mahn ピーマン peppers
p<u>eh</u>-jih ページ page (book)
PEn ペン pen
PEn-chih ペンチ pliers
peN-KIH nu-LIH-TAH-TEH ペンキ塗りたて wet paint
PET-toh ペット pet
PIn ピン pink
PIn-ku ピンク pink
poh-KET-toh ポケット pocket
P<u>Oh</u>-ku ポーク pork
POHss-toh ポスト mailbox
P<u>Oh</u>-t<u>ah</u> ポーター porter
pu-LEH-zen-toh プレゼント gift
pu-LIN-TOH プリント print (photography)
pu-LOH-GU-lah-mu プログラム program
P<u>u</u>-lu プール swimming pool

R

see **L**

S

S<u>AH</u>-BISS-ly<u>oh</u> サービス料 service charge
sah-KAH 坂 slope
sah-KAH-NAH 魚 fish
sah-KEH 酒 Japanese liquor
sah-MU-ih 寒い cold (temperature)
_____ sahn _____さん Mr.; Ms.
sahn-bahn 三番 third
sahn-bun noh ih-chih 三分の一 one-third
SAHn-gahts 三月 March
SAHN-G'lahss サングラス sunglasses
sahN-POH SU-LU *(irreg.)* 散歩する to take a walk
sah-T<u>Oh</u> 砂糖 sugar
sah-WAH-LU *(-u v.)* 触る to touch

SAHy-goh 最後 last
sahy-hu 財布 wallet
SAHY-KOH-SOHk-doh 最高速度 speed limit
SAHy-n サイン sign
SAHy-n su-lu *(irreg.)* サインする to sign one's name
sah-YOH-NAH-lah さようなら good-bye
sahy-shoh 最初 first
SAHy-zu サイズ size
s'BAH-LAH-SHEe 素晴らしい wonderful
seh-BIH-LOH 背広 men's suit
seh-KIH 咳 cough
SEH-kih 席 seat
SEh-lu セール sale
seh-MAHy 狭い narrow
seh-NAH-KAH 背中 back (body part)
SEh-tah セーター sweater
set-KEN 石鹸 soap
SEn 線 line
SEn 千 thousand
SEN-Pu-kih 扇風機 electric fan
SEN-SEh 先生 teacher
s'GOH-su *(-u v.)* 過ごす to spend time
shah-LIN 車輪 wheel
shah-LYOH 車両 car (railroad)
SHAHn-pu シャンプー shampoo
shah-SHIN 写真 photograph
shah-SHOH 車掌 train conductor
SHAH-tsu シャツ shirt
SHAH-wah シャワー shower
SHEE-tsu シーツ sheet (bedding)
shih 市 city
shih-AH-WAH-SEH *(nom.)* 幸せ happiness
shih-CHAHK SU-LU *(irreg.)* 試着する to try on a garment
shih-CHIH-GAHTS 七月 July
shih-gahts 四月 April
shih-GOH-TOH 仕事 work; job
shih-KAHK 四角 square
shih-KAHsh しかし but
shih-LAH-BEH-lu *(-lu v.)* 調べる to examine
SHIH-loh 白 white
shih-LU *(-u v.)* 知る to know
shih-MEH-lu *(-lu v.)* 閉める to close
shih-NU *(-u v.)* 死ぬ to die
shih-OH 塩 salt
shih-TAH 下 below; down; under
shih-TAH 舌 tongue
shih-TAH-GIH 下着 undergarments
shih-TS'lay-sh'mahss 失礼します excuse me
shih-YOH-CHU 使用中 occupied
SHIH-zu-kah *(nom.)* 静か quiet
shin-bun 新聞 newspaper
SHIN-DAHy-shah 寝台車 sleeping car

shin-goh 信号 traffic light
SHIn-gu-lu シングル single room
SHIN-JIH-lu *(-lu v.)* 信じる to believe
SHIn-kay 神経 nerve
shin-kohk su-lu *(irreg.)* 申告する to declare
SHIn-nen 新年 new year
shin-pahy su-lu *(irreg.)* 心配する to worry
SHIn-sets *(nom.)* 親切 kindness
shin-zoh 心臓 heart (organ)
SHOh ショー show (performance)
SHOh-goh 正午 noon
shoh-HOH-SEN 処方箋 prescription
shoh-kahy su-lu *(irreg.)* 紹介する to introduce
shoh-KU-JIH 食事 meal
shoh-LU-IH 書類 document
shoh-sets 小説 novel (book)
shoh-yu 醤油 soy sauce
SHU-jin 主人 husband (yours)
shu-kahn 習慣 custom (habit)
______SHu-kahn _____週間 week
s'KAh-toh スカート skirt
s'KOHsh 少し few; some; a little
s'MIH-MAH-SEn すみません excuse me
s'NAH 砂 sand
SOh-dah ソーダ soda
SOH-fah ソファー sofa
soh-KOH そこ there
SOH-lah 空 sky
soh-LEH それ that; those
SOH-toh 外 outside
s'POh-tsu スポーツ sports
s'PU-n スプーン spoon
s'TAHy-lu スタイル style
su-IH-YOh-bih 水曜日 Wednesday
su-IT-chih スイッチ switch (electric)
su-KIH *(nom.)* 好き like (favor)
su-LU *(irreg.)* する to do
SU-mu *(-u v.)* 住む to live in a place
sun-poh 寸法 measurement
sut-PAHy 酸っぱい sour
Su-tsu スーツ women's suit
SU-TSU-KEh-su スーツケース suitcase
su-WAH-LU *(-u v.)* 座る to sit
su-ZU-SHEe 涼しい cool (weather)

T

tah-BAH-KOH タバコ cigarette
tah-BAH-KOH OH SU *(-u v.)* タバコを吸う to smoke
tah-BEH-lu *(-lu v.)* 食べる to eat
tah-BIH 旅 journey

tah-BIH TAH-BIH たびたび often
TAH-bun 多分 perhaps
tah-CHIH-IH-LIH KIN-SHIH 立入禁止 do not enter
TAH-dah ただ free of charge
tah-DAH-SHEe 正しい right (correct)
tah-KAHy 高い expensive; high; tall
tahk-SAHn たくさん many
TAHK-shee タクシー taxi
tah-LIH-NAHy 足りない insufficient
tah-MAH-goh 卵 egg
tah-MAH-NEH-gih 玉葱 onion
tah-MEH-su *(-u v.)* 試す to try
TAh-mih-nah-lu ターミナル terminal
TAHn-ku タンク tank
tah-NOH-SHEe 楽しい enjoyable
TAH-oh-lu タオル towel
tah-SHOH 多少 a few
tahss-KEH-lu *(-lu v.)* 助ける to help; to aid
tah-TEH-moh-noh 建物 building
TAH-tsu *(-u v.)* 発つ to depart; to leave
TAH-tsu *(-u v.)* 立つ to stand
tahy-hen *(nom.)* 大変 very
tahy-lah *(nom.)* 平ら flat
TAHY-SHIH-kahn 大使館 embassy
tahY-YAH タイヤ tire
TAHy-yoh 太陽 sun
tahy-zahy su-lu *(irreg.)* 滞在する to stay at a place
tah-ZU-NEH-lu *(-lu v.)* 尋ねる to inquire
teh 手 hand
teh-BU-k'loh 手袋 glove
teh-bu-lu テーブル table
teh-GAH-MIH 手紙 letter
TEH-k'bih 手首 wrist
TEH-leh-bih テレビ television
TEH-LU-LAHn-pu テールランプ taillight (automobile)
TEh-neh *(nom.)* 丁寧 polite
TEH nih ih-leh-lu *(-lu v.)* 手に入れる to get; to obtain
teh-NIH-mohts 手荷物 baggage
TEh-pu テープ tape
teh-TSU 鉄 iron (metal)
teh-TSU-DAH-u *(-u v.)* 手伝う to help; to lend a hand; to act as an assistant
teh-TSU-DOH 鉄道 railroad
teh-ZU-k'lih 手作り handmade
ten 点 point
ten-joh 天井 ceiling
TEn-kih 天気 weather
TEN-LAHn-kahy 展覧会 art show
tiss-SHU-PEh-pah ティッシュペーパー tissues

toh *(part.)* と and; with
toh 戸 door
toh-CHIH 土地 land (property)
toh-DOH-KEH-lu *(-lu v.)* 届ける to deliver
toh-DOH-ku *(-u v.)* 届く to reach
toh-ih 遠い far
toh-KAY 時計 watch (timepiece)
toh-KIH-DOH-KIH 時々 sometimes
toht-KYU 特急 super express train
toh-KOH-YAH 床屋 barber
toh-KU-BETS *(nom.)* 特別 special
toh-LAH-BEH-LAH-ZU CHET-ku トラベラーズチェック traveler's checks
toh-LAHT-ku トラック truck
toh-LAHn-ku トランク trunk (automobile)
toh-LAHn-pu トランプ playing cards
toh-LIH 鳥 bird
toh-LIH-KAH-EH-LU *(-lu v.)* 取り替える to replace
toh-MAH-LIH-GAH-KEH 泊り掛け overnight
toh-MAH-LU *(-u v.)* 泊まる to stay overnight
toh-MAH-LU *(-u v.)* 止まる to stop
toh-LIH-MOH-DOH-su *(-u v.)* 取り戻す to recover; to get back
TOH-mah-toh トマト tomato
toh-MOH-DAHCH 友達 friend
toh-SHIH 年 year
toh-TEH-MOH とても very
toh-TS'ZEN *(nom.)* 突然 sudden
TOHT-teh oh-ku *(-u v.)* 取っておく to keep; to hold on to
TOy-leh トイレ toilet
toY-LET-TOH PEh-pah トイレットペーパー toilet paper
ts'GIH 次 next
ts'KAH-LEH-lu *(-lu v.)* 疲れる to be tired
ts'KAH-U *(-u v.)* 使う to spend money; to use
ts'KEH-MOH-NOH 漬物 pickle
ts'LEH-TEH IH-KU *(-u v.)* 連れて行く to take (a person)
ts'KU-lu *(-u v.)* 作る to make
ts'KU-EH 机 desk
ts'MEH 爪 nail (body part)
ts'MEH-lu *(-lu v.)* 詰める to pack
ts'TSU-MIH-GAH-mih 包み紙 wrapping paper
ts'TSU-mu *(-u v.)* 包む to wrap
TSU-ah ツアー tour
TSU-ih-teh ih-ku *(-u v.)* ついて行く to follow

tsu-KIH 月 month; moon
TSU-ku *(-u v.)* 着く to arrive
TS<u>u</u>-loh 通路 aisle
TSU-mah 妻 wife (generic term)
TS<u>u</u>-yahk 通訳 interpreter
ts'YOy 強い strong
ts'ZU-KEH-LU *(-lu v.)* 続ける to continue

U

u-CHIH-MIH うちみ bruise
u-EH 上 over (above); up
u-EH-s'toh ウエスト waist
u-GOH-ku *(-u v.)* 動く to move
u-LAH-GAH-KIH SU-LU *(irreg.)* 裏書する to endorse
u-LEH-SHEe うれしい glad
u-LU *(-u v.)* 売る to sell
u-LU-SAHy うるさい loud
u-MAH 馬 horse
u-MAH-LEH-LU *(-lu v.)* 生まれる to be born
U-mih 海 sea
Un 運 luck
UN-TEn-shu 運転手 driver
un-ten su-lu *(irreg.)* 運転する to drive
u-SHIH-LOH 後ろ back; rear
u-SU-ih 薄い light (color)
u-TAH 歌 song
u-TAH-U *(-u v.)* 歌う to sing
u-TSUK-SHEe 美しい beautiful

W

wah-GOH-MU 輪ゴム rubber band
wah-KAH-lu *(-u v.)* わかる to understand
wah-KAHy 若い young
wah-KEH-lu *(-lu v.)* 分ける to part; to section
wah-LAH-U *(-u v.)* 笑う to laugh
wah-LIH-BIH-KIH 割り引き discount
wah-LU-ih 悪い bad
wah-SU-LEH-LU *(-lu v.)* 忘れる to forget
wah-TAHSH 私 I
wah-TAHSH NOH 私の my; mine
wah-TAHSH-tahch 私達 we
WAHy-hu ワイフ wife (yours)
waY-T<u>AH</u> ウェイター waiter
WAy-toh-less ウェイトレス waitress
WISS-kee ウィスキー whiskey

Y

yah-BU-lu *(-u v.)* 破る to rip
yah-KAHN LY<u>Oh</u>-kin 夜間料金 night rate
yah-KEH-DOH 火傷 burn (injury)

yahk-SOHK SU-LU *(irreg.)* 約束する to promise
yah-KU-su *(-u v.)* 訳す to translate
yah-MEH-TEH! やめて！ stop it!
yah-SAH-SHEE やさしい easy
yah-SAHY 野菜 vegetables
yah-SU-ih 安い inexpensive
yah-SU-mu *(-u v.)* 休む to rest
yah-TOH-u *(-u v.)* 雇う to hire
yah-WAH-LAH-KAHy 柔らかい soft
yoh-BIH-DAH-su *(-u v.)* 呼び出す to page
yoh-BU *(-u v.)* 呼ぶ to call out
yoh-BUN 余分 extra
YOh-ih su-lu *(irreg.)* 用意する to prepare
yoh-KOH 横 side
yoh-KOH NIH NAH-lu *(-u v.)* 横になる to lie (down)
YOh-koh-soh ようこそ welcome
yoh-LIH-KAH-KAH-lu *(-u v.)* よりかかる to lean on
yoh-LOH-KOH-BIH よろこび pleasure
YOH-lu 夜 night
YOH-mu *(-u v.)* 読む to read
YOHn-bahn 四番 fourth
yohn-bun noh ih-chih 四分の一 quarter (fraction)
YOHn-ju 四十 forty
yoh-shu 洋酒 Western liquor
YOH-u *(-u v.)* 酔う to be drunk
yoh-WAHy 弱い weak
yoh-YAHK 予約 reservation
YOy よい fine (quality)
yu-BIH 指 finger
yu-gah-tah 夕方 evening
yu-KAH 床 floor
yu-KIH 雪 snow
yut-KU-lih ゆっくり slow
yu-meh *(nom.)* 有名 famous
yu-NYU-HIN 輸入品 imported product
yu-shohk 夕食 dinner
YU-SU HOHss-teh-lu ユースホステル youth hostel

Z

zahss-SHIH 雑誌 magazine
zeh-kahn 税関 customs (at airports)
zeh-kin 税金 tax
ZEH-loh ゼロ zero
ZEn-bu 全部 all
zen-poh 前方 forward
ZU-bohn ズボン pants
zu-TSU 頭痛 headache